M000087211

Honest Thoughts

You're coming across as an anarchist. - *Sister*

If I can be totally honest with you, I worry that you're going to get pushback for being a stereotypical self-involved millennial.
- *Literary Agent*

Caitlin is an insanely gifted writer! I wish I could send a copy to Gram in heaven. Also, the suburbs weren't THAT bad, but high school was. - *Cousin*

I don't want to read it all at once. I want to savor it…so I will be reading more soon, when I'm not tired. - *Aunt*

Congrats about the book, that's awesome. Did you put, like, everything in it? - *Brother*

I think you're a wonderful, talented human who can do anything she wants — including this awesome book!
- *Bestselling Author*

My biggest concern is you've never written a book before.
- *Life Coach*

Somewhere, something incredible
is waiting to be known.

-Blaise Pascal

Introduction
Love Note to the Reader

I'm so happy this book is in your hands. This is about all the different places I've explored—and by that, I mean both physical spaces and countries, as well as states of being, like the changes and transitions that feel like a place: a birth, a death, a marriage, a divorce, a disease, a move, an accident, growing up, a fall from grace—you know, the usual circle of life stuff.

I want to be totally transparent with you: this is not a well-researched textbook on ancient history, social dynamics, or really, anything. This is something I wrote from my heart as a human being on planet Earth.

Back in the day, I used to think the world operated in a clear-cut way. This or that, good or bad, light or dark, happy or sad. If only things were that simple!

In reality, there were often two opposites—and then there was everything that exists in-between, the middle ground where things aren't so easily defined.

In a way, growing up between two parents who couldn't be more opposite, it was like the world was grooming me to always exist in the in-between, to see past two sides and find a balance between extremes. To explore the gray area where things don't always "make sense."

I've spent most of my life traveling, between two homes, between who I was conditioned to be and who I really am—and to all the places I was told (or forced) to go with others and the ones I needed to go to on my own.

I believe the most important things in life can be found in the least likely places—and we have to be willing to leave our comfort zone to find them. And traveling is one way to do that. It puts you in a whole new place with all new people—and forces you to see things you may have never seen before, both within yourself and in the outside world.

I've learned more about life through my travels than I ever did in school. Every place I've been in this world has opened me up to wisdom, to the things humans have known since the dawn of time before things like slavery and war and racism even existed.

I've found travel to be a tool for compassion, a cure for ignorance and an initiation for awakening. My greatest adventures consisted of exploring three types of places:

1. the spaces on the outskirts filled with the most vulnerable people, the ones who have been pushed to the edge of "society"

2. ancient sacred sites, built all over the world, all (magically) aligning with the stars

3. the dark transitions that we all try to avoid, like heartbreak, sickness, and death

I've found that outside the rules and amongst the poor and the ancient and hidden in the dark, the truth lies snugly, waiting to be recovered and remembered.

Along the way, I discovered pieces of who I am in others. Like orphans, unwed mothers, remote villagers, the homeless, immigrants—people who have something money can't buy: integrity and spirit. It shines out of them because they're not trying to keep up with...anything. They've shown me that job titles, diamond rings, and number of followers aren't what's truly valuable in this world. Resilience, strength of character and vulnerability are.

When I've met people where they are, especially in a place that's raw and real, something opens up in me. I learn more about myself because I see myself in them. Travel isn't just about getting the next Insta-worthy photo (although, that is a perk)—it's about true connection, something we're all craving in our hearts.

And the more time I've spent exploring ancient ruins, the more I've seen that the people before us knew something we've forgotten. That they built their lives around the cosmos, and we're meant to remember what's been buried underneath skyscrapers and strip malls.

Finally, the time I've spent in life's sorrow has shown me that pain only exists to bring transformation. It's not a punishment, but more of a process. Deep, but it's true.

Wherever you're meant to go, whatever you're meant to do, whatever stage you're at in life, you have everything you need inside you. And it's okay to step away from what's expected of you and do your own thing. To stop listening to other people's opinions and start trusting your own. Or to just take a fucking break. No one is meant to *do* all the time.

I want to end this little love note to you with a story about a beautiful butterfly. This is a tale that was originally told by a Peruvian shaman, not directly to me, but I serendipitously came across it one day—and as fate would have it, later became friends with this powerhouse of a woman who originally shared it (Kylie McBeath). This story is really tender and I made a few minor edits for emphasis, so enjoy:

Once upon a time, there was a town of caterpillars. One of the caterpillars was curious about what was beyond the walls of the town, over there in the forest. She asked her family and friends if she could go explore. They all said: NO WAY! DO NOT DO IT. It's too scary out there.

This caterpillar loved her family and her friends, but one day, the pain of remaining in the town became too great and she snuck away and went exploring.

The next thing she saw in the forest changed her life forever. She saw a bunch of other caterpillars going into cocoons and transforming into butterflies. She was in total shock. She had no idea that all along, she had the capability to fly in the sky. To see from up above.

Excited about her discovery, she quickly went back to her home and told everyone she could about her findings. Still, the others around her were filled with fear. She couldn't get any of them to change. To challenge what it meant to be a caterpillar.

But instead of holding back, she went to the new place she had found where caterpillars make cocoons. The place of transformation. Even though she was scared, she did it anyway.

And shortly after, as a beautiful butterfly, she flew above the town that had told her to stay put...and said: 'Hey guys! It's me! Look, I'm fucking flying!!!'

At this point, she wasn't trying to convince anyone else or preach—she was just being. This was enough. Growth was not an abandonment of others—it was an invitation.

We all have an open invitation to explore the places society doesn't have guidelines for. You are invited to do whatever your heart desires, especially if it's outside the 'norm.'

To me, the ability to travel and connect with other people is like a sacred gift—and it's never felt more holy than now.

If this book gives you an escape, I will be glad. If it stirs up a fire in your belly, then my work is done.

In the words of Bruce Springsteen:

You can't start a fire
Worryin' about your little world fallin' apart

There's where we are now and we all know how this life is going to end...so what matters is what we do with everything in between.

With love,
xx Caitlin

Paperback ISBN: 978-0-578-68070-5
E-book ISBN: 978-0-578-68071-2

Second printing edition 2021

caitlinelizabeth.me
@lovecaitlinelizabeth

everything in between

by: caitlin elizabeth

everything in its...

for Issy + Gram

you are always with me and everything i have is yours.
-luke 15:31

CONTENTS

One

1
INDIA: HOSPITAL BEDS
(the boy at the taj mahal + home for babies)

Every man is a golden link
in the chain of my good.
- *Florence Scovel Shinn*

When I pictured myself in India, I saw a woman who was finding her truth while doing a headstand in an ashram and returning home as an enlightened being. *Namaste.*

That was the opposite of what happened, although I did find a piece of truth there. Instead, my best friend Pari invited me to visit her grandparents with her, and I jumped at the opportunity—and went all the way to India without stepping foot in an ashram.

Pari and I had quickly bonded after college, becoming fast friends over our shared love for a good time and our anxiety. We found any excuse to party, and then, would spend hours in deep conversation, uncovering the mysteries of the universe and why we often felt like we were carrying the weight of the world on our shoulders. We spent Saturdays in a bar and many Sundays on the couch together, in silence and recovery.

A typical Tuesday night out with her involved befriending the Kardashian's makeup artist and his boyfriend, inviting them back to her place for a nightcap, where her own boyfriend would wake up and wonder: *Who are those two men on my balcony with my girlfriend?* Pari was amazing.

I was constantly asking her about India and her family's culture—so I think she may have invited me with her simply to get me to stop asking so many goddamn questions that even she didn't know the answers to.

Boarding the plane, I had a case of nerves, mainly because I'm terrified of flying. Luckily, I slept for the first half of the sixteen-hour flight. At one point, I met Pari by the bathrooms, and she told me that she had a middle seat and described it as "like sitting at a wooden school desk." When we landed in India, she turned to me in the terminal and said:

I actually really fucking hate it here.

The first thing I noticed when we got off the plane was both the heat and the smell. It was swelteringly hot, and there were lots of aromas and scents floating in the air that I had never smelled before, some more appealing than others. As we got our luggage, we left the safety of the baggage carousels to enter the Arrivals terminal. And that's when I got my first real taste of India.

Imagine three hundred people standing in a space designed for fifty people and they are all holding signs and shouting and trying to get you to follow them. That was what it was like when we arrived at the airport. As we found our driver and headed to the car, he strapped our luggage to the roof and I realized I was way, way out of my element. *Excuse me Sir, isn't there a trunk?*

We drove through the streets of New Delhi at night, and I stared out the window at the lights and the signs and the motorcycles and the people sleeping on the street. I was used to a world with traffic cops and recycling programs. Where jaywalking and littering were illegal offenses that one could be ticketed for. Jet-lagged and on sensory overload, I had no idea that I was about to experience things that would forever change my (very sheltered) view of the world.

In India, it felt like the world I'd known had been shaken up and turned upside down. I was out of my comfort zone to the point where I forgot what my comfort zone even was. It was beautiful and loud and felt totally chaotic, but in the best way possible. Like one big abstract canvas of humanity built upon a kingdom of gods and goddesses.

The streets in India were filled with people, food stands, cars, dogs and garbage. I saw children with barely any clothes and old men and women begging for food. It was unlike the poverty I knew back home. This seemed vast and dense and out of control. The magnitude felt overwhelming.

My religious education instilled in me the values of taking care of those in need and loving your neighbor. I knew the stories of Jesus feeding the poor and curing the blind. I had been raised volunteering at soup kitchens and then, sentenced to the nearby elderly home when I had to do community service for an "incident" in high school.

I was taught that when you see someone in need, you help them. But here, there was just no fucking way to do that. I was in shock.

We hadn't even been in India for five hours before we were heading to the Taj Mahal. I sat in the van and just kept staring out the window at all the people we passed by. A monkey breastfeeding her baby. Entire families on one scooter. Men wearing loin cloths walking on the side of the highway, barefoot and singing, in religious processions. More and more dogs and cows and scooters and cars and people and people and people.

I knew there would be poverty in India. It's the stereotype we're all aware of. What I didn't know was that there'd be extreme luxury right alongside it. The living conditions were indescribable, on both ends, for the poor and the rich. The most expensive home in India overlooked a slum. There's the finest luxury malls made of marble with people living on the dirt street right outside.

One of the best demonstrations of this juicy contradiction was in the town of Agra, where the Taj Mahal lives. I was so obsessed with seeing the big beautiful Taj that I never even thought about what lies around it (how American of me!). The contrast between luxury and poverty was...alarming. Literally the slums of India, with piles upon piles of garbage and cows and street children and beggars and thousands and thousands of people living in poverty, all right outside one of the most decadent marvels of architecture created by mankind. The ultimate contrast.

The Taj Mahal is one of the seven Wonders of the World. It was built between 1631 and 1648 by an emperor who wanted to house the remains of his most loved wife, the one whose name meant the Most Distinguished of the Palace. She wasn't his only wife, but she sure was his favorite. It is basically an architectural wonder and a luxurious and decadent marble monument to love.

When we arrived, we were greeted by our tour guide, Ganesh. He had a large, commanding presence, and I was amazed by his ability to smoothly walk and talk with such force in the hot temperature. We went through security (where they confiscated our magazines and pens) and got our first glimpse of the Taj.

It really was breathtaking. There was an energy at the Taj Mahal that was just pure love and radiance. The surrounding gardens were perfectly manicured and the white marble shined and glowed. It was something I would call magnificent, and really, sincerely mean it, from my heart.

Something else was very white and glowing like an orb—and that was my skin in the hot Indian sun. Many villagers save their money and travel from all over the country to visit. Since they come from remote regions, many have never seen a white person before. Let alone a light-haired, pale girl in a shoulder-less dress. I was drawing a bit of attention.

At first, it was flattering. Women would come up to me with their children and we'd communicate by smiling and nodding at each other. I posed for pictures and really was starting to feel like a celebrity. My fifteen minutes of fame was (finally) happening and it went straight to my head. *Who, me?!*

But then I started to feel really, really weird. People were filming me with their cell phones. It finally dawned on me that they were fascinated by me because I was so...white. And it made me feel very, very weird inside my own skin.

The more pictures people took, the more other people noticed and wanted to get a picture too—and the more aggressive they became. Somewhere, in the digital cloud hanging above India, lives hundreds of pictures and videos of locals and me, smiling awkwardly together in front of this beautiful Wonder of the World. Somehow, the natives were mesmerized by what was different, by the color of my skin. I had become the walking representative of the caucasion empire—and it wasn't a good feeling, to say the least.

After Pari finally told everyone in Tamil to back off, we placed our hands on the building, wishing for true love back home (it's a thing) and admired the view of the river flowing behind the compound. We posed for a few pictures with Ganesh and then sent him in search of water because we were literally melting in that heat and security had also confiscated our water bottles.

After some hydration, Ganesh led us back to the van. There was lots of hustle and bustle in the streets and we just wanted to get out of the heat and find something to eat. Or at least that's where my head was at. But as we were getting into the car, I felt some scratching at my ankles.

It was a little boy, probably around three years old. He was crawling on all fours because his spine was bent in half. I had seen (and loved) *Slumdog Millionaire*, so I knew that sometimes adults will purposely harm children and then send them on the street to beg, hoping they will earn more money due to their deformity. I wish I could say that I bent down and scooped this little boy into my arms, brought him home with me and gave him a better life. Instead, I screamed and jumped in the car. It was my visceral, immediate reaction. My friend's mom gave him money, and we drove away.

That moment haunts me. That little boy was living in one of the worst situations a human being can live in: as a child on the streets of India with a disability begging for money. And I jumped away, like a complete and utter prick.

It was too much. And this tiny moment stuck with me long after I left India. I don't know how he ended up there and I don't know what happened to him. Believe me, there are nights and days when I think of him and feel all the sadness in all the world. I wish there was something I could do. I wish I could fix this world where a boy has to live like that. Or where a woman like me has been so pampered that she is too afraid to even look.

I'd been so drawn to visit India and specifically the Taj Mahal—and when I got there, it was like the world was pointing at me and saying: *See all this beauty, it lives amongst all these things that need to shift, like poverty and privilege. You cannot enjoy one without facing the other.*

I firmly believe that little boy and I crossed paths for a reason. He taught me more in one second than I learned from years of studying (heavily filtered) history.

In him, I saw that the world can be really unfair. That some of us live privileged lives while others suffer. That we're often divided by our skin color. That fear drives us apart but love brings us together. I learned that I can't turn away from little boys in need or the injustices of the world, even if it's terrifying to look at. I learned that the only thing one can do in that situation is to witness it. Because by standing witness and turning towards the situation (not away), love leads the way.

It's very jarring to be confronted with extreme poverty when you've only seen it in infomercials asking for donations. It's totally heartbreaking to see it in real life. And if we aren't used to it, our immediate reaction is often to look (or jump) the other way. At least that was mine, as shameful as that is to admit.

After much reflection, I realized the first step I needed to take was simply to witness. To not get scared and jump in a van. To look at the injustices of the world straight on with my eyes wide open.

Not wanting to know what's going on in this world is totally destructive and it's what allows unfair, sad, and cruel things to happen. The traditions of India and the Gospel of Mary (somehow slipped out of the Bible) both say that the root of all evil is ignorance. So by standing witness and turning towards an unjust situation (not away), light gets into the dark places. That seems like a good first step: to see.

That little boy has been in my thoughts for years now. The more I've thought about him, I realized what a huge service he's doing for this world and what a service he did for me. Maybe some souls are here to teach the rest of us compassion and to crack open our hearts. Maybe it's people like him that are here to show us what needs to be fixed. Maybe he's shining a big spotlight on all the things we need to work on, collectively, and truly see.

On the car ride out of Agra, as I was shaken up by how a world can contain both the Taj Mahal and a homeless boy on all fours, I desperately realized two hours into our journey that I needed to pee. And that I would probably need to use the bathroom within, say, the next ten minutes. I'd been chugging huge water bottles all day because of the heat—and it was finally catching up with me.

Due to the language barrier with the driver, I had to have Pari's mom translate and speak to our driver to explain my restroom needs. Something was lost in translation because we were not stopping. The car kept moving and I did not see any out in this situation. An hour later, I entered a full-on, tear-filled meltdown begging to be let out of the car on the side of the highway, where I proceeded to relieve myself in public, in a country where women cover their shoulders and ankles regularly. I brought shame on our driver and for that, I felt guilty—but it was much better than the alternative.

The next day, we woke up in Jaipur, the Pink City and I attempted to limit my water intake, which ultimately did not end well. We toured the Palace—and afterwards, I felt so dizzy all I could do was sleep. This led to a 16-hour stint of heat exhaustion, but really it was soul exhaustion too. My heart couldn't grasp both the extreme beauty and heartache that was all swirling around me, happening all at once in this place.

There is nothing like laying in a hotel room in India, alone and overheating, while you think about life and why you're lying there while a little boy crawls through the streets. I'm pretty sure I saw my grandfathers during this daze, it's all very hazy. Either way, it was comforting to see them and I slept a lot. The next day, we got on a plane to fly south.

Chennai was described to me as "the Detroit of India," which felt true when we landed there. We were staying with Pari's family for the last two weeks of our trip.

She described her family's home as having servants that do everything for you along with a driver. I was picturing like a mansion with five Mercedes waiting out front.

What I didn't know was that in India, most upper caste families have hired help, so their family had a driver and a maid who were both the same age as us. They reported for duty early in the morning and left late at night. It was like a 6-to-9 schedule that made a 9-to-5 look like a piece of cake. Pari and I both felt a sense of guilt seeing them work so hard while we sat back to be waited on. And chauffeured.

When we had dirty clothes, they would be waiting for us, washed and folded, the very next morning. Anywhere we wanted to go, the driver would take us there. I cannot lie and say I did not enjoy these luxuries.

Her grandparents, aunt, and cousins were kind enough to rent out a whole spare apartment for us. So thoughtful and generous. They asked the maid to sleep outside the front door, like on the ground, for extra security. Pari spoke right up and refused to allow this woman to spend the night on the floor. Her exact words were:

If she sleeps there, then I won't sleep at all.

Luckily, the servant girl was allowed to go home. And it made me understand what intersectional feminism really meant.

Her aunt's and her grandmother's homemade meals were out-of-this-world. They even made less spicy versions for the *gori* (white woman). I started to crave *sambar*—and I have ever since.

I had a really interesting deep talk (in English) with her grandpa. He was amazed that I lived on my own (not with my family) and that I paid for the trip myself. It seemed so foreign to him that I was expected to work for myself, without the financial support of my family. My mind was blown that ongoing financial support was an option? He made me think about what I'd prefer: having the freedom to live on my own or still living with my family? (I'd opt for freedom, but there was something about how connected they all were that felt appealing to my heart and my bank account).

After two weeks in India, we were running out of things to do and it was the most time Pari and I had ever spent together without any of our usual vices, like say, alcohol or cigarettes. At the end of each day, I'd sneak out on the balcony with her brother where we'd both puff down nicotine like we'd never have it again—and Pari stayed strong, too scared to be found out by her family. I admired her strength and I was not as poised or disciplined.

We'd visited temples and gone shopping and visited more temples and ate more amazing home-cooked meals and went to more temples. We visited an ancient beach town and walked through a Sea Shore Temple built in the 7th century. We saw a cobra dance and got Henna tattoos and wore saris. I finally broke down and agreed to try coconut water from off the street and it tasted like a sour armpit. I'd lucked out and gotten a "bad one."

On one of our final days, Pari's family decided to take me to a religious site they thought I might like. India is a very spiritual place. Temples are everywhere (in case that wasn't clear), and spirituality is interwoven into everyday life.

They took me to St. Thomas Mount in Chennai, a hill where St. Thomas, the apostle of Jesus, was martyred. Ironically, my grandfather, father, brother, and nephew are all named Thomas, and I went to St. Thomas grade school. So the visit seemed fated.

We hiked up the hill and visited the Church. I immediately noticed all the statues and idols, and thought of the Commandment, "Thou shalt have no other gods before me" which I had been taught meant absolutely no worshipping of statues. I've since learned that it really means not putting other things in life before your connection with something greater, like money or drugs or sex.

We wandered through the church, and after five minutes, took a group picture outside and then we were awkwardly standing at the top of the hill, not sure what else to do. At the temples, her family knew what offerings to make, when to bow or kneel, and what chants and prayers to say. I had nothing really to offer them but potentially a Hail Mary or an Our Father—both of which would have been pretty weird to start reciting randomly.

We noticed this huge tree with weeping long branches and decided to walk over to it because we literally had nothing else to do. Under the tree, we saw a building with a sign that said "Babies' Home." We didn't know what that meant, so we started poking around.

It was an orphanage. The workers were very kind to us, and they gave us a tour. We got to see where all the newborns were sleeping. Then we went to the toddler's room, and the kids' faces lit up when we entered. They were fascinated by our nail polish and kept holding our hands and looking at the color and jumping up and down. They were so cute and so happy, I wanted to hug them all.

I could have been born anywhere in the world. Somehow, by an accident of birth, I ended up smack in the middle of the United States. But I could have very easily ended up in that orphanage. Or on the streets, like the little boy. Instead, I was handed a pass to a life of privilege, straight out of the birth canal.

I had been taught to live focused on what I can achieve, what I can do, and what I can prove to others. What medals and awards I can win, what salary I can pull, and what home I can buy. All of those things were surface-level nice - but there's more to why we're all here than just that.

Inside that orphanage, I felt a pull, a tug on my heartstrings. I felt a knowing in my inner core, a little whisper that was saying: *This way, this is the way for you to follow.*

As we were leaving the orphanage, I had two thoughts:

One: I want to volunteer at an orphanage in another country, at a place like this.

Two: I want to adopt children one day. I want to give kids like this a home.

A boy on the streets of Agra, India | August 2010

2
SAN FRANCISCO: CRIMINAL
(first travel experience)

One day if I go to heaven…I'll look around and say,
"It ain't bad, but it ain't San Francisco.
-Herb Caen

The first time I packed a *Hello Kitty* suitcase was to run away. I was five and knew there was a better life for me out there.

As a kindergartener, I walked out the front door with my packed bag, quite confidently. My neighbor spotted me, snitched to my mom and my first adventure was cut short.

Upon my (forced) return, I was told I was "breaking the rules" and that my life would be hard as a "runaway."

But really, I was just trying to run towards something I thought would be better. This would become a pattern I'd repeat indefinitely. Get fed up, pack a bag, and go somewhere new.

Like every human who's ever wanted to travel anywhere, I saw something brighter in what's out there—in the places and people I didn't know yet, but had heard about.

I finally was able to write my first travel story half a decade later at 11 years old:

My Greatest Adventure

My greatest adventure was probably when I visit San Francisco. I have had many adventures there. I have met my 2 favorite actors:

Winona Ryder and Robin Williams. I have gone to my first New Year's Eve Party, my first concert, and my first time eating patte.

In reality, I wasn't eating pâté every day, but I was used to experiencing lots of (luxurious) firsts with my Aunt Sheila.

When my aunt moved to San Francisco during my childhood (otherwise known as the first major trauma in my life), I refused to get off her leg during our goodbye. She took me to do fun things and was totally obsessed with me—and I was not ready to let that go. And I let her know.

I sent her cards in the mail, on a weekly basis, saying things like: *When are you moving home? Don't you miss YOUR FAMILY?!?! Why did you abandon me?!?! Thanks a lot, I need therapy now because of you!!*

All I wanted at that point in my life was to be in an actual Baby-Sitters Club and to visit Aunt Sheila as much as possible in California.

When I actually did land on Californian soil, I could no longer walk, I was only able to skip. It was like entering a dream world. I remember thinking: *Wow, this place is, like, really on my level. It was so FUN and colorful! And DIFFERENT!*

Based on the agenda I'd created for every second of our trip, we rode cable cars and jumped on the trampoline at Fisherman's Wharf, saw hippies in the Haight, rainbow flags in the Castro, green grass at Dolores Park, drum circles at Baker Beach, and snobs on Nob Hill. We went to art museums, rolled down the hill by the *Full House* house, and saw so many different kinds of people. Every neighborhood was like a new magical gem. I ate french fries and drank hot chocolate at every meal. It was like I'd entered the West Coast gates of heaven (not the cult).

When my aunt dropped us off at the airport, she walked us to our gate. As we boarded, I once again, refused to remove myself from her leg, only this time I was old enough for this to raise eyebrows.

I cried tears I didn't know I had inside me as a mere almost tween. I was making it well-known, through hyperventilating cries, that I did not want to go back to Illinois. California was my home now and San Francisco was everything my life wasn't back in the suburbs.

The gate doors were closing and I had no choice but to get on the plane. Even my aunt said I had to. But every year, like clockwork, I went back to California, mostly thanks to my aunt's plethora of airline miles and my own non-stop manipulation of my parents.

Outside of the one million tourist things we did on these trips, our other focus was chasing divinity. In ancient times, they had gods and goddesses but in the '90s, we had celebrities.

We were obsessed with finding one goddess and one god in particular: Winona Ryder and Robin Williams. Aunt Sheila created a route that we would circle over and over again, multiple times per day, no matter where we were going.

On the most beautiful day in my tween life, WE SPOTTED WINONA!!!!!! She was so gracious, as I knew she would be, but mainly because I think she was a little shocked when she saw two children sprinting through traffic directly at her, screaming her name. My brother and I came in real hot after barely dodging an electric bus.

This was before selfies, so she signed a piece of paper for us. Sidenote: She was with her boyfriend and we ignored him. He was of zero interest to us. *Who the heck was Eddie Vedder?!* Regrets.

After that, I promptly made my AOL screen name Winona12—to symbolize the woman and the age I wanted to be. Our "accidental" meeting was a pivotal moment in my life.

Seeing her in the flesh made me believe that dreams really do come true. Celestial beings really do exist. These were pure times when she was known for movies like *Reality Bites* and *Little Women* and my personal favorite, *How to Make an American Quilt*. I not only was her #1 (stalker) fangirl, but I wanted to literally BE her. *Hi, I go by Winona now. Call me that online, please.*

My aunt encouraged me to write her a letter after we met:

Dear Winona Ryder,

I am a huge fan of yours. You are my role model. We ran into each other once on Steiner.*

My favorite town is San Francisco. I know you have a house here.** I would love to live here. That is my dream someday.

We are similar in so many ways. I can not live without Coke.*** My birthday is October 28 (just a day before yours). I want to be an actress and I am trying to start my career.

I admire you because you have morals and follow ethics and you stick to your own judgment unlike many other actresses.**** You are not in the acting business for the money, but for your true love of acting. I would really like to meet you...again!

Thank you so much for your contribution to the acting world!

Sincerely,
Caitlin

*Because I was actively looking for you there.
**And I've seen it twice today.
***The soft drink.
****Written a few months before the shoplifting incident. I went through a soft mourning period.

After ambushing Winona, we were down to one: Robin Williams. And we just casually ran into him one sunny afternoon in Golden Gate Park. He was with his son who was carrying an animal balloon, which caught my attention immediately. I remember thinking:

Hey, that kid has an animal balloon!! I want one! Where did he get that? Wait a minute, that kid has a dad who looks just like...hey, that kid has Robin Williams as a DAD!

This was right after *Mrs. Doubtfire* came out, so we were practically peeing our pants with excitement. Robin was extremely kind to us, was not dressed as a nice old lady, but was as gracious as Winona and signed our little pieces of paper. His son made him seem more human and kept us from acting like total freaks. I'd never seen my mom blush so hard.

Hanging out with my aunt and all these (two) famous people made me see that there was more to life than strip malls and softball games. Every visit to San Francisco showed me the magic of exploring a new place.

I loved standing outside City Lights, wishing to time travel and meet Jack Kerouac. And chugging hot chocolate at Ghirardelli. And feeling my thighs burn from all those hills and complaining endlessly to Aunt Sheila that I couldn't walk like this, I was used to the prairie life. And watching the Bay Bridge twinkle at night. I felt so much happiness and beauty in that city.

And even more, Aunt Sheila showed us how to take the rules and flip them on their head. I admired her so much because she was an adult who could always have fun and didn't let anything get in the way of a good time.

I hope she won't get arrested for this (*what's the statute of limitations?*), but we would drive up Lombard Street—like the well-known windy street. At night. She took us to a New Year's Eve block party when we were in middle school with drag queens on stilts spitting fire. She'd let us stay up as late as we wanted and introduced us to delivery food, well before Postmates even existed.

The only time I ever saw her get angry was when a man approached us late at night once at the counter in a McDonald's and she screamed at the top of her lungs: *GET THE FUCK AWAY FROM US!* It was sweet that she was so protective.

Our parents hated when my brother and I spent time with her because we'd come back like animals who needed to be tamed again. Everything we did with her was carefree and laidback and sometimes, illegal. But it was always, always, always fun.

She also taught us not to be ignorant brats. My brother and I used the word "gay" as an adjective because that was part of the suburban (bigoted) vernacular back then.

One day, my aunt sat our butts down and we talked about it:

Why do you use that word? Do you even know what it means?

(awkward chuckling) Um, noooo...tee hee!

Well, I think the way you say it is mean and it will hurt people. Do you want to know why?

(uncomfortably staring at the ground) Yes, I guess.

You've met my friend Mike, right? And you like him and we have fun with him?

(blank stares) Yessss

Well if he heard you call him gay, he would be really, really upset. It would hurt his feelings and it might even make him cry. Do you want to make him cry?

(feeling really bad) No, sorry.

Look, I know you guys don't intend to be mean. But just don't use words like that. You're so much better than that.

That was a really good lesson because: a. it made me super conscious of my words, especially hate speech, even if everyone else is saying it. And b. it made me aware that you might be doing things that hurt people without even *knowing* it. Until someone sits you down and tells you.

Ultimately, what San Francisco gave me was exposure and experience. That became the difference between myself and (some) people back home in the suburbs (hair flip). When you get to leave home, you see that there's a whole, beautiful colorful world out there. You meet people who are different than you. You experience things you never have before. You get outside your box and you "bump into" your favorite celebs.

And when you return home, you often find that travel has changed you (for the better). When I got back from that first California trip, I felt extremely sophisticated. I looked around my hometown and thought: *One day, I'll go somewhere great in the world, beyond this town of plebeians.* And it gave me so much hope and a sense of superiority I'd yet to find elsewhere.

Around the same time, my interest in music took on a life of its own. Fiona Apple, Sarah McLachlan, Liz Phair, Alanis Morissette, Jewel, Shawn Colvin, Lauryn Hill, Natalie Merchant, and Joan Osborne were on a never-ending loop in my bedroom.

Alanis' rage towards men both scared and intrigued me. Fiona Apple was, by far, my favorite. I can close my eyes and still picture her two blue eyes staring back at me from the cover of her album.

I would play these CDs over and over again on my boombox, memorizing every lyric and even making mixed tapes of my favorites. These women sounded sassy and strong and powerful and I just really loved their vibes. As I became a woman, their music was the soundtrack to my pubescent development. Every time I listened to *You Oughta Know*, my ovaries grew a little.

When I heard about the Lilith Fair, I knew I had to go. It was a music festival of predominantly female artists created by Sarah McLachlan, one of my favorites due to her totally dramatic and super melancholy ballads. No one in my life had passed away yet, but I would listen to *In the Arms of the Angels* and felt like someone I loved dearly had, in fact, died. It was so moving and deep. I loved crying to it.

Lilith (as we blossoming feminists called it) was coming to a neighboring suburb in Chicago, and I made it well-known amongst my family how BADLY I really wanted to go.

I was in 8th grade and my parents were in the middle of a divorce that would best be described as "brutal." My dad made a point to do one activity alone with each of us - my brother, sister, and I -

and he let us pick what we wanted to do. One of the perks of a "modern family."

As fate would have it, it was my turn in August 1998. So, I chose the Lilith Fair. My excitement was THROUGH THE ROOF and I could not WAIT to see SARAH MCLACHLAN LIVE!!!

I'd seen Sheryl Crow already, in San Francisco, of course. My aunt took me to the Fillmore with her friend Shauna. Shauna had a buzz cut, wore a leather jacket, and introduced me to gender fluidity. She put me on her shoulders during *Everyday is a Winding Road*—and then attempted to put me ON stage. I refused because I didn't want to piss off Sheryl. Basically, I was no stranger to the LGBTQ+ lifestyle at that age, which was pretty amazing given I had about the same cultural exposure as the child born in *Room*.

So, there I stood with my father at the Lilith Fair. It was he, I, and about 25,000 other female-identifying friends, many of whom would also identify with the L-word.

Homophobia was alive and well in the Midwest at that time. But I hadn't even hit puberty yet (late bloomer). And I'd already been around women who liked men and women who liked women. *What difference did it make? Why would anyone care?*

I saw Sarah perform, it was as breathtaking as one would expect, and my dad really liked Bonnie Raitt's performance. It was a very happy moment for the two of us in the middle of mostly not-so-happy times at home.

Afterward, I could not wait to brag about it at school. I marched in, standing up a little straighter than usual, announcing that I had been TO THE LILITH FAIR, EVERYONE!!

Instead of inspiring jealousy, I got called a "lesbo" and like eleven kids in my class of twenty-three laughed at me (which was over 50% of my social circle at the time).

This made me very sad because this baker's dozen of kids were taking something I genuinely enjoyed and tainting it. It felt cruel and really ill-informed.

Did they need me to bring my boombox to school so they could hear these women's voices? What about this was not connecting for them? Why was this a trigger?

But that's when I realized that people are scared of what they don't know and can be really mean about it.

If only we could have taken a class field trip to Aunt Sheila's loft in San Francisco with Shauna as our chaperone, maybe they'd have appreciated the amazing feminine gathering that was the Lilith Fair too.

My brother (left) and sister (right) hanging out with another celebrity, one of the Hanson brothers (middle).
San Francisco | early '90's.

3

IOWA CITY: CRYSTAL VILLAGE

(mistakes)

Every girl must decide for herself if she is going
to be true to herself.
- *Glennon Doyle*

I'd been beyond ready to get to college. Mentally, I'd been there since, like, the age of three.

As a teen, I was truly just focused on passing time until my real life could start. I fantasized about becoming an adult, thinking my 20s were going to be the most powerful, epic decade of my life. I'd think about having my own place and my own life in a city—and it was like my own personal mental escape room.

I used to lie in my bed at night and worry about whether or not people would like me after high school. Who would I sit with at lunch in a university setting? How could I possibly make friends in a new place? Well, 18-year-old me knew the easy answer: Drugs. It had worked in high school!

My high school friends smoked and drank and got high—so I did too. Because it was an excellent way to let loose and drown out reality. Because if I just needed to have time pass, then I wanted that to happen as quickly as possible. And I can attest that yes, time really does fly when you are having fun!

Most of the people at my (private) high school were ridiculously wealthy. We'd go to parties in South Barrington homes that had both an indoor swimming pool, a tennis court and a 20-car garage. I swear I recognized one of the houses on *Cribs* once.

These kids could get whatever they wanted and our parking lot was filled with Range Rovers and BMWs. I was nowhere near their level—and felt like an outsider because of it.

My family did not invest in luxury vehicles for teens. My dad was paying for two houses and gave a big chunk of his income to my mom. And they both were giving huge chunks of money to their lawyers and the court system. Money was more like a weapon than a showpiece for us.

I spent my high school years basically trying to fit in, doctoring my report cards at Kinko's, trying to keep up, (sometimes) shoplifting, smoking, and partying. I worked at Limited Too, where my main responsibility was to catch shoplifters (ironic!) and I realized that working in retail was my personal nightmare, mostly because I hated having a manager who treated me like I was an idiot. My closest friends were mostly kind, humble, and a little dorky too. None of us peaked in high school and that was such a huge blessing. *Who wants to peak at sixteen?!*

WWJD was a popular catchphrase back then and people even wore wristbands as a reminder to feel guilty every day: *Would Jesus smoke a joint? Would Jesus ever be tardy?! Would Jesus untuck his shirt???*

To drive this incessant need for punishment home, the main authority in my high school was our principal, Mr. Jackoff, who I knew was just a little too angry towards females—and totally had it out for me.

I'd get a detention for breathing or blinking, and he was always around every freaking corner I turned. I'd sit alone with him in his

26

office as he refused to make eye contact and grew visibly angrier with every word I spoke. I began forging my mom's signature on the detentions because I knew this was all just ridiculous. There were much bigger issues we needed to focus on as a community, collectively. Like, say, wealth disparity and abuse of power, for instance. And literally NONE of these stupid rules would matter the second I received my diploma. Also, Mr. Jackoff would later be arrested for domestic violence after I graduated, proving my point that he was, in fact, an aggressive misogynist.

My teenage rebellion was like a one-woman personal protest—and it was mostly fueled by what was happening at home and the fact that school had become increasingly less of a "safe space" to retreat to every day.

One day I woke up and decided I just really didn't want to wear the man pants (khakis, purposefully constructed for the male body) they forced us to wear each and every day. So, I put on jeans and walked through the halls that day, pretending I'd "accidentally thought" it was an out-of-uniform day (even though everyone knew that wasn't even a mistake I could possibly make). But I was just so sick of being told what to do that just wearing a different pair of pants for one day felt oddly free-ing, even if I had to spend an hour being quiet and passing notes in detention because of it.

Because I didn't care much about really anything, I spent a good deal of time goofing off and pranking others. Mostly in the form of actual prank calls, since we were given a directory of phone numbers at the start of each year and I'd started practicing at an early age with my cousins when we'd prank call 911 during Christmas Eve. *Help us, Santa's not here yet.*

In hindsight, this was not always kind and probably made other people feel like shit when they'd get a random voicemail and wonder: *Why is someone prank calling me? What did I do to deserve that?* I was the best at it because I was able to keep my cool and really commit to whatever storyline we'd decided would be hilarious that day. *I'm so sorry to tell you this, but we're going to need you to come in early and refill all the tampon machines. Please don't ask why, but you will receive extra credit on your next report card. Thank you for complying.*

It wasn't always nice—but it was never intended to be hurtful. Honestly, I didn't even consider the consequences of what those phone calls and pranks might feel like for other people because I was so desperately trying to make something in my world happy and fun, even if it came at another person's expense.

On the flip side, I was also the target of straight-up bullying, even though I never would've admitted to it back then, due to my own pride.

When I got together with my junior-year boyfriend (who was in rehab for pot, just my type), my guy friends at the time were ruthless. I didn't get why then, but later, I understood it was because they were jealous and (probably) felt rejected. *But I thought we were friends!*

They egged my car repeatedly. When I had to stand up and be in a pep rally, they got people in the audience to boo me. They smashed pumpkins on the hood of my car. They spread rumors about me, calling me a whore. And I didn't take any of it lying down, but it also didn't boost my self-esteem in any way, shape or form.

I really just knew this "religious" community had lost the plot somewhere along the way. Many of the students had access to daddy's credit card and didn't understand what the word "no" meant. Nothing (that mattered) had ever been taken from them, only given. Some people were genuinely kind and I made some really good friends. But I had a reputation as a "slut" because I made out (no penetration) a handful of times (which was not even enjoyable for me) and was constantly being harassed, usually because of whoever I was dating.

As the cherry on top, my very best friend in high school was really, really wild and made each day like a thrill ride due to her mania and total lack of consideration for anything but her own needs. Acting out became one way I could get attention. I learned to turn down my intelligence and turn up my very innate wild side when I was with her—which ultimately culminated in getting arrested my senior year for (arguably sexual) harassment.

One day we (she) thought it might be fun to heckle a group of junior high boys. Mind you, the age gap between us and them was only like two (four) years. We just politely offered them some candy that happened to be hiding in our pants. We could barely get the words out, we were laughing so hard and drove away as they started taunting us back. No one was the victim in this scenario, we were all equally acting like immature losers.

But one of those snitches told their mommy they were almost abducted (not true). The snitch's mother told the junior high principal that her son was almost kidnapped —and the school sent out a memo about a group of middle-aged women in an SUV trying to lure young boys into a car with candy (in their pants). It didn't help that the major news story at the time was about an abduction case in Utah.

We were promptly arrested two weeks later, ironically while driving around and getting high again. We sat in the double-mirrored interrogation room at the police station giggling like crazy. We got mugshots and fingerprints and a court date.

Of course, none of us told our parents because that would have been total masochism. So, we showed up in court with no legal representation and were given a "harassment" sentence and told to do 40 hours of community service.

This was actually exactly what I needed at that point in my life. A sentence to community service. It was the perfect punishment (and wake-up call) because it sparked my interest in doing something outside myself, like to understand someone else's pain, instead of just running from my own.

I started spending time in the Alzheimer's wing at the elderly home (where I'd end up spending a lot of time later with my grandpa) and it gave me a much-needed perspective check on life. Nothing teaches you to cherish every moment more than a bunch of people who can't remember any moments at all.

However, a few months later, my dad discovered my little "incident" when he happened to be in court himself (because he was representing someone as an attorney) and the judge asked him how his daughter was doing ...with her case. Oh, brother. He pulled up the police record and weirdly enough, he didn't see how funny the whole thing was! My college countdown felt more urgent, probably for both of us.

Once I finally escaped the suburbs to live amongst cornfields at the University of Iowa, I was living in a new place with a new roommate: Ellie, a lovely Mother Bear hippie-type from Minnesota with way more life experience than me.

Even though she was almost a year younger than me, she became like my college mom figure. She saw what a douchebag my boyfriend was right away and took me to my first political rally. Together, we made a new group of friends, mainly other girls who lived in our dorm and conveniently, also smoked pot too.

I fell in love with Iowa City. I'd spend hours inside Prairie Lights, the local bookstore. I chose to study film and writing (as one does in the Corn Belt). I thought I was so cool when I'd go to the Tobacco Bowl to smoke inside, trying to give off a Beatnik vibe. I also frequented The Java House, where I pretended to study and mostly, admired the funky ceramic mugs they had on sale while eating a bagel.

I was originally studying Psychology but there was way too much science involved in that. I took one film class as an elective and then, I fell in love with making movies. My major was technically Cinema and Comparative Literature, which translated to *Movies and the Books That Make Them Worth Studying.*

I signed up for a class about Bollywood because it was either that or another Kafka literature course, which I wasn't sure I'd survive. I would rather spend weeks watching an actual caterpillar grow from cocoon to butterfly than talk about *The Metamorphosis* for another second. *We get it, waking up as a bug would definitely feel isolating.*

Instead, I got to watch super long, cheesy Indian films in a dark theater...for class. It was amazing. Each movie was a minimum of three hours long and we'd often have to watch them in parts (which did mess with the flow).

There was something about these films that just drew me in like a magnet. The bright, colorful costumes and the people and the exotic places and the dancing and singing—all filled with this pure energy. There was joy and feelings pulsing off the screen that felt so open and...spiritual? I didn't really know how to explain it—but it felt equal parts magical and cheeky. I also loved being able to name drop Amitabh Bachchan to anyone that had ever heard of Bollywood. *Yeah, I know his work.*

At that point in my life, I was blissfully ignorant. My priorities were: relationship, social life, waitressing shifts, and class—in that order.

College was a non-negotiable for me, the only option and paid for by my parents with the help of my grandparents, as stated in the divorce agreement.

But I had a rather rocky start to my college experience. I ruined Ellie's birthday during our second week of school by (accidentally) trying shrooms and having not the best trip, to say the least. I kept rubbing my eyes, thinking it would help clear up my funky vision. Ellie looked after me, ditching her own birthday plans to be my caretaker, even though we'd only known each other for like a fortnight (14 days, not the video game) at that point.

There was not one moment of that hallucinogenic experience that was enjoyable. They say that magic mushrooms can be very therapeutic when administered with the right people in the right dosage and the right setting. However, in my case, it was pure trauma seeing as I didn't know what dosage meant, I was with all new people I barely knew, and in a new setting, a dorm room the size of a walk-in closet.

It was like all the fear, all the anxiety, all the worry, all the feelings I'd pushed down inside me since I was little, just came flying out of me. Like the shroom dust had opened up Pandora's Box of my repressed emotions and it was a fucking nightmare I'd never be able to shove away.

When I finally started coming down, I cried over and over again from relief. I thought I was going to be stuck feeling that way forever.

I called my high school boyfriend who had followed me to college. He lived about a mile away. I told him he had to come get me. Even though we were on the rocks, I needed comfort. I'd just been through a personal inner battle and returned. I was shaken and beaten up. Ellie walked me downstairs and when Jack showed up, he was so...mad?

I started walking away with him and telling him about what HELL was like, because I'd just been there for a night and it was AS BAD AS THEY SAY. And he turned to me, with total sincerity, and both sternly and sadly said:

I cannot believe you did shrooms without me.

I spent the rest of the night consoling him, trying to explain what a freak accident this was. I cried myself to sleep in his little dorm-size bed, which I'm sure his roommate really appreciated. Pretty sure he put in his request to switch rooms the next morning.

Within a week, my eyes were completely covered with little blisters, thanks to my non-stop rubbing and laying on a dorm room carpet for 6 hours (barf). It finally got to the point where I looked straight-up terrifying. I couldn't go anywhere without sunglasses on. And if I took them off, people visibly shuddered. I felt (and looked) like a leper version of the Hamburglar.

I called home and said:

Hi! I know I'm only 3 weeks into college, but um, I have this little face rash so I'm going to come home for like a week.

I booked a Greyhound ticket and took a bus from Iowa to Illinois, through the farms and over the Mississippi, purely out of vanity because I refused to be seen in my new college community with this horrific rash thing that was happening on my face.

If you've never ridden a Greyhound before, consider that a giant blessing. It was basically like a moving porta-potty on wheels. And the other people on the bus were a mixture of college kids in crisis and anyone without a driver's license who was desperate enough to cross state lines in America's lowest form of transportation possible.

My mom and sister picked me up from the bus station in Chicago, and I'll never forget their faces when I took my sunglasses off. Pure horror.

I spent about a week in bed, thinking about my life. How was I finally given freedom only to end up back in this godforsaken place again, and so quickly? Did I really love my boyfriend? Or was he just an asshole?

Turns out, he was definitely an asshole. He cheated on me that week with a sorority girl, who he introduced me to over the phone, as if that would somehow make me approve of what he was about to do. *"This is Mindy, you guys will be friends!"* No, we fucking won't, Jack. You're an idiot and I know what you're doing.

Finally, my facial issues started to heal and I went back to Iowa. I never tried anything else after that, aside from weed. I was too scared. And after that enormous explosion of anxiety, I learned to never talk about it or show it to anyone so I would just numb it out, quiet it in any way I could, instead of listening to what it was trying to tell me or like, accepting it as a part of me, not all of me.

I finally got up the nerve to dump my boyfriend when I started hanging out with another guy from our high school, who was a year older (and therefore, cooler). We started flirting—and he asked if I was still with Jack?

Of course, my answer was *NOPE* and I sent the final break-up text right then and there.

But the new guy was fun and became one of a few I had on a rotation for a while. I liked having options and also, not having to really be vulnerable at all. As soon as there were feelings with one, I'd just text the next one and repeat the cycle as needed.

I remember the older guy once, very seriously, told me that he really, really liked me, but he was not looking for a girlfriend. And as I was secretly reading texts from my other options, I tried to match his sincerity when I said:

I'm so not ready for that either.

Guys became my band-aid. If I was in a relationship, of any sort—casual to serious—I felt wanted and needed. It felt good to feel attractive. I weirdly understood the power I had and that I had something they wanted. Desperately. I would walk into a party and scan the room until I locked in on my target and would think to myself: *That one.*

Most of the time I just flirted. Maybe I'd make out. Once in a blue moon, it'd go further. But I liked the attention and it made me feel good about myself—which is the opposite of where true self-esteem is supposed to come from.

I finally did start a real, committed relationship halfway through college. My friends and I became friends with the guys who lived across the hall, so it was literally like a very drunk, college version of *Friends*. We'd play pranks on each other (my favorite) and go out all the time. They did not appreciate the day I filled up a garbage can with water, gently perched it on their door and knocked—that kinda ended the prank war, awkwardly, I might add.

But they were genuinely kind-hearted people and I started dating one of them. It was a foreign experience for me because for the first time, I felt...actual feelings.

Bear was the one we all had a crush on—and when he and I became a thing, it caused tension with my group of friends, who I quickly realized were not my friends if they were actively trying to sleep with my boyfriend. I spent the rest of my time in college in a place I'd never thought I'd actually be: in love.

Our relationship wasn't perfect, but the way I felt about him was different than anything I'd felt before. He made me feel safe. And he got me to do things I never would have done for anyone else and actually find enjoyment in these activities, like camping and fishing. For the first time in my life, I didn't even have eyes for anyone else. My days of hunting for male attention were over because I'd discovered something new: a reciprocal relationship.

Mostly, I needed someone to both accept me and put me in my place. When I'd freak out on Bear, lashing out for one thing or another, he'd sit me down and explain to me that I couldn't treat him that way. And I'd actually apologize and really mean it. For once, I realized I really cared.

Outside of him, waitressing was my other saving grace. First, I made a ton of cash and it felt good to be able to spend it at other bars. Second, it gave me an excuse to not party 24/7—my waitressing shifts were like my day off, my time to just be nice to people and not drink my face off. And third, waitressing was a humbling, fast-paced, work environment. I think every human should have to serve others for at least a day.

One day while I was working a particularly busy shift, the Beatles' song, *Here Comes the Sun* came on—and I found myself getting really, really emotional. Like having to fight back tears. The song reminded me so much of my dad—and I realized I missed him. Like really, deeply missed him. I'd wanted so badly to get away from home that I never thought I'd actually miss it. And maybe those tears weren't just about being homesick, maybe it was ALL the change that happened so fast back there in Illinois. But like most things, I stuffed my sadness down somewhere deep inside. As one *does*.

Iowa City was like my safe haven in many ways. It was the first place I lived on my own and the first place I truly fell in love. It was the first place I knew I'd be okay and could even be loved by someone else, even if I made (lots of) mistakes along the way.

The Pentacrest, Iowa City | sometime in the early 2000s

4

ADULTING: CHICAGO

(european vacation)

She refused to be bored chiefly because she wasn't boring.
- Zelda Fitzgerald

Miraculously, I graduated from college in only four years, despite my rare attendance in an actual class. I skipped my graduation day for two reasons: 1. I had no interest in having both my parents in Iowa City at the same time (hard pass) so 2. I intentionally booked a flight to London on the same day.

My friends from high school and I found this trip to visit eight countries throughout Europe in 21 days! I saved up my waitressing tips and told all my family members that I didn't want any graduation gifts, just donations to my European travel fund.

When I landed in London, I was by myself and had to take the Tube to the hotel where I'd be meeting my friends. I lugged my suitcase up the Underground station stairs and finally made it to the hotel lobby where I waited...and waited...and waited.

Two hours later, my friends finally showed up—and they were fucked up. They'd flown in earlier that day and had mixed sleeping pills and wine (an often lethal combination). So, they completely "forgot" when I was arriving. But we still managed to go out that night and every night after.

For the next three weeks, we traveled via ferry and bus from London to Paris to Amsterdam to Germany to Austria to Florence to Rome to Athens and then, the Greek Islands. Every night, we partied like it was 1999 and every morning, we got on a bus and passed out. Our tour guide was a man in his mid-twenties who most definitely had a crush on one or all of us. When we'd arrive at our next destination, he'd get on the bus speaker and mockingly say: *Wakey, wakey...* and we could see the twinkle in his eye, the joy he felt in ruining our one chance to sleep.

We saw the Eiffel Tower, toured Anne Frank's house, floated down a canal in Venice, saw the Colosseum in Rome, and ate enough gelato for a lifetime.

My least favorite part of the trip was when my (wild) friend ate space cake for breakfast in Amsterdam—and then we were promptly stopped in Belgium for a thorough bus search where she was forced to eat the rest. Not a highlight. My favorite part was the day we spent touring Salzburg, Austria and then, we headed to a town in the Alps called Zell Am See.

I had no clue what it would be like and slept on the bus ride through the mountains.

I remember getting off the bus in this little village and thinking:

I'll stay here for the rest of my life.

The hotel was on a small, crystal clear lake that was surrounded by green grassy mountains and views of the Alps.

Words can't begin to describe how truly beautiful this place was, like *The Sound of Music* meets *Blue Lagoon*, only without any Nazis or incest.

We rented bikes and rode around the lake, where we saw horses and butterflies and the sun was shining. We went out in the town that night and danced our hearts out. I woke up the next day and couldn't even feel hungover if I tried—it was just too beautiful.

I felt this sense of....joy washing over me. I felt happy. Sincerely and truly happy.

Life wasn't magically perfect. I got an emergency call from my family while I was in Amsterdam, telling me that my brother wanted to join the army. At that time, there were active wars happening—this was in the years after 9/11.

I used the hotel phone to call my brother, telling him:

Under no circumstances whatsoever can you do this right now. Do not sign up. Do not pass go. Do not do this, I do not want you to die in the Middle East. You need to seriously think about if this is what you truly want because you cannot change your mind once you make this choice.

He didn't enlist—but he did become a fireman and have three beautiful children instead. Thank the Goddess I didn't sample the space cake before that call!

But I was happy. I had graduated. I had a better relationship than I'd ever had before. I had a job waiting for me back home. I was living. And my life was filling up with...joy?!

The trip ended in the Greek Islands, arguably the most beautiful place on Earth. The ferry ride to Poros was like a dream—the sun over the Mediterranean, the beer in our veins, the smiles on our faces.

We saw Greek ruins and beaches and a pier that literally faded into the sea. We went into town for lunch and on the way back to the hotel, we all jumped into the sea fully clothed, on a whim. We were so young and excited and free. *Adulting wasn't so bad after all!*

I had to leave Europe a few days early because my new boss wouldn't budge on my start date. I reported for duty on my first day, jet-lagged, dehydrated, and covered in bug bites from the Athens airport. The picture of a modern, successful businesswoman.

Even though I was starting my first "adult" job, I wasn't really sure what I wanted to be when I grew up, because I couldn't really pick one thing, another recurring theme in the *mise en scene* of my life.

I'd studied film, but my friends and family were all living in Illinois—and film jobs were hard to come by outside of L.A. So I started working at a production company that made commercials. It was owned by a man whose interests included motivational quotes and doctoring contracts with at least an 80% mark-up.

At my interview, I met with his #1 minion, Waldo—who was ten years older than me and extremely serious about the interview. He looked at my resume, searching for holes. He asked me about my work experience in my early years:

Did you work in high school?

Um yes, I've been babysitting since I was thirteen. I've babysat for tons of families.

So, it sounds like you're great with kids, but how are you with adults?

(awkward pause) I'm good with adults too...

We would later laugh thinking of how he had never interviewed anyone before—and I, in turn, had never been (properly) interviewed.

Waldo kept his desk meticulously clean and used his hands for emphasis. We became fast friends and I babysat his cats when he and his fiance got married in Napa—but I didn't clean the litter box correctly and his new wife was devastated to come home to a clearly unhappy cat. I was later allowed to babysit their human daughter, so all was forgiven.

My main responsibility at this "film" job was to burn DVDs. I watched the same shitty commercials, over and over and over again, and edited them together, over and over and over again, to put on DVDs and send to ad agencies, over and over and over again.

Within eight months, my boss called me into his office. I knew something was wrong.

I guess anticipation is the worst part. So, here goes. I'm shutting down the company. They're hiring me back at the ad agency. And I want you and Waldo to come with me.

I wasn't even a year into my first job and our country was heading into a major recession. There was only one answer to that offer: *Yes, PLEASE!*

Weirdly, I'd had a premonition of that moment. I'd been sneaking a cig in the back alley after lunch one day when I had this thought that came barreling through: *I'm going to work at an ad agency.* I remember finding it so odd I would even think that—because I didn't even know what an ad agency was!

That summer, I still went to the office every day, by myself, and did nothing. Waldo came in sometimes and we would sunbathe on the roof and watch movies. We both felt anxious because we were promised jobs, but had no signed offers yet. It was a tense time.

The weekend before our job offers were to arrive, our boss invited (summoned) us to his family cabin in Michigan. Both of us did not want to go, but we also felt like we had to. I mean, our future jobs were on the line here. It was the first trip I ever sincerely did not want to take.

I intentionally "forgot" my bathing suit. Mostly because I felt incredibly uncomfortable being in a bikini around my boss. I wanted to shield my body from his gaze.

When Waldo and I arrived at the lake, it was time to go on the boat and go tubing—and I did my best impersonation of "girl who is totally sad she forgot her bathing suit and will now begrudgingly spend a day in the sun in street clothes."

My boss was not having it. When I say he forced me to wear his 10-year-old daughter's bathing suit, I mean he verbally forced me. I tried to say no, but he was adamant—and this man was in charge of my ability to pay rent for the foreseeable future. Waldo looked at me with sincerely apologetic eyes and he knew, that I knew, that he couldn't speak up either.

I put on the one-piece and went tubing. When the jet-skis came out, Waldo and I took off at full-speed to the other end of the lake. We had to spend the night there and I slept in a musty room in the basement. I was sure to lock the door. Thankfully, I was undisturbed.

The next day, we stayed for breakfast and then left as soon as humanly possible. When we got in the car, Waldo looked at me and said: *Is it okay if we just don't talk?* I nodded. We drove back in complete silence, which was comforting. Silence amongst friends truly is golden.

The next week, we got our job offers and a tiny piece of me felt like I'd compromised myself to get it. *Was this because I looked decent in his daughter's one-piece?!*

At first, everyone at the new office hated us because we were hired by the new boss and they thought we were probably narcs (we were not). I started getting emails like this:

From: Boss
To: Me
Subject Line: Not feeling good

Can you pleese run down to the kitcn and bring me a glass of OJ, three advil and some hot tea? Stat.
Thanks. :)

I'd walk into his office holding his remedies, with a smile on my face.

His response: *Have you never heard of ice?*

Me: I'm sorry...I didn't realize you liked ICE in your orange juice....

His response: (Looks at me like I have a tree growing out of my head)

OR this:

Text from boss: See me now.
Phone rings.
Voicemail: Need to see you right now.
His assistant runs over to my desk: *He really needs to see you right now.*

Enter his office.

Him: (Waving hands to shush me out of office) *No No NO not now not now not now.*

If I was a "success" with my cubicle and my salary—then why did my life not feel like me? Why did scenarios like that make me want to run screaming from the building?

Even though my life looked like an episode of *Sex and the City* (ok, *Girls*), it didn't feel great.

Like most relationships that start when you're barely an adult, my college boyfriend Bear and I broke up. Internally, I was devastated, but I couldn't even begin to process that, so I scorched the Earth, defriended almost all of our mutual connections on social media, and buried the loss so deep inside myself that I didn't even know it was there. I convinced myself that I had no part in the demise of the relationship—and I shoved myself forward, leaving a chunk of my heart behind.

I proceeded to jump from the next guy to the next one and then the next one, with no space in-between any relationships, like a romantic version of leapfrog. I wasn't sleeping with all of them but it didn't matter. I was trying to fill something inside me, even if I didn't understand what that was, and I was trying to deny the reality that maybe love doesn't just disappear overnight, that it couldn't be willed to go away.

The majority of guys I was with at that time never passed the "what" test. Meaning, if there was a circumstance or something I thought they might be lying about, I'd ask them about it:

Are you texting another girl right now?
Did you just cheat on me?
Are you having sexual relations with that woman?

And without fail, each one would immediately respond with: *What?*

The quicker the what, the more guilty they were. My heart would sink a little bit every time I heard the *what*. Because it was a way for them to deflect. To say: I know the answer to this question, but I don't want you to know the answer to this question, so I'm going to instantly respond by pretending I don't comprehend what you just said. *What?!*

I didn't even truly care because I was not (emotionally) committed, but it was the lying that bothered me. I couldn't stand being lied to. I was picking some real winners and that was because any guy who was sincerely nice to me, I ran from.

I thought this one intern at the office was so cute and one night, after a concert, I made out with him. He was so kind. Like he actually wanted to get to know me, not just my body. And he had a very hipster vibe, even wearing a jean shirt with a rose embroidered over his heart.

The next day at work, I was mortified. He was sweet and quirky— and I did not know how to handle that. I locked myself in my friend's office, hungover and about to cry, claiming that I was "just drunk" and now I had to "break it off" with him because he was "too clingy." The reality was I knew he actually liked me and I knew he was exactly the kind of guy that would be good for me and that scared me more than anything.

One night, a few months after Bear and I ended things (and five guys later), I was having a cig alone on my balcony, staring at the moon. I heard my roommate get home.

She had been raised in one of the only small towns in Indiana with a country club—and let everyone know it. She loved mixing cheese, mustard and lunch meat in a bowl for dinner. It hurt my stomach and my eyes. My instant reaction when I heard her was: Shit. She's coming out here.

Did you take my cheese?

No. Why is it missing? (Flashback: Putting cheese on chips and into microwave late at night with friends)

It's not in the fridge.

Huh. That's so weird.

Is that my shirt? (Flashback: Taking shirt from her closet)

I borrowed it from Mallory.

Oh well, it's mine. I need it back.

Okay, no problem.

The porch door slammed. I sat there thinking about my life and what the fuck I was doing. All I knew was that I wasn't happy anymore. And I knew the last time I felt happy was when I was with Bear. Even though things weren't perfect, they were better.

I looked at my phone. One voice was telling me:

WARNING! MAYDAY! DO NOT GO FORWARD. STOP!!!

The other voice was telling me:

Just do it. You have nothing to lose at this point.

I put in the number (*Would I ever forget it??*)

My fingers started to type and I didn't stop them:

I still love you.

My thumb was dangling over send. I took a drag. I looked back at the moon. And I hit send. The next morning, I woke up to the sunlight coming through my window, slowly over my legs and finally onto my face. I thought about how I really needed to get some better curtains.

I reached for my phone. 1 New Text Message. HOLY SHIT!

I still love you.

To which he replied... (drum roll)

Please don't text me. My new girlfriend doesn't appreciate it.

I slammed my phone down. Put my pillow over my head. FACKKKKKKKKKKKKKKKKKK. Time to plan another trip. To anywhere but here.

The beautiful hills of Zell Am See, Austria | May 2007

5

CHICAGO: POLYESTER BRIDE

(weddings)

Being proper and sweet and nice and pleasing is a fucking
nightmare. It's exhausting. As women, we get the message about
how to be a good girl – how to be a good, pretty girl – from such an
early age. Then, at the same time, we're told that well-behaved girls
won't change the world or ever make a splash.
So it's sort of like, well, what the fuck am I supposed to be?
I'm supposed to be a really polite revolutionary?

-Phoebe Waller-Bridge

Throughout my twenties, everyone told me I was "living the dream."
And by that, they meant the American dream, not my dream. I was
"happy," mostly in an alcohol-induced kinda way. I kept telling
myself: *You should be HAPPIER!* But I was, in fact, increasingly not
that happy. At all.

In my culture, there were certain expectations for how I should live
and who I should be, laid out neatly in a straight line:

School > Job > Marriage > Kids > Suburbs > Kids Leave > Retire >
Travel > Die

To me, this timeline felt...colonial and outdated. I decided I liked
the Travel part, so I'd like to do that well before Death, if possible.
Travel felt like an option for me because I'd spent my childhood
reading about Laura Ingalls Wilder and playing Oregon Trail—and I
wanted to be a pioneer too, only without dysentery and with a
window seat.

But the rules didn't align with that vision, especially where I was from. I was raised in Palatine, Illinois, a suburb of Chicago. Our town was made famous in the early '90s for the Brown's Chicken Massacre (my grandfather went through the drive-thru right before it happened). Outside of the occasional murder, it was a very safe place to grow up.

In the nineties, there were many spoken (and unspoken) rules— a.k.a. the social norms—that told us how we needed to behave in order to "fit in." Slowly but surely, I saw how each rule didn't really match up with...reality?

The Rules I Learned vs. The Truth

We compete against one another to see who is the best.
Truth: Everyone deserves the best.

Diversity is dangerous and scary.
Truth: Diversity is natural. Racism and prejudice are scary and dangerous.

God is a Man, and He is judging you. Always.
Truth: God is personal and universal, male and female and loves everyone.

Wear your uniform. Don't look different.
Truth: Wear whatever you want. Express yourself.

Success means making lots of money and buying nice things. The more money you make, the more respect you deserve.
Truth: Success is whatever fills your heart up the most. It's defined by you. The more money you make, the more you have to give. Money is a tool, not an end.

Boys are strong and tough and don't cry. Girls are quiet and pretty and take care of everyone.
Truth: All humans are strong and tough and cry and have a voice and are beautiful and need to take care of themselves and one another.

Choose one thing to be when you grow up.
Truth: You can and will be many things when you grow up. It's okay to be all of them.

Sex is bad for women, except inside a marriage. If a woman is overtly sexual, she's a whore.
Truth: Sex is a natural part of being human, the highest form of love and creation. Share it wisely.

Getting married is the next step after college—and it's only for a man and a woman.
Truth: Marriage holds many attachments outside of love—mostly financial. A committed partnership between two equals is between anyone who loves each other enough to build a life together. Sometimes people choose to get married too.

Divorce means everyone in the family is going straight to hell.
Truth: Divorce happens because people change. Some relationships aren't meant for a lifetime.

Being gay doesn't really happen here, but maybe in other places.
Truth: People can share their bodies with whomever they want in the spirit of love. There is no right or wrong way.

Be grateful for what you have. It can go away in an instant.
Truth: Everything is temporary—it is all a gift. There is enough for everyone.

If you disagree with authority, punishment awaits. Or you'll be shunned.
Truth: If you disagree with authority, you're thinking beyond the status quo. Hallelujah!

People are born with bad things called sins inside them. People should feel guilty for sins and ask for forgiveness.
Truth: People are born deserving and worthy. There's nothing for anyone to prove.

Death is sad and scary.
Truth: Death is a natural and sacred part of life.

We live in the best country. We are the best at everything.
Truth: There are hundreds of countries in the world. Each is different and each has value.

Luckily, there were three rules I learned that didn't need to be revised:

Treat yourself and others with kindness and love.

Faith, hope, and love are the most important things in life.

Respect your elders. And everyone.

But it's the little things, the seemingly meaningless nuances that added up to create a set of rules which fed a system that favored those in privilege and repressed those that weren't. *Boom!*

Being born into this world on the all-white end of things, it was (sadly) a challenge to even be *aware* that privilege existed. Because when I was surrounded by everyone else who was just like me too, I didn't even know what was out there beyond my bubble. It wasn't until I got my first whiff of the stank of racism and greed that I even realized that something was very wrong with the way things were structured. This happened when my sweet little sister Emmy had her first crush. I was in 8th grade when she was in 1st grade, so I used to pop into her classroom during lunch (or whenever I felt like it, which was often) to see how she was doing and be the helicopter sister-mom I was born to be.

There were two things I could not bring up with her because I knew they'd make her upset:

1. The book that had a painting of a guy with a top hat on and an apple in front of his face—it used to terrify her.
2. Her first crush, Jamal. She was made fun of so much for having a crush on him that she was permanently scarred.

It turns out my sister had a thing for snooping through her older sibling's rooms. One day she found a list from our brother's girlfriend Martha (potentially a direct descendant of Martha Washington, given her tendency towards blatant racism).

It was a list of all the things she loved about our brother (cute). And one of the things on that list was: For making fun of your sister for having a crush on Jamal...because he's black (*what the actual FUCK, Martha?!?*). My poor, sweet innocent sister was horrified when she read that. She ran downstairs and cried her little eyes out to our mom, trying to understand why any human would write that???

My brother and I did make fun of our sister for everything. When she upgraded from Happy Meals to Quarter Pounders before we did, we let her hear about it for the next twenty years. When she kissed a little boy in her Barbie car as a toddler, we tried to film it with our dad's old-school video camera. So, when she had a crush we had any knowledge of, we used it against her, mercilessly. That's how siblings show their love for each other, through endless torture. But Martha didn't know that and because she was, um, very racist, she completely misinterpreted the root of our mocking.

Emmy's early love affair with Jamal fizzled, mostly because it never really heated up—they were seven. And any hopes of rekindling as they aged died too because he was kicked out of our Catholic school. The other parents kept calling to complain about him. And by 3rd grade, Jamal was gone. He was expelled because he "threatened someone with a sharpened pencil"—a storyline that reeks of...discrimination based on skin color. That's the sick and sad truth.

Even though the general rules of the community had an overtone of prejudice, thankfully, they had an underlying depth of love and acceptance in my family. And luckily, my parents taught me that all people were equal, no matter what they look like.

But I still didn't even know what "civil rights" were until I was like 13—and that's only because I got to take a "college" class at Northwestern University on the weekends (I was a closet genius). All the other kids were ridiculously smart and I felt incredibly inferior. For our first lesson, the teacher put on Marvin Gaye's *What's Going On*—and I remember thinking:

Huh. He's really on to something here...

Basically, my growing up experience had a very noticeable lack of color. And when you live in a world where everyone is basically the same and there is a certain way we do things 'round here, then inevitably, like osmosis, the rules of that place creep into your being and everyone becomes expected to follow them.

In reality, once I was over the age of 18, I felt duped by the world I was raised in. When I finally got out into the real, diverse world, I was so pissed off. *You mean to tell me that all these people don't have equal rights?!? What the fuck is this, adult preschool? Why don't adults know how to share and be nice to each other!?!?!?!?*

In my own (very privileged) adult life, I tried to just focus on "fitting in" at work for a while, ignoring my urge to travel and think for myself. The ad agency felt like a grown-up version of high school, except everyone was (mostly) nice to each other.

In between meetings and emails, we'd prank each other ruthlessly by stealing each other's office supplies or leaving voicemails that the gym membership you tried to cancel just auto-renewed. Being in the office was fun and the people were amazing, it was just the actual work part and being trapped in a cubicle that I didn't like.

I thought grad school might be the answer. A PhD in Counseling seemed legit and like a shiny accessory for my name. I did my research and took the GRE. There was just one last step before my grad school journey began: an interview with a professor.

I walked into his office and knew right away how this interview was going to go.

We didn't make eye contact, mainly because he was too busy pedaling on his office chair that was actually a recumbent bike. Which is cool and very wellness-oriented, unless you're a total dick. The chair must have been on a high setting because he was really putting his back into it (the opposite of what you're supposed to do on a seated bike). It took everything inside me not to react. He didn't smile, so I didn't either.

What makes you think you're qualified to be a counselor?

Well, I've always had an interest in mental health and I'm a very empathetic person.

(curtly) *Well, that doesn't mean you'll be a great counselor.*

I wasn't finished, sir. I feel that working one-on-one with people to alleviate their suffering will have a positive impact on this world. And I have experience with mental health issues...

(speaking over my voice) *Oh. So what does that mean? Do you have mental health issues?*

I've experienced situational anxiety and depression, but I also believe that's part of being a human. And carries an unnecessary stigma with it (awkward laugh). Like most mental "illnesses" (yes, I used air quotes). I know how hard it can be to find the right treatment and support. Which is why I'd really like to be able to help...

(in the middle of my sentence, again) *So do you feel mentally stable enough to help others?* (increases pedal speed)

Yes, absolutely. I'm really passionate about this work and know I'd be...

(staring fondly at the pedals) *I don't think you're aware of what this profession entails.*

I'm not sure what gave you that impression, SIR. But it seems I can't really finish...

(takes a delicate sip of water while still pedaling) *I don't think counseling is the best fit for you.*

Needless to say, when I walked out of his office, I did not want to become a counselor anymore. He did me a solid favor, because I clearly wasn't meant to be a therapist if all it took was one guy on a chair bike to throw me off course. Back to the drawing board.

Back at the office, I went into this older (quite attractive) producer's office one day—and he had a map on his wall with pins in all the places he'd been. I thought that was so fucking cool and he encouraged me to travel, while I could. *Noted.*

My co-worker Ina also encouraged me to get out there. To see the world. And she was the first Black woman who talked openly to me about being white and what that meant. One thing she explained to me really stuck out. She said: *You are literally as white as they come*— and it was a message I (really) needed to hear. She opened me up to the possibility that maybe the life I'd been living was skewed in my favor because of the color of my skin—and it was something I would never unsee after she shone a light on it for me.

When I decided to switch ad agencies, I wrote Ina a thank you and she wrote me this card:

Dear Caitlin,
You are the one that has continually inspired me. You have given me a world vision again. I know that you are someone incredibly special. I hope you realize that about yourself. You are SO WONDERFUL and I am so glad you've sprouted your wings and are going to put them to good use. Please follow your heart and your passions. This world needs you to live your Purpose...I love you lots chica and hope and pray for greatness to constantly surround you.

Love love,
Ina

Her words were like a boost of happiness in my heart—and meant so much to me. Sometimes, all it takes is a person in your life to see you, like really see you, and give you words of encouragement.

Yet even after making a switch to a new agency, within a year, slowly but surely, it felt like my soul was being sucked from my body in my cubicle again. Don't get me wrong, the perks were wonderful. I had a salary, paid time off, and free LaCroix. But the work itself was monotonous and pretty blah. It was definitely not what I wanted to do forever. I was starting to hate waking up every day and going to my job (like much of America).

Here's a little secret no one really tells you: it doesn't really matter what you major in or what your GPA is (unless you want to work in medicine or law). What matters most in the corporate world is who you know (and your willingness to sacrifice your personal life). What matters most in your actual life is your passion and your gifts, which are already inside you (and often not easily defined on a resume).

When I looked around and saw where my future was heading, it wasn't really somewhere I wanted to end up. Waiting for client approval until 4am and working every weekend. Never leaving the office and missing time with my hypothetical future family. It didn't seem worth it. I'd rather make less money and be a waitress again— and not be chained to a cube.

As the months went on, my quarter-life crisis was brewing, but it really kicked off with my next break-up. Technically, it was break-up number like 17 with this particular dude. I stayed on the merry-go-round that was that relationship because I didn't want to be alone.

I'd known Preston since we were teens (he was one of the "friends" who egged my car, ironically!) and when our mutual friends started getting married, we started "dating." We talked all day long and hung out every night, but I wasn't his "girlfriend." *Okay, sure buddy.*

He expected me to be able to do certain things, like to cook for him and pick up after him, and even when I tried, I could never do it to the level he required. Like when I tried to make bacon and burnt the shit out of it and his feedback was: *I like it crispy, but not like that* (followed by maniacal laughter).

At the same time, he also intermittently respected my creativity, even if it was only fleeting. My main reasoning for why we were together was because he also liked indie movies and concerts. *Great call.*

When he went to Asia on a business trip for a few weeks, he cut off all contact with me because of his "phone bill" and his need to "focus." I felt like one of those astronaut girlfriends, awaiting the first sign of contact from space. Except it was the 21st century and WiFi was definitely available internationally.

When he finally landed back in our stratosphere near L.A. for a layover, I felt relieved. I thought: *Now, he's in the States, the trip is over, we can finally talk. Hallelujah!*

But, instead, I got one text:

Hey, going out to dinner with Juliana. Will call tomorrow. Sleep well!

My slow simmer of rage was now at a full boil. After weeks of waiting and putting my needs for VERY BASIC communication aside, this was what I got?! No way, not today.

I sent a break-up text response and cried in bed for three days, mostly because I was mad at myself. On the fourth day, I rose again, in fulfillment of my own destiny, and went to my work holiday party, which wasn't dinky. It was at a five-star hotel in downtown Chicago. Fancy as fuck.

I proceeded to get a little overserved, smoked a joint with some co-workers on a balcony, and then scanned the room. And cha-ching, I found a match. He was a Peruvian guy with flawless skin and big brown eyes. He had a boyish charm (sounds creepy, but was enchanting) and we had been in a few meetings together.

We hung out for a few weeks after that. He was like this cuddly teddy bear who reminded me that guys can be sweet and kind too. I also spent most of our time together quizzing him about Peru, which I'm sure was odd to him.

On our first official date, he wanted to take me to a Peruvian restaurant on a Sunday. I was so stressed out because I despised formal dates, but I wanted to come across as carefree and, like, totally up for a Sunday evening dinner date. I made Pari coach me beforehand. We sat on our balcony (we were living together at the time) and had multiple drinks, enough where I felt my nerves melt away a bit. Pari was a fixture throughout most of my dating life, always there to talk to me or help me self-medicate, when needed. I left her to go on my date—and sobered up enough by dinner to remember all the things he was telling me about his mother country.

Things faded between us and by that, I mean a new girl started at the office and he clearly had a crush on her. Even I could admit that they were adorable together. I wanted to be mad when they hit it off, but I genuinely felt happy for them.

While all this was happening, of course, Preston suddenly decided this would be the best time to tell me that he loved me. Interesting timing. So, I did what I always did when strong emotions came up, I ran away and stopped talking to him.

In the midst of my twenties, I found myself...single. For the first time since basically grade school. Ironically, my friends were all sprinting in the opposite direction to the nearest David's Bridal. The women's lib movement had come so far, and yet, it seemed to still be catching on in Chicago. It was like after twenty-five, this internal switch went off, letting everyone know it was now time to wed. My switch must have been faulty because it didn't go off.

As my friends started dropping like (wedding-themed) dominoes, I was becoming more and more single. The majority of my time, I was alone and trying to figure out what I wanted from life. Really getting deep into my quarter-life crisis.

If you are a woman and you've been single for more than a few months in your mid-to-late 20s in the Midwest, people transition from asking:

So, who are you dating? (wink, wink)

to

So, how are you.....doing? (confused look)

It's as if they've reached a glitch in the matrix, encountering a strange species yet to be observed in this area. Spotted: North American female, seems uninterested in following the pack and settling down with a long-term mate. Has "dreams" and prefers to be alone at this time. Very odd. Must observe further.

I'll never forget the day I was talking to a guy in my social circle and he said:

Well, no one wants to marry the wild girl.

Like I had to learn how to sit and roll over in order to be lucky enough to get married at twenty-five, which I knew was very, very young. I was surrounded by guys who were searching for a trophy, not a partner. *Yuck!*

Here's some other truths about that time in my life: I was not very healthy. I drank and smoked way too much. Like a pack of cigs a day and when the doctor asked, over 10 drinks a week. My life was on the same cycle: Work. Party. Repeat. I kept thinking: *Is this what adult life is? Every single day? This can't be it...*

I wanted my life to be full in other ways. I wanted to travel and see the world. India gave me a taste of that. And as far as marriage, I was starting to realize that...it's not the only option. I knew lots of people who were getting married that were far from happy. And I knew I would never do it for the wrong reasons.

Yet, I found myself not only attending, but being in wedding after wedding after wedding. The lowest moment was when my (slightly neurotic) BFF from high school got married and I was her maid of honor. On the big day, my other best friend at the time, Corona (the beer), helped me survive. Things were tense and not fun at all. I snuck out for one tiny cigarette in the 8 hours we were trapped in her house and I got a full-on death glare upon return (probably because she wanted one too). The big moment was when she was putting on her dress. She wanted close-up shots with her maid of honor (me) snapping up the last buttons.

Except this maid of honor had finished a six-pack and needed to run to the bathroom as the photographer was preparing the lighting— but no one had put up a sign that this particular toilet was broken. As two inches of water filled the floor, I opened her family's linen closet and used every last towel to soak up the water. Another bridesmaid came looking for me and by some good fortune, knew how to get the water to stop running. We threw all the wet towels in the bathtub for the bride's family to find later because I didn't know what else to do, I had buttons to close!!

I missed the dress buttoning pictures and the bride simply said: *Don't worry, Mallory stood in for you*...as she slowly turned her back to me. And that's when I knew I really needed to take a break from wedding duty and probably needed to find better friends.

After being a forever bridesmaid, never the bride—and my own faulty attempts to be in a loving relationship—it started to feel like there was a pea under my mattress, but I wasn't a princess in search of a prince.

Metaphorically speaking, I felt very uncomfortable in what was supposed to be a cozy life. I lived a privileged life, but it didn't always feel that way to me. It felt like I was sleeping on something. Like I couldn't fully rest because there was something rubbing against me. There was a voice in my head filled with all the shoulds from everyone:

I should be happy. I should just find a nice guy, let him put a big, fat diamond ring on it, and live that cozy life in the suburbs, with the facade of safety and predictability wrapped around me like a warm blanket. I should just take my college degree and find the highest-paying job and white knuckle my way through it. I should just be HAPPY with what I have.

It felt like I was drowning in a sea of shoulds. Like everyone was shoulding all over me.

And when I asked other people about the things that actually made me happy, like traveling somewhere exotic and starting to write more, most of them told me why I should be focused on getting married instead. *I mean, what else was there in life?!?*

And because of this, it always felt like I was doing something wrong. Like I was breaking some rule, just by being who I was. Like there was something wrong with me that I couldn't just sit in a cube and pull a salary and shut the fuck up and marry the nearest investment banker.

I felt guilty—and I wasn't even really sure why. Maybe it was the years of Catholic schooling? Or because I felt like I had all these things that I should just be grateful for—and I felt guilty that I wasn't happy with what I had. I knew I'd been handed all this privilege—and was this really what I was going to do with it?!

But when I tried to just blend in and smile and party a lot, it wasn't really working and I could feel something coming up inside me that I'd been trying to ignore for far too long.

And then, it finally hit me. I came home from work one day and had a major revelation:

Dear Diary,

I have the crazy idea that I want to quit my job and volunteer in Peru for a long period of time. Am I nuts? Is this insane of me? I just have this gut feeling that I should. It's almost creepy. But I feel like I need to think this through a little more.

Reasons I Want To Go to Peru:
I want to help people
Life experience
Live in another country
Nothing holding me back
Good timing - no lease, no boyfriend, all my friends are paired off
Good for me
Learn another language
Get out of my comfort zone

Reasons Why It Might Be Dumb:
Financially
No job when I get back
Miss time with family and friends

So, clearly the good outweighs the bad. I think I'm going to do it!

When I told other people, most were excited and intrigued. Some would praise me for my "adventurous" spirit. *Oh, you're so adventurous.* And there was a little zing that (sometimes) came along with it.

In Illinois, it translated to: "not fulfilling the traditional role of a woman." They might as well have patted me on the head afterward. As if I was wandering hopelessly around the globe, hoping to stumble upon a man who would finally put a ring on it. *Omg, I knew you had to be SOMEWHERE! Thank God I found you, now let's go put this on social media immediately!!*

Or that I was so foolish that I'd shunned the unspoken duty I was born into, of becoming a wife and birthing and owning some goddamn property. It felt like there was a red alarm going off somewhere, telling me I was in violation somehow, of some social code or rule I was breaking.

When I told my grandmothers I was going to Peru by myself, they both said (at least to me):

How wonderful! Go. Do it. You'll do great, kid.

But lots of other people...did not reply that way. They asked questions, like:

What about your 401K?!
Your lease?
Weren't you dating that guy?
Will you even be working??
Aren't you worried about being abducted by a cartel?
Is South America even safe for someone like you?

The answers were: my 401K was coming with me, my lease was up, we had broken up, I'd be working for free, no that's probably from a movie you saw so please read a book, and did you mean for a white person? That's pretty racist.

The truth was:

I didn't really have a choice. The world gave me two options: follow your purpose (out of your comfort zone) OR ignore it and try to be like everyone else in the comfort zone you don't even really like. I chose Option 1. The fact that my choice (maybe) would have a positive impact on others, was just a bonus. The cherry on top.

Still, doubt would start to creep in. Some of the things that floated through my brain were:

-Everyone will think I'm insane. And then I'll spend the rest of my life in an institution, and I won't be able to handle that because I can't handle being confined.

-But I'm also kinda afraid too. It's scary out there and what if something bad happens?

-It's never going to happen. This is just a pipe dream. I smoked way too much pot in high school and now I'm unable to properly discern what's right and wrong for me.

-I'm going to look like a total fucking idiot. I know what people are going to say about me.

-What the fuck am I even thinking?!?! None of this makes sense. I just need to stop with these fantasies, settle down and get my shit together.

-I'm just failing. I'm trying all these things and they're just one failure after the next. I'm just failing my whole way to South America where I will end up lost and alone and most likely on an episode of *Locked Up Abroad*.

All of these things were coming from how I'd chosen to define success. If success came from being liked by others and getting their praise, then yes, I would feel like a total idiot when I dared to step away from that and do my own thing.

What I didn't realize was that I was starting to make decisions from something bigger than my mind. My mind was telling me: Stay here. stay safe. That's scary. But something else was telling me: *I can't tell you why now, but you need to go to Peru and leave everything behind. Just trust me. This is the next right step.*

When I listened to my mind, I felt like: *Ok, everything will be ok and I can stay here.* And that was quickly followed by a wave of misery and feeling stuck and like I was doing nothing with my life and that my soul would continue to seep from my body each day as I rotted away in a cubicle farm.

When I listened to the other voice, my intuition, I felt alive. I felt lit up. I felt excited and thrilled and like I had rocket fuel in my veins that would carry me through, no matter what highs and lows might come my way. It made me feel like I was living. Like I wasn't wasting a second of my precious time.

I flirted with the idea of going to Peru until it became the only option because everything else was like a brick wall I was slamming into. It was the only way forward.

Choosing to listen to this inner wisdom is a courageous act in the modern world. Because it often runs in the direct opposite direction from what we've been taught to do. And that's where it's really hard, exhausting, tiring, fear-filled, and gut-wrenching to follow your heart as much as it is also natural, exhilarating, soul-filling, and enhancing.

All my friends were getting married, but I just couldn't do it at the time. I didn't want a wedding. I wanted real love. I wanted the most beautiful and warm feeling in the world. And in a romantic sense, I just wanted this person that loves me—all of me—my mind, my body and my soul—and who chooses to be with ME. And to me, love is really, really beautiful when it's true and it's real and it's not something you're trying to fake. Love is like the candy of life (and I really love candy)—it's so sweet and it's so fun and it's so amazing and it's so worth finding. And it doesn't always fit into a box and sometimes it stretches beyond the labels and rules we may have been taught and sometimes it involves a wedding and sometimes it doesn't—and it doesn't matter, because it's love.

I knew, deep down inside, that I was meant for something else, something different from the path all my friends at the time were on. That I'd actually be insane to try and get married when I knew it was not what I wanted. That drinking and smoking my life away felt like such a waste of my potential. That I couldn't find love and fulfillment in another person until I was able to find it in myself first.

I'd been taught my whole life that my decisions were basically made for me. But this was the first time I was making a major life choice based on a gut feeling. It was risky, but I was into taking risks. Making decisions based on how they felt...*just felt right.*

Chicago skyline | Sometime in the early 2010s, not really sure, it was all a blur of fun and growing up.

Two

6
MACHU PICCHU: GIRL FROM THE NORTH COUNTRY
(energy)

> Not I, not any one else can travel that road for you,
> You must travel it for yourself.
> -Walt Whitman

A guy I met in a cafe in Cusco was telling me that the energy was different in Machu Picchu. That people came from all over the world just to soak it up.

I was minding my own business, sipping my 19th cup of coca leaf tea (it was becoming a problem). I honestly tried to avoid talking to random men, seeing as I was alone and didn't want to advertise that to many strangers. I shifted my hand so the Claddagh ring on my wedding finger was visible as we talked, a signal I hoped would let him know that I was not "available" (even though I was).

He looked me in the eye when he said:

You know, there's a special energy there, especially right now. 2012 is a very important year and this is a big energy shift, especially in the next few days. You're going to feel some pretty cool things when you go there.

I nodded and thought to myself: *This man has lost his marbles.*

It wasn't until a few days later, when I was sitting there, on a rice terrace in the farming section of Machu Picchu, that I realized he was right. I *did* feel something different.

I was one in a million to visit Machu Picchu in a year and one in a few thousand that was allowed to hike the trail in October 2012. I was also deathly afraid of heights and had never been "trekking."

The Inca Trail began near a town called Ollantaytambo, which in Quechua means "a place to see down." That intimidated me right off the bat.

The trail most turistas climb, with a guide, was used for royal Incan pilgrimages to Machu Picchu back in the day. It was considered a "knowledge path" and there were numerous stops along the way for the Inca pilgrims, and now, for the global tourists.

All these rest stops, which my hiking group and I saw the ruins of, had "showers" which were used not to clean the body, but to clean the soul. This way, the Incas reached Machu Picchu being as clean as possible.

Ironic, because on the modern-day Inca Trail, there were no showers. The endless layers of sunscreen and bug spray mixed with intense cardio for multiple hours a day made our hiking group quite the unclean bunch, actually. But our guides woke us up with a hot chocolate delivery in our tents every morning, something I'm sure the Incan pilgrims did not get to enjoy. Or maybe they did.

I met some really nice New Zealanders who pretty much adopted me into their little trail family for the hike and let me hang with them for the three-day adventure.

This was really nice because I was alone—and had been for the past few months in Peru. I was doing the Inca Trail as the victory lap of my time in South America—and there wasn't a better way I'd want to spend my last few days in this country I'd grown to love: on the Inca Trail, going to a place I'd dreamt about, Machu Picchu.

Day 1

The first day of the Inca Trail was only a slight ascent. It was nice and easy. I'm convinced they arranged it that way because it's the only opportunity to turn back and they don't want to scare anyone off. We hiked for a few hours on mostly flat land from Kilometer 82 to Wayllabamba.

Once we reached camp, there were porters who had already set up our tents and who had carried most of our stuff for us.

We had 16 porters for our group and they ranged in age from 18 to 48. These guys were such hard workers and made the Inca Trail seem like it was nothing as they raced past our group with tons of crap on their backs. The most hilarious (embarrassing) part was they would obviously beat all of us to camp every day. By the time we arrived, they had everything set up and ready. Whenever our group finally strolled in, out of breath and red-faced, they would break into applause for us. It was meant to be encouraging, but one of the New Zealanders joked that they had to be thinking: *Wow, great job finally catching up to us! We've already carried all your shit and done everything for you! Yay!! You are so terrific!*

Day 2

Physically challenging to say the least. We hiked from 9,842 ft. up to 13,779 ft., which was known as Dead Woman's Pass. The name sounded quite welcoming so I was really excited to make it up there.

As we got higher, the air thinned and it was a whole different experience to climb once we passed the treeline. I was very thankful for the New Zealanders and their movie and music games on this day because it was a great distraction.

The physical strain was completely worth it. Every time I remembered to stop staring at the person's feet in front of me and actually look up, it was breathtakingly beautiful. The feeling of accomplishment when I reached the Pass was pretty exhilarating and not one I'd felt too many times before in my limited fitness history.

Day 3

The longest day of the Inca Trail. We hiked for about 9 hours through two more mountain passes, which seemed like nothing compared to Dead Woman's Pass. Also the prettiest day of the trail. The landscape became like a rainforest and it was gorgeous.

After lunch, we visited Phuyupatamarca, which is a temple that overlooks Machu Picchu mountain. It was really exciting to see that peak and know the end goal was just on the other side.

After the temple, the afternoon of Day 3 featured the "Gringo Killer" – a 2,952 ft. descent down Inca steps. I'd like to know how many broken ankles have occurred on those things.

The porters literally sprinted down the stairs. We'd have to yell *"Porter!"* when one was coming and quickly move to the mountainside of the staircase so we didn't get taken out.

My most memorable moment on the trail was near the end of this day. Camp was at Winay Wayna, which meant "Forever Young." There were some Incan terraces about 20 minutes before our campsite where our group decided to take a break. We soaked up the gorgeous scenery while sitting on the ledge of one of the terraces. And then, three llamas approached us. I like animals, but I've heard stories of llamas charging people. When they got to be about three feet away, I blacked out because I don't remember this at all, but I was told that I started screaming: *OH MY GOD, OH MY*

GOD, OH MY GOD, GET THEM AWAY FROM ME! and looked like I was going to jump off the terrace. They stopped and ate some grass and I scooted away, regained consciousness and all was completely fine. I made it through Dead Woman's Pass but almost lost my zen during an encounter with some llamas.

Machu Picchu Day

The last day began bright and early at 3:30 am. Usually if I was awake at that hour, it involved beer and a cute guy in my bed, but things change.

I hung by the New Zealanders as the dark sky drizzled all over us. We had to line up and wait—not exactly the highlight of my life.

Once we got the all-clear to start hiking, the final stretch of the trail proved to be the most treacherous in my humble opinion (as a rookie mountain climber). It's 95% original Incan, which meant it hadn't really been restored at all. Very vintage.

At one point, our guide stopped us and took our trekking poles and said there was a "surprise" for us. When we looked to our left, the Inca stairs had become more of an Incan ladder, which we had to crawl up using our hands and feet. I never moved so fast in my life.

When we arrived at the Sun Gate, it was quite foggy, making the whole scene all the more dramatic. We waited. And just like that, the clouds lifted—and there she was.

Machu Picchu. In all her glory.

The last hour went by in what felt like ten minutes because everyone was so excited to finally arrive after three days of hiking through the Andes and years of anticipation. Reaching Machu Picchu was everything I could have hoped for and more.

It truly was a magical and mystical place. I sat on that farming terrace, overlooking the ancient city buildings and the mountain peaks, and felt totally in awe of the natural beauty.

As I sat by myself for the first time in days, I felt it. The energy of this sacred place that had always been there, since 1450 and before—and that had probably been like a magnet calling in its "discovery" in 1911. It felt more holy than any church I'd been to.

My attraction to Machu Picchu was really about being attracted to something ancient and something sacred. I realized, at that moment, that that part of my life was missing.

I had been raised to be religious, but the feeling of connection to something greater than me had somehow faded into the background. And it's something I clearly wanted. And now, it was presenting itself to me again, almost as if this place was whispering *Remember* right in my ear.

This was just one of many places created long ago, around Peru and around the world, that were built to perfectly align with the stars. I'd spent a day in Qorikancha, the temple at the center of the Inca Empire that the Spaniards built a church right on top of. All the exploring of Incan ruins made me ponder: *What did the ancients know that we don't? What was buried in these places in the name of religion?*

I learned the Incas believed the purpose of life was to celebrate every part of it. It was a heritage based on living with a cosmic awareness. They believed that all human beings are Children of the Sun. Each person is like a unique ray of sunlight. They had three main laws:

The First Inca Law: Munay – Divine Love
Speak the truth and act with love. This will nurture the divine within you. Creation provides all we need to live, like food and clothing. In order to reciprocate, we must care for creation with love and gratitude.

The Second Inca Law: Llancay - Work
Work is the ultimate service to the divine and it is seen as a privilege. It is an opportunity to replicate the divine. To express your unique gift is the best way to serve yourself, your family, and your community.

The Third Inca Law: Yachay – Wisdom
Know who you are. Keep your energy clean. Wisdom is experienced with the heart, not the mind. It allows you to feel connected to everyone and everything.

Most importantly, the Incas believed in *ayni*, reciprocity with nature. For everything you take, you give something back. I realized I'd done a lot of taking from the world, but not much giving. And I actually liked the latter better.

Being in Peru and learning about these ancient people felt like I was getting a crash course in spirituality and reciprocity, in living in communion with the earth—and I felt ready to be baptized as an Inca. And yet, as I looked around at what Peru had become, I saw all this beauty with all this smog on top (literally, from the pollution and fumes and motorcycles).

But at least I could still see the past there. I realized a part of what I'd been looking for was like a calling for roots, wanting to know the history of who I am as a human. It's something I didn't see (or feel) yet back home because 23andme hadn't been invented yet.

In the United States, everything was wiped out and rebuilt. It's not like in South America or in Europe or in Asia where you can see the past mixed in with the present. We can see what was before in the ancient sacred places. At home in the U.S., the past was (mostly) bulldozed. Joni Mitchell said it best: *They paved paradise and put up a parking lot.*

There were pieces of my identity as a North American that were coming to light in South America—and that didn't look so pretty. I made friends from all over the world during my weekend tours in Peru before I went to Machu Picchu.

From the perspective of foreigners, being American wasn't...the best. People from other places saw things in the States a little more clearly than I did. I learned more about being an American from getting outside of my country than living in it.

It wasn't all bad. But I realized how brainwashed I'd been that everyone wanted to be like us, and that no country was better. And I wondered: *Where did I even learn that from?* It's just the American culture—loud, ignorant and proud.

The defining moment for me was at the start of the Inca Trail. Our guide was Quechan, a native Peruvian. We all stood in a circle and introduced ourselves. There were people from New Zealand (my friends!), Germany, England, and other Americans. We had to say our name and where we were from. What happened was my worst nightmare:

Hi, my name is Caitlin and I'm American. I'm from Chicago.

Which America are you from?

(getting nervous) Um, you know, America.

There are two Americas, my dear. Are you from this America or the other one?

(feeling like a total bellend - that's a British word for the tip of a penis) The other America. The north one. I'm from the North America.

Never made that mistake again. And I learned to listen and absorb other cultures. To respect them and to realize that I'm being changed, for the better, by interacting with these new people and these places.

Outside of all this, the ancient ruins and the different people and the Inca empire, the greatest gift I received in Peru was time alone to think. Sitting in a window seat on bus rides through Peru, staring at the mountains and valleys and sun, it felt like a blanket of truth was being wrapped around my being, a truth that I may have been avoiding for some time. The distance allowed me to see my role in this world. To see that I'm here and a part of something so much greater than myself. And it allowed me to dig into my own experience (and my own neuroses).

I'd always internalized all the not-so-pretty experiences from my childhood and thought it meant there was something wrong with me. I thought I was broken and I was so afraid of being judged. And for the first time since, I felt a sense of peace in my heart. I looked out the window on the way back to Cusco from Machu Picchu and I let myself actually cry for once. Because it was all so beautiful and sad, everything, all at once. For the first time, I felt compassion and understanding for...myself?

And after feeling all these deep but necessary feelings, it was a good thing I was leaving Peru because I had been on Inca overload. I thought I might start worshiping the sun and carrying rocks around if I stayed there. (Note: I did start doing both of those things).

80

The whole path to Machu Picchu, also known as the peak of my human experience thus far, was like preparation for arriving—both the actual trail and my life leading up to that moment. Valleys and peaks, ups and downs. And now that I'd arrived, it felt so...heavenly. Mystic. Majestic. All I knew was that it was easy to believe in something greater. There was something ancient, I could feel it in my bones, like my soul knew this place.

The concept of a trail leading to a spiritual site is very common and found in all cultures and religions. The trail is the preparation for the sacred. Walking the ancient Inca Trail opened up a part of me that I had not been in touch with. It made me see that the connection between the human (earth) and the holy (heaven) is closer than we think it is.

The energy I felt in Machu Picchu was really one of connection to something greater than me. Ironically, never in history had humans been as "connected" as we were in 2012, on a global (and probably sexual) level.

When I was born back in the '80's, there was no Wi-Fi and no cell phones that weighed less than a brick. My dad (a digital pioneer) first showed me this new frontier, this thing called the Internet, back when it was still in DOS format, a.k.a. unreadable.

I saw all the little bright green letters flash on the screen, saying things like:

```
C:\ mode
MODE PREPARE
C:\>
C:\>
NERD ALERT
C:\ mode
```

And I thought: *This is confusing and very hard to read. I will never use this.*

Until Prodigy was launched, with a digital Baby-Sitters Club might I add, and I was quickly banned from using it because I sent way too many emails and they each cost one dollar. *Who knew?!* By the time I was a working woman, I made a living by sitting at a laptop, day in and day out—and luckily, computers evolved to using words, instead of only nerd code. What barely existed when I was born became an essential element to my existence.

I'm part of the bridge generation of hyperconnectivity—the one that developed right alongside technology, moving from Prodigy + cordless phones (primary school) to AOL + *69 (junior high) to Instant Messenger + Nokias (high school) to Facebook + Motorola Razrs (college) to Instagram + iPhones (adulting)—a new way to connect and to stalk your crush, with each stage of life.

In this modern age I'd grown up in, things had rapidly changed—and we could learn about the world in real-time from anywhere. I could potentially have a boyfriend in Austria and our relationship would be considered "long-distance," instead of "impossible."

This was the world we lived in. A world where we're connected, all the time. But what I realized in Peru was: *Maybe we aren't as connected as we appear to be?*

Just because I can tweet to someone in Botswana doesn't mean I actually have any idea about the reality of living there. The world was transforming rapidly. From eating habits to borders to technology to health to education, there was hardly anything in life that was not changing, quickly. And as someone who had grown up in the "land of the free," what I started to realize was:

Were we really as free as we'd like to be?

We'd made great leaps of progress as humans and life was infinitely more comfortable (for some). And yet, we'd kinda forgotten to create a place in "modern society" for the most vulnerable among us because we were so busy trying to get ahead.

But if people, hundreds of years ago, learned how to live in union with nature, how to feed and clothe everyone, how to create community, even on a mountain top—then surely we could too?

Machu Picchu told me the answer: *Yes, we can and we must.*

I'm not a scientist, but if I were to break each one of us down into what we're made of, it's all ultimately energy. And when groups of people gather in a place and create things, there's a certain energy that goes into that place. And in nature, there are certain spots, like ancient ruins and Machu Picchu, where the energy is just different.

When we go to new places, we are brought into new energy, some that might feel familiar and some we might have even been fearful of—and all that will alter our lives and change the very energy we are each made of.

Each place holds a different kind of energy and when we go there, that energy becomes a part of who we are—and dare I say, can be healing, whether by reflecting light on something we've left in the darkness or by feeding us with more light and opening up new levels of awareness.

Thereby, I am personally convinced, from my own experience, that travel is the key to compassion, enlightenment, healing, and making this world a better place. And even if we might not have the means to travel to remote exotic locations, we can just go somewhere different in our own town or even in our own head.

When we show up in a place we aren't "supposed" to go, we change the place and the place changes us. (Of course, always be safe, duh).

What I felt in Machu Picchu was...love. Working together. Communion. Being a part of a community. Feeling a connection to something we can't explain but can only feel.

There's a theory that Machu Picchu was a royal retreat for an Incan king, but our guide said historians don't really know what it was.

Around eight hundred people lived there and the city was divided into three sections: farming, spiritual, and urban.

Even though the true meaning of Machu Picchu was unknown, there were wonderful guesses as to what occurred there. I liked the belief that it was a place to receive the first light of daybreak, which opens your heart spiritually. *Namaste.*

Our guide pointed out a significant underlying meaning, which I had never thought of:

Machu Picchu, and all the Incan ruins in Peru, were a clear reminder that nothing lasts forever. He said the Incas were fully aware of their downfall—accepted it and may have even predicted it.

And yet, they still worked hard to create this vibrant and beautiful community in the clouds.

The remains of an Incan home at Pisac in the Sacred Valley of Peru | October 2012.

7
AREQUIPA: BACK DOWN SOUTH
(orphanage)

Produce your own dream.
If you want to save Peru, go save Peru.
It's quite possible to do anything, but not if you put it on the leaders
and the parking meters. Don't expect Carter or Reagan or John
Lennon or Yoko Ono or Bob Dylan or Jesus Christ to come and do it
for you. You have to do it yourself.

-John Lennon

To say I "stuck out" when I first arrived in South America would be an extreme understatement. I felt like a glowing white flashlight as I walked down the street. Like there was a stage light following me everywhere I went.

Being in Peru was like stepping back in time. To get my hair dyed, they used one of those plastic caps my grandma used back in the day. It's like this in many places around the world, I guess. You go there and it's not just like traveling to a new place, but also, to a different stage of human "development."

When I landed in Lima, it was what I expected: congested and overcrowded and a lot going on at all times. I didn't feel unsafe but I didn't feel totally comfy there either.

I went to a park in the middle of the city that was really pretty and well-maintained. Like a nice little section of solitude amongst all the craziness. There were stray cats everywhere. They looked cute but if one came near me, I knew I would scream—and I was trying not to draw any (more) attention to myself.

When I ventured out on my lonesome for the first time that morning, I went to the LarcoMar, a mall on the edge of a cliff overlooking the ocean. I felt this was a prime setting for my first solo adventure in South America seeing as I'm from the U.S. so retail franchises made me feel safe, I guess.

There was a lookout spot above the mall so I attempted to take pictures of the cliffs and ocean and then decided to treat myself to Starbucks, because when in Lima. I was standing in line, thinking:

Geez, I don't even feel like I'm in South America. I can totally do this alone in another country thing.

Literally, the moment these thoughts crossed my mind, the man standing in front of me suddenly turned to his left, slammed his face into the shelves on the wall, and fell onto his back in a full-blown seizure. Luckily, he came to and medical help arrived. I stood there not knowing what to do or say—and decided that maybe I didn't want a hot tea after all....

I slowly walked out of the store and decided to walk a mile through Lima to get to the park with all the stray cats. A black stray cat did walk directly in front of me, but since I was in a new country, I didn't think that omen applied.

After a few days and a wonderful bike tour of the Barranco district, I flew to Arequipa on a Saturday night from Lima. The flight through the Andes was super short. Eduardo the driver was waiting for me with a sign. I could see him from baggage claim because the walls were missing in the airport. He didn't make eye contact with me or say hola. He just grabbed my bag and led me towards his taxi, which was basically a glorified go-cart. *Donde esta el casco?!*

We started driving through the streets of Arequipa and I realized that I had no idea where I was or where we were going, and no working cell phone—so my life was pretty much in Eduardo's hands.

Thankfully, he dropped me off at the volunteer house. I met some of the other volunteers, but I think the altitude and the concept of communal living got to me because I went right to bed.

Arequipa was the second-largest city in Peru and was at like 13,000 ft. elevation, or something crazy like that. The volcano El Misti provided quite the scenic backdrop and there were tons of little cobblestone streets. It reminded me *mucho* of Italy.

The other volunteers were mostly from Great Britain. I loved their accents and weirdly found myself starting to say "Brilliant" a lot within the first 24 hours.

My roommate was one of the Brits, was the same age as me and worked as a teacher. She let me shadow her completely and I felt like her student. She was truly a saint. She took me to the orphanage for a visit on my first day, so I'd know how to get there.

It was about a ten-minute walk up the road, then we got on one of the local *combis* which was really an old van (down by the river—literally) and people crammed in it. They are banned in many places around the world but because of Peru's limited restrictions on imported used vehicles, they were used as a way to provide public transportation (instead of a regular bus). It cost 1 sol to ride (that's about 30 cents). We got off at the La Posta stop, which means little stopping place. That's when I started noticing lots of *banderas rojas...*

Red Flag #1: The overarching theme in my initial conversations with other volunteers was illness. Each of them was either currently sick, just getting over being sick, or fearful of getting sick again. In such tight living quarters, it was not shocking that germs spread fast. It was even less surprising once I visited the orphanage. The volunteers swapped sickness stories as if they were badges of honor. I was not really looking for any badges.

Red Flag #2: The orphanage was really a three-bedroom apartment with 19 children living in it. Nineteen!! In the words of my dad, there was crap everywhere.

The main room was for the babies. There was a bunk bed (used as a changing table), a crib, and a bassinet on the floor. I noticed there was no garbage can. I thought: *But where do all the dirty diapers go?* How incredibly naive.

The first bedroom was for the older kids, jammed full of beds and clothes. At least eight kids slept in this room, sharing beds and mats on the floor.

The two other bedrooms were for the toddlers (monsters) and for the babies with disabilities. There was one bathroom for the children with only a shower and a toilet (no bathtub or door). The bathroom appeared to not have been cleaned since it was built.

Basically, the sanitary conditions were absolutely appalling. I saw a *Tia* wet a onesie with water and use it as a wipe for a baby with a very dirty diaper and then toss said onesie in a hamper. Ten minutes later, she returned to the hamper and started pulling out items she believed to still be clean. I gagged.

Red Flag #3 (a.k.a. the GRANDE red flag): On my first official day of volunteering, all volunteers were banned from the orphanage for two weeks because four children were diagnosed with Hepatitis A, as well as the numerous other viruses which were being passed around, like rotavirus. The oldest child in the home, who was 9 years old, was hospitalized because his symptoms were so bad.

Considering I was not even one week into being there, I hightailed it out of the volunteer house and stayed at my backup location. It was a good thing I was such a neurotic planner and hypochondriac.

This was not the grand start of my volunteering adventure that I was looking for. It was sad and I felt helpless so I did what I always do and I made a plan. I was going to DO SOMETHING to change this situation—and what a miracle that I was there to do it!

Even if I had to go in full-jumpsuit style (like the end of *E.T.*), I wanted to know that positive change was made after this outbreak. I was given a glimpse of life for children with no parents in Peru. And I was ready to help, I just wasn't sure how to do that exactly.

It was scary when I thought about where I was. Alone, unable to volunteer and potentially sick after only six hours of volunteering. But I knew I'd rather be there, really living and experiencing the world than feeling like a robot back home.

I had to do something with myself so I went to the Santa Catalina monastery. A bunch of cloistered nuns lived there for hundreds of years. I weirdly felt like a cloistered nun myself since I refused to leave my room once the sun had set (for safety reasons, I'm not a vampire).

The buildings on the monastery compound were really old and brightly colored. Beautiful place, but it gave me the creeps. I got this vibe of repression—very hard core repression—which wasn't shocking considering a bunch of nuns and priests had lived there. Many took a vow of silence. So a lot of things *were* repressed, like for one, their voices.

One thing I found fascinating were these tiny little confessionals they had. What does a cloistered nun possibly have to confess?

It was interesting to me that someone would choose to leave their family and seclude themselves from the world, for religious purposes.

In a weird way, I felt like my trip was the antithesis of the cloister nuns' world, but usually extreme opposites have way more in common than they'd ever like to admit. I chose to leave my loved ones and seclude myself from the world I'm used to—but in order to go out and see a different part of the world.

The surrounding landscape around the monastery was very scenic. I climbed up to the roof in a few places and I got some great views of the local volcano, El Misti.

Arequipa was really beautiful. I loved just sitting on a bench in the Plaza des Armas. But I had a hard time letting myself truly enjoy it because I couldn't stop thinking about the kids.

One thing I realized during my deep thoughts on the Arequipian bench was that the world was both large and different and small and similar at the same time. It's a weird phenomenon. I felt so far from home and like I was on another planet yet there were so many things that were making me feel connected and at home too. Quite bizarre.

After a week, we were finally let back into the orphanage.

As a female volunteer, I was responsible for the babies. There were nine babies, with six having special needs, and two volunteers per shift. We spent our time changing them, feeding them, consoling them, getting them to sleep, playing with them. Two volunteers for nine babies meant at least one baby was always crying. It was like a game of whack-a-mole that no one could ever win.

The babies were dressed in so many layers of clothing and the windows were not allowed to be opened. The *Tias* (local women who worked there) were fearful that the babies would get *enferma*, so they insisted on keeping them very warm at all times. The babies were sweating and urinating through their clothes and bed sheets constantly. And the smell was definitely not healthy for any human to breathe in, all day and night.

The older children played on the roof during the day with the male volunteers. There were toys, but no games or activities for them. They didn't leave the orphanage, except for once a month. The highlight of the children's week was when the garbage man came because his truck played music, similar to the ice cream truck in the States.

The kids were fed all fresh food—fruits and dishes made by the *Tias*. I never saw one kid drink any water. The babies and children were all coughing and sneezing non-stop. Many of the children couldn't walk correctly and would trip frequently.

I spent about 4 hours a day on cleaning each room in the house – scrubbing down every wall, crib, floor and surface I could get my hands on. It was humbling, yet totally satisfying. I was able to clean every room but the bathroom, which I was actually okay with. The kids who were sick were looking and feeling better too.

In between my volunteer shifts, I'd try to explore and see the sites in and around Arequipa. It was a welcome distraction from the sad parts of spending so much time in an orphanage.

I went to the Museo Sanctuary to see Juanita, a frozen Inca girl who was found on the top of a mountain. She was a human sacrifice.

The Incas believed the mountains were gods—and they kept a relationship of reciprocity with them. By offering sacrifices of children to the spirits, the mountains would treat them well back.

One interesting thing was that I got to see these pins that Juanita used on her clothing. And there were other, smaller versions in another display case. Apparently they signified social status - the larger your pin, the "higher up" in society you were. It's crazy to me that even back then, social status was important. We've evolved in a lot of ways and become more "civilized"—but we're still hung up on being bigger and better than others. *See, my pin is bigger than yours!*

I went to Colca Canyon, one of the deepest canyons in the world—and I climbed in and out of it. It was gorgeous and so beautiful, but that canyon made me face two of my demons: fear of heights and pushing myself physically.

I spent three days hiking on paths I would normally only have nightmares about. It was a huge feeling of accomplishment to get up and out of that canyon, alive.

I really was only able to do it because of my friend Alastair. He was another Brit who stayed with me when I was struggling. On the last day, we woke up at the bottom of the canyon at 3am and by 11am, we were at the top. Literally went straight up and out. I seriously doubted my ability, but Alastair stayed by me, even though he could have run up the canyon by himself. It was extremely kind.

Mentally, I was in a kind of transitional place. I felt really far removed from my life back home. Yet little things could still bother me. I guess distance gave me a bigger perspective. And I could see a lot of things more clearly—which caused some pain, but it was really just growing pains.

I was able to jet over to Lake Titicaca too. And by jet, I mean take a local Peruvian bus (not one for tourists) – which was not a highlight. On the overnight ride to the lake, I was lucky enough to get a seat next to a broken window. Sleeping on a bus with the cool mountain air howling in your face is quite soothing. I think my seat was on a jet stream.

On the way back I was even more fortunate because this time my seat was conveniently located on top of a heat vent! While my organs slowly roasted, there was a salesman who stood in the aisle and presented a lengthy pitch for an Inca-inspired herbal weight loss supplement. If I never get on a bus in South America again, I will have lived a good life.

Lake Titicaca is the largest lake in South America and is located on the border of Peru and Bolivia. At 12,507 ft. elevation, it is considered the highest "navigable" lake in the world. It is also the "Birthplace of the Incas" and the "Birthplace of the Sun." There's 41 islands in the lake.

About twenty minutes offshore, there are a bunch of man-made, floating reed islands. It's crazy that people created these and actually live on them. They were first created by the Quechan people (Peruvian natives) when the Incas started expanding their empire. These Quechans weren't really interested in bonding with the Incas when they showed up at Lake Titicaca so they took some reeds and made islands to live on.

Each island has a watchtower to look out for Incas, pirates, etc. There was no electricity because that would obviously be a huge fire hazard. The residents of the floating islands now mainly survive off the income they receive from curious "Westerners" like myself.

I was able to do a homestay with a family on the Amantani island. My mom-for-a-night was so sweet and really made me feel at home.

94

She spoke only Quechan so there was a bit of a language barrier but we smiled at each other a lot. She made three meals for me and my friend Mia, which were all super tasty. Mia was another Brit who had a big crush on Alastair and asked me lots of questions about him during our stay.

There were no cars on the island and no grocery stores – so everything we ate was from veggies our house mom grew herself. We shared a room with electricity that we paid extra for (which meant a single light bulb with about a 20-watt voltage) in a dirt hut.

Since there was no light pollution, the stars were unreal. The most beautiful stars I've ever seen. I wanted to stay up late and just stargaze, but our island Mom was pretty strict about bedtime.

The society on the islands of Lake Titicaca were based on one basic principle:

Ama sua, ama llulla, ama ghilla which means "Do not steal, do not lie, do not be lazy."

I really liked the simplicity. Short, sweet, to the point.

The islanders also had an interesting take on marriage. First of all, the islands get together for three different celebrations a year and these are the only times you can meet a potential suitor. This really takes the pressure off for the rest of the year.

When you decide you want to marry someone, you first have to live together for three years. If it goes well, you tie the knot. If not, adios. Personally, I thought this built-in trial run was brilliant!

Finally, there was only one day on which you can get married a year. So everyone whose getting married does so on the same day and celebrates together. This really drives down costs and embraces a "the more, the merrier" attitude. Big fan of this concept.

Also, if you had any problems with anyone else in the community, you'd just meet in the town square on Sunday. I really loved this because it forces people to be real and deal with their issues— something I'd been notoriously horrible with. Also, the hot chocolate was the best I've ever had in my life. Heaven in a mug.

The neighboring island of Taquile was famous for having men who knit. I even saw two men knitting away in the main plaza. Women made the yarn and the Taquilen men used that yarn to knit. I loved the fluid gender roles. *Looks like you need an extra purl, Bob.*

I saw a pack of boys going around and singing songs and asking tourists for "money, money please." I couldn't say no so I gave them each 1 sol (Peruvian dollar). Little did I know what a riot this would cause. They became quite rambunctious and gathered more of their friends and kept pointing me out. A local store owner then clued me in that under no circumstances whatsoever was I supposed to give the local children any money ever. *Lo siento, pero no lo siento.*

The islands of Lake Titicaca embraced the simple life. They lived off the land and had a very close-knit community. They didn't have smartphones. A lot of the "stressors" I was used to back in the States (traffic, deadlines, weak WiFi signal, cable bills, etc.) simply didn't exist there. But they also didn't have many of the comforts (running water, a non-hut bathroom, dishwashers, delivery food, etc.) which I'd taken for granted my whole life. As my grandma always said: *It's not better or worse, just different.*

When I got back to Arequipa, I was trying really hard to look at the bright side of things. It's not hard to do that considering it was sunny and clear skies every single day there.

I knew that working in an orphanage in South America would be challenging. But I never thought my presence would be rejected. I'd done many stupid and rebellious things in my life, but getting kicked out of an orphanage was not one I'd planned on.

Karla was the boss of the orphanage—and she did not take a liking to me. When I deep cleaned, she entered the bedroom I was in and changed a baby's diaper. She threw the unsealed diaper in the middle of the floor I just mopped and said:

You are too slow with this cleaning.

Things can get lost in translation, so I interpreted that as:

It looks really clean in here, this cleaning will be good for the children.

I did not go to Peru on a quest for a new best friend, so I bit my tongue and put my cleaning supplies away when she asked. But I watched as the orphanage slowly slid back to the state it was in when I first got there. And one morning, she finally had enough of my ambition for cleanliness.

Around 7am, I was in the little babies' room with 4-month-old twins and a 9-month-old baby boy. I could tell Karla had been watching them prior because the room was noticeably stinkier so I opened the windows and went hunting for the culprit(s).

All three babies had dried diarrhea in their diapers, which meant they'd been sitting in them for hours. I changed them and then noticed a dirty diaper on the ground. I then found a few more, one of which had leaked onto the floor. I cleaned it all up—*SO asqueroso!!!*

Enter Karla. She slammed the windows shut and started moving the babies into the back room. She told me she'd asked me numerous times not to clean and I'm just not listening and this is the final straw. I tried to explain the situation, that she'd left babies in an unventilated room full of feces, but as I was talking, she slammed the back bedroom door, screamed *GET OUT!*—and never spoke to me again.

I couldn't believe this woman was putting her own personal issues with me over the best interest of the kids. Admittedly, I became a bit neurotic with the cleaning supplies. I did want to be the hero volunteer who magically eliminated all germs. I couldn't fathom that anyone would resist cleanliness, no matter where you're from.

What it really boiled down to was a complacency with the way things were, regardless of how bad the current state actually was. Like trying to move a pig out of her sty. She liked it and didn't mind the smell so who was I to make her change?!

It truly broke my heart to see how these kids had to live. They were so helpless and were just stuck there. And this was not the only place in the world where this was happening. It wasn't right. There had to be a better way to care for our babies in need.

What I witnessed was that humans can survive and adapt to almost anything. It's pretty amazing. I saw toddlers eating out of dustpans and some of the grossest living conditions I've ever witnessed. But everyone there just adapted to it because they had no other choice.

And of course, these kids needed better resources to live a healthier life. But they still laughed and smiled, which was seriously the most beautiful thing I'd ever seen, mixed in with the ugliest environment I'd ever seen.

I had so many special moments with those babies. They'd smile and stare at me. They would cling to me for dear life or do something adorable or new for the first time. Every moment I spent with them was seriously a gift. I'd feel so many emotions as I watched them, knowing they'd grow up in this world, possibly without ever having a parent. I felt like I used to doubt my ability to be a mother, but I realized I could do it. If I can watch nine babies at once, I could handle one (at a time).

Mostly, the orphanage made me deeply appreciate all the material comforts I had growing up. I'd taken much of it for granted, as if I was entitled to access to Nickelodeon and Fruit Roll-Ups on demand.

After getting fired from the orphanage, my thank you gift was a mutant stomach virus which really got me the closest I will ever come to having abs. It was very hard to be alone when I didn't feel well. All I wanted was someone to bring me water or to find a helicopter to rescue me from my hotel room. I had a full-on pity party for myself as I chugged Pepto Bismol for five days. But I realized that, actually, there were definitely worse things that could happen. Like feeling so sick, but being a kid living in an orphanage, with only strangers to look after you.

There's no magical way to fix things. All I could do was my best. The problems of the world may seem overwhelming at times, but step by step, and little by little, positive change can happen. Viruses do pass. And kids do grow up. Even when it seems impossible.

And amongst all the things that hurt my heart, there was so much light and beauty there too. Every smile, every laugh, every squeeze on my fingers made it worth it, just to let those kids know they were loved, even if I could only do it for a little while.

Mostly what I learned in Arequipa was the power behind the kindness of strangers, more so in receiving than in giving. I went there with such high (and naive) hopes of saving the world. I was going to work in an orphanage and be like a modern-day Mother Teresa and just save some children and feel so fulfilled and life would be grand.

But then I got there and realized there was not a damn thing I could really do once those kids were sick. But that didn't stop me. I got money from back home and went to local markets and haggled and bought a shit ton of cleaning supplies and then went in like a one-woman Haz-Mat team and fucking scrubbed that orphanage from top to bottom. And it just kept getting dirtier and dirtier. And I was in this place, trying to "do good"—and there was nothing I could do. I couldn't change it, even when I kept trying and trying and trying.

And I sat on a bench in the Plaza one day, alone, really just feeling down about life in the midst of all this. I missed my friends and family and my life back home. And I was questioning every decision I'd ever made up until that point. Like what the fuck got me THERE. To that point where I was just useless and doing nothing and not even helping ORPHANS?!?!

And as I sat there on this bench, an old man came up to me and handed me a little red heart. On the back of it, he'd written the name of the town: Arequipa—and I swear, his handwriting looked just like my grandpa's and he looked like him too.

It was that small moment of kindness from a complete stranger that shifted the entire experience for me. He didn't know he looked or wrote like my grandpa. He didn't know what my deal was, other than I probably looked gloomy and I wasn't from around there.

But it was that small, simple act that snapped me right out of my own sense of despair and helped me see the good in people again. The purpose in trying to be kind, in giving to others, in doing something nice with no expectation of any return.

That little heart really warmed my heart—and I took it as a sign that my actual heart was in the right place, even if it didn't always feel like it. That even though I couldn't see the way things would get better, there was still the possibility they still could, if only by the kindness of strangers.

Strangers and sunbeams in the Plaza des Armas, Arequipa, Peru.
August 2012.

8

CUSCO: BLANK MAPS

(pachamamas)

The present moment
is a powerful goddess.

– *Goethe*

After the orphanage, I flew from Arequipa to Cusco through the Andes. It was only an hour flight, so the plane stayed nice and close to the mountain peaks!

Cusco was literally like night and day from Arequipa. The change of scenery was so needed. I could eat again and I loved where I was staying, a hotel with a center for street kids. The woman who founded it had visited Cusco, noticed all the kids on the street and decided to come back and create a hotel that would fund a program that gives the kids healthy meals, tutoring, medical care, basic hygiene (showers + toothbrushes), and even, a gym to play sports in, a little movie theater and a reading library. It was...AMAZING.

And they didn't accept volunteers. Even when they told me that, I pushed. *C'mon, really* (wink wink) They actually employed 81 local adults in the hotels and children's facilities. If they accepted volunteers, those jobs would have been obsolete. *Touché.*

The lovely worker who gave me the tour, Gloria, told me they have a weekly meeting every Friday afternoon for all the staff. At the meeting, each worker must answer 3 questions:

1. Why are you happy right now?
2. What is bothering you?

3. What are you going to do for yourself this week?

Gloria said that working there really changed her life, not only because of the steady income but because for the first time, she was learning to think about herself and see herself as a person, not just a mother or a sister. I wanted to give Gloria a huge hug at the end of our tour, but she was very modest and I didn't want to embarrass her.

Overall, I was just absolutely thrilled to be in Cusco. The Plaza des Armas was gorgeous and the streets were all cobblestone. I was really surprised by the weather. Cusco was at 11,200 feet elevation, so the sun was really, really strong during the day. But at night, it dropped to 35 degrees (Fahrenheit, I'm North American).

Propane-fueled motorcycles were quite common on the streets. And I noticed that Peruvians loved both 80's music and Adele. I knew that because headphones hadn't caught on there yet. If you wanted to listen to music on your phone, you just played it on speaker for all to hear. Peruvians also loved hill carvings. Like they literally carved words or pictures into the sides of hills.

Peru was also really carving a special place in my heart. I could feel a part of me opening up there, and it was mainly because of the children. The wall I'd built around my heart was starting to fall down. The kiddies I saw outside my door every morning, and the ones I worked with, something about them (and this country) felt so pure and innocent, yet also so wise and ancient.

Although I went down there on my high horse (much like the Europeans before me), I started to see that as much as I gave, I also received, that and more. Like my favorite Shakespeare quote: *The more I give to thee, the more I have, for both are infinite.*

That's what it felt like Peru was giving me. A taste of the infinite. It also gave me (many) reality checks. Like when I almost become a Peruvian godmother.

I couldn't walk through the Plaza des Armas (the town center) without being asked for *dinero*. Notably, that exact spot was once the literal center of the Inca empire. Now, it was filled with tourists and street children and unhoused adults selling trinkets to said tourists, like myself, to make money.

Since I walked through it multiple times per day, I started to recognize almost every vendor and knew some by name. And every single day, they all acted as if it was the first time they'd ever seen me. I either blended in with the cloud of foreigners, or this was a sales tactic. Either way, it was working. I was embarrassed by the number of llama keychains and alpaca finger puppets I bought.

I was sitting in the Plaza on a bench one day, thinking about if my little niece would even like all these finger puppets?! Thinking about her started to make me homesick. Like very homesick. Like I would have given anything to teleport home and play with her. It was the first time I experienced this feeling that strongly since I left.

My whole experience in Peru had been so fulfilling, yet I had to admit that every moment was *not* utter bliss and it was difficult to process it all on my own. So I started to (gently) cry a little bit, sitting on this bench in the old center of the Incan empire.

One of my vendor friends, Sonya, noticed my emotional state and joined me on my bench of sadness. Her gesture was sweet and I was in need of a morale boost.

She started to share her story with me. She grew up in Ayacucho, a city in Peru known for terrorism in the '80's and '90s. I almost went there but then a Google search told me there were still active terrorist "cells" at the time—which I was not interested in exploring.

Her entire family was killed one night by these terrorists. Everyone except her. When she asked why I was sad, I felt more than a little silly when I told her why: *Um, I miss a toddler? You don't understand, she's, like, really cute...*

Sonya was a single mother of four kids and she sold paintings to support her family. But the police had confiscated her paintings, because she was using an expired permit.

And now she was crying too.

My feelings of isolation vanished and were replaced with a deep yearning to help this woman. I did what I always did best: replaced my own issues with someone else's.

I gave her the money I had with me. She expressed her gratitude for ten minutes straight and said she wanted to repay me. She invited me to visit her home the next day and meet her children. Not wanting to be rude, I agreed.

The next day we met in the Plaza and I took the combi bus with her (I'd like to note that I was now a pro at riding local transportation). She and her children rented one room in an apartment owned and shared with a couple. She was emotional as she showed me the mattresses in the corner of her room, which they rolled out on the floor each night.

I met her 10-year-old daughter, Estefani, and her 7-year-old son, Jefrin. Her two other children were not home. The kids played on my iPhone while I chatted more with their mom. I noticed the kids' shoes were broken, so I asked for their sizes.

Sonya mentioned she was scared she wouldn't have enough money to pay rent. I offered her the difference, as I happened to have the same amount with me. It's like she had x-ray vision and could see into my wallet. She wept tears of gratitude.

Before I left, she gave me a small gift and asked me if I would be her daughter's godmother. Estefani had never been baptized and needed a *madrina*. I felt deeply honored by her request, and with my Catholic upbringing, *sí* was my instant answer. I made plans to meet Sonya in the Plaza the next day.

Before our next meeting, I went to the shoe store and the sweater store. I had a strict budget for my trip, but I made adjustments for Sonya's kids. I mean, they needed shoes and sweaters!! I found Sonya in the Plaza later that afternoon and dropped off the goodies.

She told me the baptism would be in two days. I asked if a madrina needed to bring anything to the ceremony? Sonya said we would go to the Baptism store together.

We met again the next day and she led the way and we happened to run into one of her friends...who was magically carrying the shoes I'd bought?

Sonya explained that the shoes were *un poco grande* and needed to be exchanged. Luckily, we happened to be right down the street from the store I had purchased them from. We headed over to make the swap. The timing and ease of all this seemed almost too good to be true (probably because it was).

As the saleswoman was pulling new sizes for us, Sonya explained that she wants to start selling silver in the Plaza, instead of paintings. I agreed that this might be more lucrative.

But she needed a start-up investment of 3,000 soles to get started. I thought that was a bit steep, but maybe I could do some fundraising from friends and family to help her.

The saleswoman returned after a 15-minute vanishing act and said she didn't have the new sizes we were looking for. She'd return my money, but we would need to come back in two days for it. I thought this was odd, but many things were very different to me in Peru. So, we headed to the Baptism store.

When we arrived, Sonya picked out a pageant-style dress for her daughter with matching shoes and a peacoat. All for the low price of 400 soles (about 122 dollars). At this point, I finally realized I was being hustled. Not a second sooner.

Things became awkward quickly. I told her I could not afford this baptismal clothing, because I honestly could not. I no longer had an income and had stretched my budget already.

Suddenly, Sonya could no longer understand my English, Spanish, or Spanglish. She attempted to shame me into making the purchase by announcing to the store, over and over, that THE GRINGA SAYS SHE HAS NO MONEY followed by scoffing, foot-stomping, and eye-rolls.

She gave me a guilt trip that Estefani was going to cry without her pageant dress. I stayed strong and said I'm sorry, but no.

Then she said Estefani must have jeans for the baptism instead. So I bought the damn jeans. Shamelessly, Sonya asked me for my change from the purchase to buy Estefani a new hoodie for the baptism. I came to my senses again and said no, lo siento. She turned on her heels and ditched me.

I was left standing in a crowded, locals-only market at night. I assumed the baptism was canceled. And I was in tears again. I cried the whole walk back to my apartment for the following reasons:

1. I was scared out of my mind of being mugged. Every guidebook tells you to never go to a locals-only market area unaccompanied at night as a tourist woman. I thought maybe if I cried like I'd already been mugged, I'd trick any possible attacker.

2. I felt really, really dumb. How did I fall for this?

3. Mostly, I was really sad. Even after my ride on the Hustle Express, I still wanted to help Sonya. The codependent in me was desperate for a fix.

Were those really Sonya's children or actors? Do Peruvian girls wear pageant dresses to baptisms? How did the jeans do during the ceremony? All of these questions will forever remain a mystery.

Honestly, I probably would have done the same thing Sonya did, if I were in her shoes (maybe). She did what she had to do to take care of herself and her family, whether those were her real kids or not.

At the time, Peru was the second poorest country in South America. Much of the economy depended on tourism and curious people willing to spend *dinero* to see the famous sights. Sonya was one of the women in this country trying to get by. And she lived in a very different world than what most visitors see when they come to Peru. I know because I saw it (or at least, a staged version of it).

But I really did see the areas of town that *turistas* don't usually (ever) go to. I accidentally took the van-bus in the wrong direction and ended up in a poverty-stricken area of Cusco. It was a real eye-opener. Blocks and blocks of clay homes with plastic tarp roofs. The poverty seemed almost unfixable, like India. Not to mention, the pollution was out of control. I hate to break it to all my fellow environmentalists, but I am pretty sure there was some serious damage being done. The fumes were nauseating. And I used to smoke.

Peru was a country with so many beautiful things to see if you had the money to do so (like many places). Many people that lived there did not. There was so much *need* there, as there was in so many other places around the world, including the States. Need for safety, security, homes, money, health care.

Even though I never saw Sonya again, I did have another volunteer project to focus on, thankfully. I started working at a home for teen moms in the San Jeronimo neighborhood, a solid *45 minutos* commute from downtown Cusco. The ride was just a straight shot down the Avenida del Cultura with one to fifty-five pauses, depending on how many *BAJAS!* we had. It was kinda difficult to tell where your stop was because there weren't many landmarks. It made things exciting!

I can still picture all the locals' faces when they'd hear a random, soft-spoken baja, said in a Chicago accent, coming from the back of the bus. They'd all look perplexed as a random white girl was getting off in a random neighborhood, alone. I never felt unsafe because people were usually just so confused to see me in a place not many other (blonde) tourists went.

The home for teen moms was on a calle tierra. On my first day there, I took a cab because I wanted to be on time. My cab driver and I got completely lost as I used a mix of charades and Spanglish to direct him around dirt roads with no signs, using the directions I'd been sent in Español.

The *simpatico* cab driver had to get out of the car and remove a few rocks from the middle of the *calle tierras*. At one point, I'm not kidding when I say, we had to ask an old man and his *flock of sheep* for directions. I couldn't contain my laughter, *how did I end up here?!* Luckily, we eventually spotted the purple gate (with painted cute little angels).

The facilities were *muy, muy bueno* at this casa for teens. Rita was the owner and she lived on the grounds. It was basically one large house that Rita and her family shared with 15 mothers and their children.

One in four mothers in Peru was under the age of 18. That meant 25% of all the mothers in that country were TEENAGERS. The girls living in the casa didn't have the support they needed at home. Some of the girls fell in love and then the baby daddy headed for the hills to do carvings once he heard the exciting news. (Trigger warning:) Another volunteer told me that, sadly, the majority of the girls had been victims of sexual abuse, sometimes within their own family.

The *mamacitas* were between the ages of 12 to 18 and their children ranged in age from newborn to 6 years old. There was a large kitchen and eating area, a TV Room, two classrooms, a huge laundry area, a sewing room for the girls, one *grande* bathroom, and a nursery. And they were all cleaned, daily. I wanted to kiss the ground. *Beso!*

Spanish was solely spoken in the Casa, so I was improving on a *muy rapido* basis. Except for the day when I ran out of soap in the kitchen. I ran around the house asking everyone:

Donde es más sopa??!? (while using hand motions to simulate washing dishes)

No one would answer me so I just kept going from room to room to room asking around.

Finally, another volunteer overheard me and let me know that sopa means soup, not soap. *Muchas gracias.*

I worked with the newborn-to-toddler group so I spent most of my time in the nursery. There was a playroom, access to the outdoors, a changing room, and a bedroom for the babies. With twelve children under the age of 3, the space was perfect. *Not too grande and not too pequeno.*

As a volunteer, we basically provided an open-door daycare service all day so the moms could meet with a tutor, study, and help with other tasks around the house.

In comparison to the orphanage, volunteering there was a piece of *pastel.* I was there as a supplement and to allow the mothers some free time to work on other things for themselves.

The rule of thumb there was "get the Mom." If a child was crying, hungry, cranky, or had a dirty diaper, I always tried to find the mom first (especially with the diapers). Only if she was busy did I step in and feed or soothe or change her *bebe.* My main job was to play and keep the *bambinos* smiling and happy.

The youngest mother was 12 years old. Twelve. Like a 6th grader. She was 9 months pregnant and due the week I arrived. Most of the other *mamacitas* were 14-15 years old. So, like a freshman in high school. At 18, the girls moved out of the home and found work. However, it was not like they got kicked to the curb on their 18th birthday. They spent months preparing and honing their skills and Rita helped them. It was seriously beautiful.

One of the moms had really taken a liking to me. Lisa was fifteen and she called me Señorita. She liked to walk around the house holding my hand. She was a person with a learning disability and (trigger warning) she was raped. Her son's name was Francisco and he was so attached to her. She was one of the most doting mothers in the house (not that I was comparing but just saying). She'd always be coming around to check in on him. Watching them together melted more of the ice in my heart.

I fell head over heels in love during my time there too. I had a favorite baby, and although I should've been ashamed to be playing favorites, I was not. I couldn't help it, my heart couldn't be tamed. Her name was Candy. She was the *gordita* of the group and I was (weirdly) obsessed with her. I loved to squeeze her because she was just so pudgy and perfect. I couldn't get over her cheeks.

She was so stoic for a baby. She sat and quietly observed everyone, like such a cute little nugget. Sometimes she would literally give people the stink eye. I saw it with my own two eyes. You had to earn her love and respect. She didn't give smiles away to just anyone. She was sassy but sweet. Like my soul sister, in baby form. I could hold and squeeze her all day.

I had to tell Candy's mom how obsessed I was with her daughter and I know I freaked her out. I think she was genuinely concerned with how into her baby I was. I had a vision of bringing Candy home with me, walking off the plane with her in a Baby Bjorn (obviously it never happened, her birth mother was wonderful).

Candy's mom was so shy. She wasn't super talkative and she was so gentle with Candy. She came to check-in as much as Lisa did, which was cute. But also slightly annoying, because I really wanted as much one-on-one time with Candy as possible. *Don't worry, I've got her! Go take some "me" time, por favor!*

(Trigger warning, again) I found out Candy's backstory through one of the other volunteers. Candy's mom was raped. I was so taken aback and I cried so hard that night when I got back to my apartment. I couldn't believe Candy's dad was a rapist. I couldn't believe her sweet, soft gentle mother had to go through that.

How could this beautiful child, who I loved so much, come from that kind of violent beginning? Why was she born into these circumstances? These were the questions I couldn't stop thinking about. The only answer I could come up with was that something beautiful must be able to come from something awful. Candy was a chunk of love who came from something painful and violent. But now she was here and that was all that mattered.

I learned about Pachamama during my time there. The Incas worshipped her as a benevolent, giving fertility goddess who embodied the mountains, looked over planting and harvesting, and even caused earthquakes. There wasn't an equivalent word in English to sum up what Pachamama really meant. I guess the closest concept would be Mother Nature, but the word really embodied the universal feminine with creative power to sustain life on Earth. *Can't think of a word for that in English...wonder why?...*

I've prayed all my life to the male God I learned about in school. And to Jesus. And to my Grandpas. But I was learning that God was a woman too. (Side note: If only I'd written a pop song about this.)

And it felt like something I'd always known all along, even if I wasn't able to put words to it. There's male and female, yin and yang—and I was definitely hardcore tapping into the feminine side of things there. Seeing all these young mothers surrendered to their fate yet embracing it with so much love in their hearts. And so much trust. Things I'd been lacking in, but was learning from them.

I went there to "help" these girls and I was the one learning. So really, it seems, I went there to be helped. If I'm honest, I'd had such a complicated relationship with my own mom—and if I'm really honest, it's the thing I'd been most afraid of in the world:

Becoming a mom.

But there, my maternal instincts were in overdrive—and not in a *I want a baby right now* kind of way. I felt this soft, nurturing, gentle, kind and motherly side of myself just opening up. It had always been there, but was now flourishing in this estrogen-filled environment.

I brought in nail polish one day, per Lisa's request, and I think that's when the girls decided I was cool enough to hang with them. It felt good to fit in without having to do drugs. When I was in my teens, cruising around in a car, smoking cigs (okay, pot too), I wasn't even close to the maturity level of these *mamacitas*.

These girls had to deal with so much that it was easy to forget that they were just a bunch of teenagers. All they wanted to do was paint their nails, laugh, listen to music and talk. They listening to the radio and got so excited when *Gangnam Style* came on.

On my last day, the girls got in a circle and individually thanked me, which was such a sweet gesture. I was so sad to say goodbye to everyone (especially my *favorita*, Candy).

I came back to the house the day after my last day because I was packing up my bag and realized I didn't need all the sweaters and sweatshirts and leggings I brought. I also wanted an excuse to go back just one last time. I took my last *combi* ride back out to the casa and wrote notes to each of the moms on the way, giving them my email address to stay in touch. When I arrived it was after lunch. Most of the girls were in class so I left the clothes outside their rooms and went to the nursery.

The babies and toddlers were taking naps while the volunteers watched on in the sleeping room. Except for Candy.

She was in the playroom, sitting in a swing by herself. She gave me the biggest smile when I walked in the room. I spent almost half an hour alone with her, swinging and laughing and smiling and playing. It was like *cielo en la tierra*. Walking away from her felt like Rose saying goodbye to Jack at the end of *Titanic*. I couldn't let go.

With more than a few tears in my eyes but a big goofy smile on my face, I gave Candy one last squeeze. I also went against protocol and added her mom as a friend on social media when I got back to my room, because the truth was I really couldn't let go. Candy, and all those girls and their babies, would always be in my heart. And I needed to be able to stalk their lives for the rest of mine.

The purple angel gates to the home for teen moms in San Jeronimo, Cusco, Peru | September 2012.

9

COSTA RICA: SAD DREAM

(sorrow)

To dance beneath the diamond sky with one hand waving free, silhouetted by the sea, circled by the circus sands, with all memory and fate, driven deep beneath the waves, let me forget about today until tomorrow.

-Bob Dylan

I'd said 'I love you' romantically to only three people in my life and meant it only twice.

ONE
To my high school boyfriend. This was a pretty cliche "I love you." He said it first, and I don't even remember when—so that demonstrates how deeply I was into it. It was that real needy, but also ready to discard you when needed kinda "love." Recyclable, if you will.

TWO
To my college boyfriend, Bear. I knew it was love when he let me keep watching *LOST* instead of the Super Bowl. I knew it might not last when he told me I was "overreacting" during an actual (F2) tornado. To my utter dismay, he sat NEXT TO A WINDOW, casually eating leftover ribs while refusing to seek shelter with me near a bathtub. But I couldn't really think about him after it all ended because it actually hurt—and pain was something I avoided.

THREE
To the guy who met me in Costa Rica. Preston. I finally said it back

to him in the months before I left for Peru, even though my intuition was trying to tell me: *Danger ahead!*

I literally had a dream one night that we were on a rollercoaster together—and suddenly, were sucked backward into a pond, sinking. I woke up thinking: *Whoa, that was wild*—and completely ignored the very clear message.

Saying "I love you" can mean lots of different things to people. I personally believe we say it with more than just our words. And when I speak it, I mean: *I feel deeply connected to you, I care about you and who you are, and I always will. You live in a space in my heart.*

There's different stages and types of love too. Like I've felt *passionate, I want to be with you forever* love. And I've also felt *you're like a good companion* love.

I have no regrets when it comes to my "I love you's" in life (okay, maybe one or two of them). They were all what I needed at the time. I had to experience each of those relationships, from fleeting to committed to tumultuous, because they each unlocked a different part of me.

My relationship with Preston unlocked a very deep part of me. I mean this when I say that it was a karmic connection, with an emphasis on *karma.*

After a few months in Peru and a very large phone bill, he decided to meet me for my golden birthday (28!) in Costa Rica. I was heading there to volunteer and would take a few days off to be with him. He booked the trip, then threatened to cancel about seven times before deciding he would keep the reservations.

When I saw Preston at the airport, I felt so relieved. It felt so comforting to see someone I knew after spending so much time so far from home and having so many foreign experiences. The familiar felt like a warm glove in a Chicago winter, comfortable.

Within 24 hours, we got into our biggest fight ever. I surprised him with a massage. Not from me, with a professional. And right afterward, we got on a bus to go to the rainforest.

As perfect as this plan sounds, it did not go so smoothly. He decided he needed to spend his sweet time in the sauna. And we started fighting because he felt rushed and I thought: *Who gets angry after a fucking massage?! In Costa Rica?!* And (I'm guessing) he thought: *Can't this chartered van wait while I open my pores?? Why doesn't time bend at my will?*

When we were about an hour into the bumpy and very tense road trip across the jungles of Costa Rica, after the driver repeatedly told him to *tranquilo, amigo,* Preston asked:

Where's my jacket?

To which I replied:

What jacket? It's 85 fucking degrees outside.

Turns out, it was a raincoat and it was hanging in the closet of the hotel room we'd just checked out of. I did not grab it when I single-handedly carried both our luggage to the lobby as he was pampering himself—because I didn't know anyone actually uses the closets in a hotel room during a one night stay.

His passport was in the pocket of the jacket.

The next 24 hours were terrible. He dug into me in the van, really going for the jugular. He kept threatening to leave and refused to even look at me. I'd gone from a state of blissful comfort to pure agony in the matter of one day.

Finally, I found a cab to drive his passport across the country and meet us at our next location. And I broke down and had a cig, even though I hadn't smoked the entire time I was in South America. He kept repeating: *Just remember, you smoking is not my fault.* Sure.

Once the passport was returned, things got "better." He started looking me in the eye and speaking to me again. We laughed a bit and drank smoothies. He didn't complain when I couldn't hang at the beach all day because I got heat exhaustion after like ten minutes.

When a local tried to lure me into a boat down the beach, he stepped in and pointed out that I shouldn't do that. He made me think about safety. My naive trust and his severe paranoia balanced each other out quite nicely.

He was the third person to tell me I was beautiful (and he also told me I'm "no Cindy Crawford" once). He wrote me a letter and apologized for things that happened in the past (and also would ignore me for days when he needed to apologize in the present).

But I needed someone to say sorry to me so badly in my life. His apology letter meant a lot to me, even if it was for things from years before. It was a major revelation for me—people do this. They can say they're sorry after they hurt you. So I clung to him because I chose to see his bright side, instead of reality. That's what love was, right?! (Wrong).

The upside of this time was my golden birthday was in such a beautiful place. I'd never seen sunsets like the ones in Costa Rica. They lit up the whole earth and sky.

On my birthday morning, he banished me to the other bed in our room for being "annoying." Not sure how one can annoy another while sleeping.

On my birthday night, we went swimming in the pool. The stars were so bright and I just remember laughing and swimming under the night sky without a care in the world.

What I didn't know then was that this relationship was so unhealthy—actually, destructive and toxic. I'd kept rose-colored glasses on, choosing to look at the good things and tuning out the bad. I hadn't even heard the word "codependent" yet.

I didn't know that after this, he'd hit close to rock bottom, and I'd be propping him up *Weekend at Bernie's* style, as if none of it was even happening, because I knew how to do that so well. I knew how to function in the world as if everything was normal, even when it's not.

The truth, that I never told anyone, was I was scared to leave. I felt guilty, knowing things would get worse if he didn't have me care-taking him. No one saw the fits of rage, the holes in the wall, the night in the E.R. after he smashed a glass in his hand, the sketchy drug dealers, the lies, the very dark reality. And I chose not to see it either. I didn't realize how much of myself I was losing either.

When I'd finally get the courage to walk away, he'd keep circling back, pulling me back in anytime he wasn't getting the attention he needed. And I didn't know how to say no. I didn't know how to not put someone else's pain first. I didn't know then that I would finally see it, all of it, the truth, for everything it really was. That this relationship had never been the thing I so desperately wanted it to be. And I realized the small scraps he was throwing my way weren't even close to enough and would never be enough. And I deserved so much better—and would never be able to save him from himself. I'd only be dragged down with him. Just like on the rollercoaster.

Before I knew all this, he left Costa Rica, and I went to a small beach village and tried to teach kids English.

I was living in an apartment complex with a pool with three other girls who were great. Obviously, we all had something in common: we left home to come there and teach.

I worked as a teacher's assistant with a teacher who had been volunteering for nearly a year and was about to head home and relinquish her classroom to me. She was clearly having mixed emotions about this transition because she treated me like I was her hired help, something I was used to from spending so much time with Preston.

But I was not a fan of this young woman's attitude, to say the least. It made the experience unpleasant, especially because attendance was super low in her class, due to the fact that it was optional and she was more-than-kinda controlling.

My roommates and I rode bikes everywhere around the town—to the fruit stand, to the beach, to volunteer events. I went out one night for drinks at a bar with the other volunteers and decided to go home early by myself because I just wasn't feeling it that night, which may have been the first time ever.

I rode my bike back home in the pitch dark down the dirt roads. It was like a darkness I'd never experienced before. I literally couldn't see a thing at certain points on the road. I had to just go slow and keep riding, which felt a lot like my life at the time.

I called home to check on my grandmother and she didn't sound so good. She'd been getting sick a lot and was going in and out of the hospital for tests.

And then, one night the earth rumbled, both literally and metaphorically. After my first-ever earthquake (which was probably a 1.0), I spotted something that made my inner world shake on social media. It was a picture of yet another girl in Preston's apartment, just two weeks after he visited me.

Between the earthquake and my grandmother and that doomed relationship, my heart wasn't in it anymore. Being in Costa Rica didn't feel right. I wanted to go home, mainly because I couldn't truly enjoy paradise.

I was literally in one of the most beautiful places on Earth, but I decided to go back. I didn't think I was worthy of living in paradise, so I pulled myself out of it.

I didn't fully understand why, it just felt like I didn't deserve to be there. Like why would I get to lead this life? Why did I think I deserved to enjoy paradise?

This was an age-old conundrum, and it all began with the story of Adam and Eve who were thrown out of a world filled with life's wonders into a world of suffering. And what they really felt was shame. Shame for their actions, for being human.

Shame is what keeps us apart—and ironically, the time we spend in separation from each other is what allows us to become the people who can be kind to each other. When we feel shame, we don't feel worthy of the sweetness of life, so we run from it. Without shame, the gates of paradise and goodness swing open for us. And the only way we can feel and spread this joy is if we let go of our shame.

It would take me a few years until I learned that I was letting shame hold me back. That I was refusing to look at the things that made me feel shameful from my past, so they just kept playing out in my present, especially in my (horribly traumatic) relationship.

When things would get too good, I would shove it away before it could hurt me. Because being hurt was something I knew, it was the version of love I'd learned. Because I felt I wasn't deserving of being treated well. And I felt ashamed for thinking I might.

I'd ripped myself out of happiness before—and I realized that the "karma" I was dealing with was...self-created. Before that, I'd been the one who was hard to love. I was the one who let my emotional baggage get in the way. And now, there I was, trying to salvage love in my life with someone who wasn't able to love me back.

I was so blinded that I "fell in love" with someone who was clearly, all wrong for me. And I refused to see the truth and I pushed and forced and tried as goddamn hard as I could and made myself into a total martyr in the process. *Like a good Catholic girl does!*

I made this mistake because I thought that love was fixing someone else and making them see your brilliance. And boy, was I wrong. That was actually a fucking nightmare. I was mistaken because I didn't understand myself and what I wanted from life. So I gave my light away to someone else and it took me a while to get it back. But after losing myself once, I knew I'd never hand my heart away again like that. I'd look for someone else who was shining brightly too so that our lights could shine together to be even brighter.

Love and the ideas we have about love can sometimes provide the hardest lessons. I learned that you can love everyone else, but that doesn't mean they'll love each other. Or even themselves. And it's really disheartening. Because what's a life with all this freedom and all these things and all this opportunity—but without love. Without joy. Without learning how to get along. Without respect, especially for yourself.

When I left Costa Rica and I broke up with Preston, I found myself in a place called Sorrow. The place where love gets lost, where the sad truth resides, where the things we bury wait for us to mourn them. What I'd been looking for was an apology, any kind of an acknowledgment from Preston that his behavior was the worst.

What I didn't realize was that I was really the one who owed that, but not to him.

I'm Sorry

Dear Bear,

I am sorry.

This is so long overdue that I'm not even sure it counts. I get it now. And I want to tell you a few things I've realized, even if it took me a long time to figure it out:

I fucked up. BIG TIME. With you. I was so terrible a lot of the time and the memories used to haunt me. I am so sorry. I was a shit more than I wasn't.

You were mostly so good to me and I am so deeply grateful for that. You weren't perfect but you treated me with respect and you made me feel safe. It was the first time I ever felt that way, in my life.

I had my heart smashed, over and over again, for years. You opened it back up again and made me see that the world is a beautiful place and that people can love me. You made me feel accepted and you gave me a sense of stability that I so deeply needed in my life.

When problems came up, I couldn't deal. It's something I deeply regret. I can't rewind the past and I can't change anything.

All I can do is say I'm sorry.

I am sorry.

It's really about knowing that my actions and behavior and choices sent you a different message than what was really true.

The truth is: I do believe in miracles and you were truly a miracle that came into my life. I could never be who I am if it wasn't for you. So please know that:

I'm deeply sorry and all I wish for you is to know that truth. And obviously, happiness in your life.

All my life I've chased after things, I've pushed and pulled and forced and manipulated and always tried to get what I want— except with what actually mattered.

I'm sorry.

With Love,
Cait

P.S. I also wish I would have agreed to being friends, like Jerry and Elaine. I was too selfish back then to be that cool. I'm sorry.

Fishermen coming in for the day in Tamarindo, Costa Rica. Oh, and a pretty sick sunset | October 2012.

10

THE PAST: EVERYBODY'S CHANGING

(clashing of energies)

Forgiveness is giving up the hope that the past can be any different.
-Oprah Winfrey

I threw my diaries in a dumpster once. As a teenager, I packed everything I'd ever written in my suitcase and brought it with me on a family vacation. From the balcony of a rented condo, I snuck outside with my notebooks and dropped them, one by one, into the trash below. I wanted to make sure no one would ever find them (again).

As I heard the whack of each diary hitting the trash, I was symbolically letting go of my childhood. I was done with hard feelings, with trying to understand and make sense of things that did not, in fact, make any sense at all. And I definitely did not want another soul to ever read what I had written.

From that point on, I knew I had to just bide my time and do what had to be done to get to high school graduation and pass Go and collect my freedom. I was totally done with following all the B.S. rules—because in my experience, all they caused was pain. I mean, I still obeyed traffic lights (mostly, except for the day I rear-ended a priest), but I was done with all the pretending. With posing for portraits when the reality was...anything but pretty.

At that moment, I decided the world hurt too much and I had to find ways to tune things out and to bury the truth.

But, the truth doesn't like to be buried. It turns out, repression has an expiration date and when you try to shove a ball of emotions underwater, one day, they come flying out into the open and refuse to be hidden any longer.

It was hard for me to piece together the truth because I'd been young and things just happened and then they changed so quickly and I never knew what the truth was because I always had different sources with mostly opposing versions.

I don't really remember what it was like to be with my mom and dad together. It was the first ten years of my life, but I'd forgotten (read: repressed) the memories, both the good and the bad. And I don't really remember much from the years of 11 to 18 either. I was kinda like a ghost who was just floating in my own life, having fun where I could—but I don't really remember much of anything at all. All I did know, for sure, was that what I wanted more than anything was to just be normal, whatever that meant. I'd look around at other perfectly polished families and think:

What is it like to live like that?

What I didn't realize was that, behind closed doors, lots of other kids were experiencing the same thing I was. In fact, as a human, it's almost impossible to make it to the end of life without experiencing trauma in some way—it's just that when it happens when we're little, it tends to stick with us and shape the way we approach...everything.

I couldn't even talk to my closest friends about what went on. Because my biggest fear was being judged. I didn't want to be labeled as "broken" or anything else. I just wanted to be *normal*. Sidenote: I'd later learn that there was no normal.

Ironically, my childhood *was* mostly sweet and filled with so much love. As one of the first grandchildren in my family, I was showered with attention and gifts and praise. It was so pure and loving—and I was given so many privileges, from the best education to food to *American Girl* dolls. In summary, I was spoiled and used to a world filled with rainbows and sunshine.

But the skies got cloudy—and then what felt like a never-ending storm set in. I started having my first recurring dream around 10 years old. I was climbing a tower of scaffolding and just as I'd reach the top, the whole thing would come crashing down. Very symbolic.

When I was just old enough to form memories, my brother and I were playing (I was bossing him around) in the family room. My mom was multitasking: vacuuming and making dinner. My dad was still at work.

The doorbell rang—which was odd because usually, we knew if someone was coming over?

The vacuum stopped and when my mom answered, there was a woman standing on our front door stoop. She said:

I didn't even see him. My kids are in the car.

My mom ran out the front door and this random lady was crying in our hallway. I remember standing there staring at her, as if she was an alien. *A stranger in our home, crying?! What does this even mean?*

Our house began to fill up with people, mostly firemen and cops. My brother and I were so excited, because to us (suburban white kids), anyone in public service was like a celebrity. We talked to them and I'm pretty sure I may have asked for a few (discreet) autographs. I've always been great with celebrities.

What was actually going on was the woman who rang our doorbell had (accidentally) hit a man with her car. He was walking home from work and he was killed. My mom was the only "witness." She had to be a part of the (vehicular manslaughter) trial for a few years.

We moved exactly three blocks away and I was conditioned to forever be terrified of the doorbell. *Who died?*

Life went back to being kinda vanilla again, at least to me. I was desperately trying to become a ballerina (and star in *the Nutcracker*) and my mom took us to do lots of things, like going to the pool every day in the summer. The rest of the year we went to a religious school and watched *Hey Dude* and *Salute Your Shorts* religiously.

A few summers later, my mom stopped taking us to the pool. She stopped doing a lot of things with us. I remember going with her to drop off something at the hospital and she was being real weird about it. Of course, I was nosy and wanted to know:

Mom, what's in that bag, though?

Don't worry about it.

Okay, but what are we dropping off?

I said don't worry about it.

Mom, I just want to know what's in that bag and why we are at the hospital??!!

It's my POOP, okay. Do you want to see that?!

(silence)

I concluded that something was wrong with her stomach, and so, something was wrong with her.

A few weeks later, my brother and I went to visit Aunt Sheila with our grandparents (score!!), and my little sister stayed back with my parents.

But when we came home, my dad didn't live there anymore (major, earth-shattering loss) because my mom had kicked him out. He lived with my other grandparents a few blocks away.

I was really into *Harriet the Spy* at the time, so I remember trying to piece together the clues I'd missed. I realized I'd dismissed three critical pieces of evidence:

ONE:
I'd woken up one night and heard my parents speaking loudly to each other in the kitchen. I sat at the top of the stairs and had a thought conversation with myself:

What if they get a divorce?

No way, that's impossible.

But isn't this exactly what happens to kids whose parents are about to get divorced? They quietly listen in on a fight from another room?

Ugh, you are so dramatic. That would never happen.

TWO
My mom spent the majority of her time on the phone—and it was hard to get her attention. And the bits I heard of her conversations were usually things I didn't want to hear, so I pretended I hadn't heard them.

THREE
This was the big one and it really hurt the most to think about. The day my dad was changing my little sister's diaper in her room—and I went in to talk to them. I sat on her little playhouse bed, looking up at my dad, who was holding and bouncing her, and he was...sad? It was the first time I ever saw him cry. He told me he didn't know what was going on but he was trying his best to work it out. And that he was sorry this was all happening.

It wasn't the only time an adult would tell me that. My grandmother also did the same thing that summer. She pulled me in the kitchen and told me she was always there for me and started crying. All I knew was the adults in my life were sad, but I didn't really get what was happening?! Would anyone like to explain what exactly was going on here?!

As expected, my parents got divorced—and let's just say it wasn't swift or amicable and would definitely qualify as traumatic for everyone involved. And for the cherry on top, with my dad being out of the house, my mom found a new outlet for her frustrations: me.

I became her dumping ground for everything she was going through. It was about as fun as it sounds. This was nothing totally new, it just became exponentially worse. Each and every day became like an emotional warzone. Non-stop drama. And after every episode, she'd hand me the phone and say:

Call your Dad then, have him come get you.

I was twelve years old. And I was very tempted to do that. But I didn't. Because I wasn't able to process reality. And I couldn't leave my brother and sister. I'd willingly put myself in front of her, like a little Joan of Arc, because I refused to let my siblings experience her wrath. If she even looked in their direction, I'd basically throw a lit match on her so she'd go after me instead.

I had a very "come at me bro" attitude because I knew how she was treating me was wrong. She'd start in on me—and I was like a brick wall. I'd say my piece back to her and then run like hell to my room. I rearranged it so my dresser was right by the door, so I could pull it in front, like my own little DIY security system. Worked like a charm (almost) every time.

One day I made her too mad, so she refused to drive me to school. I stood by the window, crying, and watched as she drove off with my siblings. Then I had to lie to my teacher and say I was sick the next day. Every day was an incident. Dishwasher soap down my throat. Doors slamming. Being slapped. Chased around the house. Broken fingers. Locked outside in the cold, barefoot, during Christmas tree decorating. The constant threat of being kicked out. It's really no wonder why I got really into *Dashboard Confessionals* later in life.

I felt ashamed, like there must be something so wrong with me, because my world just wasn't as "normal" as everyone else's, mostly because I never saw my friends' moms act like that. I was hard-core grieving not only the breakdown of my family, but also, the total crumbling of the relationship with my mom. My home experience became a total fucking nightmare, to put it best. And I couldn't tell anyone about it.

The only person I did tell was my aunt. I'd call her sometimes when my mom was having one of her episodes. I'd beg her to get my mom help. I'd write her letters, saying my mom needed treatment. And she'd listen and console me, and then give my mom money to fight for sole custody of us, as my mom (extremely ironically) accused my dad of being physically abusive (when the truth was, the opposite). It was *that* messed up. The only help my mom did get was from the pastor of my school, who she also developed an odd relationship with because (from what I picked up on) my dad had found a Valentine's Day card from this priest to my mom? The priest started coming to every holiday at our house (really normal), a cute extra rumor to have circulating at my junior high! *We heard your mom's dating a priest?* Real fun.

At the time, I was in my prime awkward years, not a girl but not yet a woman (thank you Britney). I was a late bloomer, the last girl in my grade to shave my legs and get my period. I was friends with three girls, and the rest weren't always so nice to me.

One of my only vivid memories from this dark period of my life was during recess in the winter. A girl tripped me, held me down and "whitewashed" my face in the snow. I couldn't breathe and it felt like the world just fucking hated me. Like the two places I spent the most time, at home and at school, someone was waiting to smack me down and remind me how small and meaningless I was.

It was hard for me to admit anything that was going on to anyone else—or to even say that it was a problem for me. Because I saw so many families looking so happy and daughters smiling with their moms and having these beautiful, loving and supportive relationships —and I always felt like:

Well, what's wrong with me that my own MOTHER doesn't seem to even like me?! Like she actually actively hurts me, tells me it's my fault and then pretends it never happened?

The worst part was really the things she'd say to me. I'd easily repress everything else, but sometimes, I'd hear the phrases ringing back in my ears, the sounds of her voice, even years later. The one that stuck the most, that I still work to believe is not true was:

"You were a bitch from the day you were born."

Imagine your own mother (consistently) saying that to you (at 12) and then trying to develop any kind of self-esteem. It's quite tricky, let me tell you! I knew she loved me inside, because she could be nice. But I often questioned if she even liked me because she wasn't always so nice to me, to put it lightly. And when she started treating me that way, it made me decide that: a. I didn't need anyone, b. I could take care of myself so c. I built a fortress around my heart.

I felt like there must be something *really* off with me if this was how my own mother feels about me. And, um, society reinforces that shame. I'd hear things like:

Why are you so mean to your mom?
(Because she's often been really mean to me).

Your mom would never do that.
(You have no idea what she's capable of).

I'm sure she didn't mean it.
(Doesn't change the fact that she did it).

What I didn't understand was that my mom was going through her own pain, but since I was young, I thought it was all about me and had no concept of the fact that she was just a human being—all I knew was she was my Mom, this god-like person who I looked up to for...everything.

I never knew what would set her off, but it seemed to just be me and my presence. She never got mad at my brother and sister the way she did at me. And on the outside, everyone thought it was just my parent's getting divorced, but on the inside, it was much, much more than that. So much suffering, in silence, behind a closed door.

Everyone always asked: *Why did your parents get divorced?* And it's really hard to answer when:

a. you don't fucking know the answer
b. there is no clear answer
c. you never knew the (full) truth
d. you were like 11 and couldn't understand

The little bits I did know were complicated and as fun to put together as a dresser from IKEA. The only thing I knew for sure was how it affected me—and I was in complete denial that it ever would for many, many years.

I was absolutely determined to not let any of it affect me. I was not going to be marked with any scarlet letters and I was not going to be labeled as anything other than "normal." I went about my days and stayed in my lane and kept my head low, except when I had to eat because I couldn't hide in my room forever.

It was a confusing time, to say the least. Life went from Happy Meals and endless fun to custody agreements and split holidays. From stability and financial security, to fighting over bills and never going to the dentist.

My mom was my main source of information at the time—and she was very vocal to us kids about her opinion of "our father." She painted this picture of a single mother, forced to protect her children and kick out her husband—and I believed her, even though my actual experience with her was...different. Again, I was like twelve.

My brain compartmentalized everything, so what happened at mom's house, stayed at mom's house and vice versa with dad's house. Those two worlds became COMPLETELY separate and never, ever mixed in my head because if they did, then I'd have to face, like, reality. Much better to just turn one off when you enter the other one. *Exiting Planet Mom, Entering Planet Dad. All systems erased and refreshed.*

The turning point happened when I made a card at school for "someone I appreciated." I wanted my mom to love me and stop chasing me around the house, so I made it for her. I knew what she wanted to hear so I thanked her for "fighting for us kids in court." But I went to my dad's house that night and the card fell right out of my binder and onto his kitchen floor.

He asked to talk to me privately after dinner and he was holding the card. If you ever want to feel your heart drop out of your body, just do something to make your father, who rarely shows any emotion, cry. He asked me why I thought my mom needed to fight for us? Did he ever do something that would make me think that?

At that moment, everything changed. It was like my reality started spinning, the two worlds I'd tried to keep apart suddenly collided— and they didn't add up. I realized my mom was...lying—not only to me, but to everyone else too. That the smear campaign she was running against my dad wasn't accurate or fact-based. And that the real facts told a very different story. That maybe the way she was treating me...wasn't okay either? It felt like the rug had now completely been pulled out from under my feet. *What planet was THIS ONE!?! Take me back to five years ago when I was little and everything made more sense, please!!!*

My mind and body hit pause after that. I was falling asleep during school and for a few months, I just couldn't stay awake. The doctor said maybe it was mono (even though the test came back negative), but really it was just a case of acute sadness (depression). Everything in my being just needed to deeply, deeply rest. I loved my parents so much and I could not even begin to accept reality. So, I just went into Sleep mode, like a laptop. Before I even hit puberty.

I was living my best life as a tween planted on the couch in my mom's living room. My grandparents brought over a little TV with a VCR. I would read and watch movies and learn about making movies and becoming an actress. This was where my obsession with Winona Ryder really took on a life of its own...

The only place I went was to my dad's, where I would also just lay on the couch and not move much. Until one day he said:

Maybe you aren't sick. You might just be sad. You should get up and do something. It'll make you feel better.

I went back to school and all my months of studying acting on the couch paid off because I was given the lead role in the 6th-grade play. Which was definitely a pity gesture from my teacher to try and make me feel special. I starred as Electra—a Greek heroine who plots revenge against her mother to avenge her father—which felt weirdly fitting.

When my mom and I would fight (every day), I was being told that my mouth and my voice was bad and wrong and sassy and needed to shut up. It definitely was sassy, but it's also really no shocker that one day, my subconscious picked up on that and was like:

Yeah, you know that sounds about right. You don't have anything worthwhile to say. And if you do have the balls to say it, get ready to be attacked. No one wants to hear you speak and everyone is judging you. Best of luck sharing how you really feel to anyone ever! Muhahahaha

About a year after my groundbreaking debut performance as a lead actress, I developed a crippling fear of public speaking and learned how to protect myself by being edgy, kinda rude and anything else I could do to (hopefully) never be hurt by anyone I loved ever again.

In the midst of all this fun, my siblings and I had to visit a court mediator in Chicago who asked: *Which parent do you want to live with?* I knew this was a really fucked up question to ask a fresh teenager. And even worse, I knew they were probably asking my sweet siblings the same thing—and I was so pissed off. I wanted so badly to protect my brother and sister. Can we please think about the children before we speak?! THANK YOU EVERYONE.

We also had to go to Rainbows, the group for kids whose parents were getting divorced. My siblings and I came to school early once a month and got to eat McDonald's Sausage McMuffins. And they'd try to make us talk about our feelings. I talked about anything but what was happening at home. *And feelings? What were those?*

If you ever go to a shaman, one question they might ask you is: *When did you stop dancing?* For me, the answer was: I stopped (sober) dancing when I was fifteen. This was mostly because the Orchesis group I joined wanted us to perform during school mass (hard pass), but it was also because my heart wasn't in it anymore. I became so self-conscious (and self-critical) that I couldn't do it. I couldn't move my body without judging myself.

138

I made two close friends my freshman year of high school. Two. Karen and Lauren. Lauren had a popped blood vessel in her eye, so Karen and I quickly realized it was because she was bulimic. We were good little Catholic girls, so we went to the school counselor and said Lauren needed help. Lauren stopped talking to us. So then, it was just me and Karen.

We'd mainly spend time at her house. And we'd make funny videos and prank calls and I think I peed my pants from laughing almost every time we had a sleepover.

And then Karen got to see what was really going on at my mom's house, even though I tried so desperately to hide it from the outside world. We'd gone to the movies and my mom was supposed to pick us up. When she was late, I knew it was going to be a disaster. She was always early. When she pulled up and her tires screeched as she stopped, all I could think was: *oh fuck*.

The car ride home was terrible and Karen got to see this totally dramatic mess that I desperately wanted to *not even be a part of!!* I didn't choose this drama! I preferred my drama on the stage, not in the home!

I moved in with my dad the next day because I'd reached my breaking point. I called him balling my eyes out and asked him to come get me. I still went to my mom's like every other weekend, mainly because of my siblings and because the rules were way looser there. It was mostly good living with my dad but I was acting out a bit because, um, my home life was a little rocky.

I went to a few counselors throughout those years, but none of them really helped much, if I'm honest. My mom took my siblings and I to one who would then report back to her everything we said—not exactly "HIPAA compliant." My dad took me to one who held her sessions in a dimly lit basement. Sometimes I'd go in alone, sometimes he'd come with me. But when we had a session where BOTH my parents joined in at the same time, it did more harm than good in one hour, so I decided therapy was *not* a helpful tool for me at that time.

I also saw a psychiatrist at one point who told me I was "okay" and just "really smart." *Thank you Sir, I already knew that, but clearly, you cannot see past my facade of "okay-ness," so I'd actually like to prescribe more schooling for you.*

I knew my mom was struggling and that my dad desperately wanted things to be okay when it started to fall apart—and that the mom I'd known seemed to have been replaced by a woman I did not recognize anymore.

My parents went to court. A lot. They sent nasty emails to each other. They stopped talking on the phone. My mom and I fought every day. They kept going to court. And then, they stopped talking altogether. Thousands of dollars and many years of emotional trauma later, the divorce was "settled" and they had joint custody.

The silver lining was that it was actually really nice to spend more time with my dad and I felt better, knowing he wasn't alone. We got along well (when I wasn't sneaking out a window) and he took care of me. I was worried about leaving him alone when I went away to college.

But, turns out, I needn't worry about that. He met my stepmom right before my senior year. They were engaged and married before I graduated. I was genuinely happy for my dad and very relieved that he wouldn't be by himself when I left for college, even though my brother and sister would still be rotating in and out, per the custody agreement (every other weekend, every other Monday and every other Thursday). But a small part of me was also sad because I knew things would be different, again.

I ended up moving back in with my mom during the final few months of my senior year as my dad and my future stepmom's whirlwind romance gained speed. In October, I lost my virginity— and my family found out within days—and not because I told them.

I'd gone to church, all by myself, the morning after because I'd been taught sex was terrible and I'd now be going to hell since I was not married. I thought maybe one Mass might give me a bonus point or two?! Maybe if I repented enough, I'd still have a shot at getting into heaven?!

What actually happened was a few days after my 18th birthday, I was getting ready for school and my dad called me outside. My first thought was: *Omg, I am getting a new car for my birthday! Thank you JESUS for answering my prayers! I am not a whore after all!*

Instead, I found my dad on the driveway, with a broken garbage bag, and the evidence of my lost virtue, along with a time-stamped receipt proving I'd snuck into his house when I was supposed to be at my mom's. It was absolutely horrific, for everyone involved.

The worst part of the situation was that my punishment was: 1. I was no longer allowed to drive (a.k.a. my freedom was taken away) and 2. I had to find my own ride to school.

Except the second part was a bit tricky, because there was only one option for that and we both knew it: my mom.

I never told my dad the full details of everything between her and I, mostly because I knew it hurt his feelings to even talk about my mom and honestly, it hurt mine too. We'd both essentially been kicked out—first him, then me. It bonded us, even if we never spoke about it. And now, he was mad enough that he was basically saying:

Call your Mom then, have her come get you.

So, I found myself, once again, randomly calling the other parent to come pick me up—and having to move back in with my mom. Things weren't as bad, mostly because I was barely ever home.

All I knew was it felt like I was being ping-ponged between two homes, tossed to the other one whenever I fucked up, whether I actually did or didn't. This time, I was left with no option than to go back to the house I'd once begged to leave.

My dad and I had been close and now, he was mad at me and getting remarried, and it felt like both my parents weren't exactly in my fan club anymore—and they didn't like each other, so there was just a whole lot of everyone being mad at each other and everything changing, all the time. And my way of processing that was by generally not giving a fuck about...anything. Why would I care?! Caring hurt.

I skipped out on Christmas shopping with my Gram that year because I didn't know how to explain all this to her and I knew I couldn't fake it. She called me and scolded me, and in my teenage angst, I just added her to the list of "Adults Who Are Currently Mad At Me." I wasn't going to my stepmom's bridal showers because I just couldn't fake it there either. So, she got added to the list too. I couldn't sit at these things and pretend everything was okay, when it very much wasn't. I'd held it together for like seventeen years, dressing up and smiling and pretending—and I just needed a little break from it all for a month.

But I did start to attend family gatherings again at Christmas. When I went to dinner at my aunt and uncle's house one weekend, my aunt pulled me upstairs. All she'd heard was that I was a hot mess senior who was not showing up to stuff and having "issues." She didn't know the details, but she cared enough to try and talk to me.

She asked me what was going on—and I completely broke down. I couldn't even talk, I just hyperventilated and cried. It was the first time someone asked me if I was okay and really meant it. I didn't even know what to say or where to begin. There were so many years of things I'd bottled inside, I couldn't even begin to voice them. She definitely didn't expect my reaction and had to spend the next ten minutes trying to calm me down enough so I could rejoin the dinner table and breathe.

The next month, I got my hair done, put on a dress, and walked down the aisle at my dad's wedding, with a smile on my face because I was still happy for him. It was a really subtle, understated ceremony at the Chicago History Museum with 200+ people and an ice sculpture of a penguin. My (underage) cousins and I happily helped ourselves to the champagne on the tables and had a very happy time on the dance floor.

For the rest of that last year at home, I increased my daily dosage of street-bought marijuana, and counted the minutes until college. I went to my orientation for college by myself and I counted the days until I could finally just get out on my own. My dad got me all the things I needed for my dorm and my mom drove me there—and I even decided to rush a sorority, just so I could leave a week early. That's how desperate I was for freedom. Enough to join a sorority I knew I would instantly quit.

I shoved everything inside and refused to even acknowledge any of it. And in a world of nuclear families, I got to see what it felt like to be the outsider. And where did I put all the things that hurt? Deep inside where I'd never find them!

My life became divided by one giant wall with two camps: Mom v. Dad. I'd try to solve this equation in my head:

If ½ Mom + ½ Dad = Me
and Mom no longer equals Dad and Dad no longer equals Mom
so Mom + Dad = PAIN/HURT/SADNESS
and Mom = sometimes nice, but mostly scary
and Dad = mostly nice, but sometimes scary
Then what the bloody hell am I?

That's a pretty deep and complicated equation for a teenage girl to try and solve all on her own. I never knew the answer to "Who am I?" because it depended on where I was. Because I was one person at mom's house (POW) and another person at dad's house (supportive daughter / rebel teen) and I was this person in ballet class (serious ballerina) and I was this person at school (prank queen). But I was really this person inside (sad, seeking love).

All I knew was that truly, deep, deep, deep down inside, I just wanted everyone to be happy. I wanted everyone to be okay—my mom, my dad, my siblings, myself. And when I couldn't make that happen, I learned how to numb — because it hurt too much to see the people I love, hurt. And to have them hurt me too.

When shit like that happens, you see the flaws in the system. Situations in life that cause pain expand your sight. It's an amazing phenomenon. You see how goofy all this pretending is. You see that there's a whole world out there beyond all this trying to fit in. Here's the good things about all this (because nothing is ever all bad):

It made me adaptable to new environments.

I've always looked out for my siblings and we have each other— when you've been through war together, there's a bond that can't be broken.

I can live out of a bag anywhere, anytime. I can pack at a moment's notice.

I don't feel a sense of attachment to a house or an apartment. I can move around easily.

I've learned the art of diplomacy.

I'm very good at dissociating and compartmentalizing.

I learned that there are unseen forces protecting us. That is how we all survive anything tough.

I have loads of compassion and empathy.

I see the truth in the world and past facades.

I have respect for people and their pain.

The worst part about those years was not what actually happened. I was in shock for most of that, so my little developing brain protected me. It was how, in our tiny suburban bubble, it was <u>not</u> to be acknowledged. I spent so much time and energy trying to pretend everything was ok, when really, it was very much not. What I really needed was an outsider, someone from outside my family, preferably even someone my age, to tell me: *I see you. I see what's happening. I know what's happening. I know you are hurting. I know.*

I got that in a letter from my first-ever boyfriend. We were briefly "together" during junior high, so you can imagine what that was like. He tried to kiss me and I turned my cheek, a visceral reaction when I saw anyone heading towards my face. We "broke up" and went back to talking again.

In high school, we grew apart, mostly because he was responsible and I was not. But I went on a Kairos retreat and it was basically a bunch of people giving speeches on why partying will ruin your life. And when you're in it, you really drink the Kool-Aid and I remember thinking: *This is it. I'm never smoking pot or touching beer again. Thank you for saving me.* That lasted approximately 48 hours.

But the best part of the retreat was the night when a "big secret" happened, except everyone already knew the secret: you got handed an envelope full of letters and sent to your room to read them and cry. Every letter ended with: *Hope you brought your Kleenex!* And I couldn't help but roll my eyes. This shit was for wimps. I had already been through the emotional trenches, did they think a fluffy letter was going to break me?!

The first letter I read was from my boyfriend at the time and he wrote about how "I really complimented him so well." I'd deal with that later. But the others from my peers were mostly a mass template they wrote to everyone.

Until I got the letter from Bob, my grade school friend and first boyfriend. He wrote:

Dear Caitlin,

Let me just say that I am so glad you've decided to come on this retreat. Even though we've gone our separate ways in high school, I still think you are a great person and I wish only the best for you in your life. I know you have had a tough past. Try to open up these next 2 days, they will fly by. Trust me, you'll be happy you did.

Love,
Bob

It's the first time anyone, like any other person who was my age, acknowledged my pain. I kept reading that line over and over again: *I know you have had a tough past.* I remember thinking: *Wait, how does he know?!?!*

I'd never read a sentence that meant more to me. Whenever I think back to my deeply, deeply repressed teen years, I think about that letter. And I think about how I didn't know what was going on and I was so sad and felt like my world was crumbling but I had to pretend it wasn't and everyone else pretended too. But one sentence of acknowledgment, eight words, meant so much to me.

Even though those years were painful, they shaped me. They made me stronger. And they helped me to not become a totally spoiled brat later in life, which I've always been super grateful for. I got a crash course in life's ups and downs at a young age—and that's something I'm glad I got to learn early.

I never, ever hoped for my parent's to get back together. I knew that was outside the realm of possibilities and I would have disowned them if they even considered it after all that. People would always tell me "you know it's not your fault, right?" and I would brush it off like, *yeah yeah, duh, I didn't make this choice, I know that!*

But it wasn't until I was much, much older that I realized that maybe, just maybe, all of this *did* have an impact on me. That maybe I couldn't just will my way forward without looking at the things I'd avoided for most of my life. It wasn't until I was able to look at the whole truth and nothing but the truth that I could accept everything and start to heal up any leftover wounds that had festered.

It wasn't until I was older and went through my own break-ups that I understood how the heart can be so hurt that the world becomes like tunnel vision. My Gram always told me that everyone does the best they can. And I realized that was resoundingly true for my parents too. They did the best they could at the time—and they had their own lessons to learn with each other—and as the oldest, I was fated to exist right in between them. *What luck...Just kidding. Kinda.*

We can all bond over our horror stories in childhood and to be honest, I don't enjoy reliving mine (*who does?!*), but I also don't let them dictate my life anymore. At a certain point, we have to let go in order to move forward—but we can only do that when we have the courage to face the truth head-on and accept reality for what it is.

As tough as life's challenges can be, those seeming disasters offer the greatest gifts. Any loss, any heartbreak, any divorce, any disaster, any accident—it's incredibly painful and there's no denying that pain. But there is beauty in knowing that right on the other side of that pain lives joy. The more pain we feel, the more joy we can access too. And that is really, really beautiful when you think about it.

It's really easy to tell a story about far off lands and the vulnerabilities of strangers—but it's something quite different to share the truth about your own vulnerabilities.

Before I was ever born, there was a story already unfolding around me. We're each born into a story, whether we realize it or not. Sometimes the circumstances are idyllic—but that's honestly pretty rare. I've yet to encounter a human who had a perfect childhood. And the ones who claim they did...are usually not telling the truth.

My experiences made me who I am and were a big motivator for me. It's the only way to explain what gave me the empathy to be drawn towards the vulnerable, the emotional issues I'd try to outrun, the nudge to do something different with my life, the ability to see that I had the option to make a different choice than "the norm." That I could go after the life I desire and I could put myself first.

From a generational standpoint, I was born into a world that taught me that the way to deal with trauma was to not talk about it. For instance, my grandmother's dad left when she was a toddler—and it was something that was not to be talked about. Anytime I asked her, I could see the pain all over her face, so I'd stop. I didn't even learn much about my other grandmother's dad, other than he was sick. The only thing she ever said to me was: *You're very lucky to have a dad who wants to spend time with you.* Period.

This tradition of pushing things under the rug wasn't exactly sustainable, though. When things get shoved in the dark, what comes up instead are things like: depression, anger, and anxiety. If the skeletons stay in the closet, we each silently suffer in order to keep the status quo.

As a female born on planet Earth, there's a whole other layer to this inherited story too. To be honest, I never believed I couldn't do something because I was a girl.

But like socially and generationally, women were taught to sacrifice (and oddly enough, so were men). And that we're selfish if we put ourselves first. As little girls, we're taught to be nice, to be polite, to act like a lady, to stay quiet, don't be too loud, and to be a helper. And to never, under any circumstances, reveal the family secrets.

So, in the big picture, what happened with my family was a huge blessing for me because it helped me step out of those inherited patterns of abuse and pain. It gave me a more expanded view of life at a rather young age.

We're not supposed to stuff all the shameful things in the dark. We have to put light on them and bring them out.

We're supposed to talk about those things and sometimes, it's painful. But we don't get to healing without getting to the truth first.

Before I acknowledged the past, I never made a choice just for me. I never trusted myself enough because I thought the reality I had was invalid, because it didn't align with the narrative I'd been given. I never honored how scary it was for me and how confused I was.

Until I started to heal. What I went through growing up was hard. It was not easy. I cannot lie and pretend everything magically got better one day because that wouldn't be true. But I can tell the truth that as an adult, my life is much better now. Things are better than I could ever have imagined they'd be, back then. That is something I am eternally grateful for.

We cannot change the story we're born into. I cannot change my past—and I wouldn't want to (okay, maybe, like, a lot of it).

The only story I can actually change, though, is my own. And the only way to do that is by owning all parts of it, the good, the bad, and the stuff I used to shove under a rug. Because I learned that once I gave it a little air, it actually felt better.

The only way to heal, to break the chain of what gets passed down from generation to generation, especially between women, was to focus on healing myself, not anyone else.

And most importantly, I want any girl who struggles with how her family treats her to know that it's okay to tell the truth. That acknowledging pain is not a weakness, but a sign of strength. And that they don't have to be a "good girl" in order to be loved. Those days are over, thankfully.

Is it bad luck to open an umbrella indoors? This was taken one month before the accident, so you decide. December 1988.

BONUS! The Next Level of Hell

It seemed like a really sick and cruel joke that whoever was planning all this out, whatever higher power, decided:

You know what? You thought that was tough, let's spice things up a bit, here's a "bonus mom" — have fun!!!

I inherited a stepmother who hated to be called a stepmother and always referred to me has "her husband's daughter."

The woman who always managed to make me feel like I was an old accessory from the past - a living, breathing reminder that this wasn't her husband's first family.

The only reason I ever even tried to foster a relationship with her was out of respect for my dad and my little brother. It's his wife and his mom, so I thought I had no choice. Until I realized that trying to do that was costing me something far greater: respect for myself.

After many years, I realized I'd just become an understudy character in her play. Someone who was expected to attend mandated events, and be on the ready to perform. To show everyone in the room that this was a happy family, even when it wasn't. Sometimes we were invited to events for our littlest brother—and sometimes we weren't even told about them. But if invited, attendance was mandatory, no matter what. And if I didn't show up, even when sick, I'd be shunned, barely even greeted for months afterwards.

She only ever called me when she needed something. As if I was an on-demand servant to meet her needs, for whatever her latest crisis of the moment was, all while treating me like a second class citizen.

When we came over for dinner, she made sure to announce to the neighbors that THE WHOLE FAMILY was over tonight. If I showed up early, before my dad was home, I wouldn't even be greeted until he arrived. Not even a hello, just open disgust that I'd arrived before she was ready. I spent hours of my life sitting silently in their family room, being ignored until the garage door opened. (Mostly because I'd commute from the city, leaving early to beat traffic, only to get stuck in...that).

She had an opinion for everything I did and always thought I should be doing something else. And was sure to let me know that.

The worst part was watching the toll she took on my little sister, who was right around the same age I was when my parents divorced, for my dad's second marriage. This woman came into her life, at eleven years old, and showered her with attention. Kissed her feet, doted on her, showed her all the love in the world.

And the moment she became pregnant and finally got what she wanted (a child of her own), she dropped my little sister like a bad habit. I was already away at college, but my sister had to spend her teen years...with that. Demoted in her own family. Alone. And one of my only regrets in life is the example I set back then.

I would plead with my sister to just follow my lead, suck it up, it's *our dad*, just kill her with kindness, etc. I didn't truly understand because I didn't have the capacity to understand. And I chose not to. It was too much for me to handle at that point in my life. I could only handle one mommy issue at a time.

This woman didn't look at what would make us happy as individuals, but was solely focused on how her son (my littlest brother) would perceive us. What impression we were making on him and if it was acceptable, according to the standards she chose to live by.

Nothing would ever be good enough and slowly but surely, I saw my dad's opinion of me change too, as he absorbed her constant remarks, her judgments, her telling him how it "should" be, and how she was always, very conveniently, the victim.

Until many years later and I didn't recognize my relationship with my father. She'd so deeply entrenched him in the new family of her dreams, trying to prove it was so much better than the old one he had before.

But the worst part was the fakeness.

The performance for other people.

The moment anyone else was around, her charm sparked on. She'd pretend to know about my life. Pretend to be on good terms. Pretend she hadn't driven a giant wedge between my dad and I.

Really, it was the watching the relationship with my dad fade away that hurt the most. In my desperation to make sure he was okay, I overlooked how this new woman in the family was good for him— but like a living nightmare for me.

It wasn't until she entered the picture that the awful patterns started. It happened all the time with my mom, but as a bonus, now it happened with my dad and his wife too. Silence, being cut out, not spoken to for weeks, sometimes months. Five different times since they got married, to be exact. Where something would happen that was not approved of—and instead of talking to me about it, I'd be ostracized. And during these periods of being iced out, on both sides, I'd be labeled as crazy, the problem, too much, overly dramatic, and my personal favorite, "probably a lesbian."

This cycle would repeat, until I couldn't handle it and would contact them, apologizing for whatever "grievance" I'd caused, like missing a St. Patrick's Day party, or being sick, or moving away, or daring to ever speak up and say, "Ouch, she hurt me." I'd either show up and shut up, with the agreement to say nothing and never stand up for myself—or I was cut out of the family until I got back in line. So I kept quiet. And apologized, so they'd speak to me.

There's really no way to illustrate what this added family experience was like, for me, so I will let her words speak for themselves (with the responses I wish I'd had the strength to say, at the time). Mind you, this is only a sprinkling, and I just silently took it all in, because I was afraid of losing my dad if I didn't.

On my parent's divorce: "I know families where the parents got divorced and they still talk and the kids are angels." (Oh, honey.)

On why my father married my mother in the first place: "Your dad was attracted to your mom because she reminded him of his mom. Crazy." (I'm their....daughter. You know that, right?)

Whenever I mentioned my dog: "When are you gonna get rid of that thing?" (Oh, the feeling is mutual—my dog doesn't like you either).

When she decided she wanted a dog: "With everything I've put up with from you kids, the least I deserve is a dog." (Love that for you).

When she named her dog "Emory" and my sister's name is "Emily": "Ems, Ems!! Sit, Ems, go to your cage." (No comment).

When I mentioned maybe wanting to live in London one day: "You could move to London if you worked in insurance, but you won't be able to afford it any other way." (Please stay out of my finances, I've literally never been included in yours).

On my decision to not work in corporate America: "I'm going to tell you what your parents won't. You need to get a real job. My friend works at Big Bank and you'd be a great teller. You need to grow up." (My parents would never say anything like that to me).

When I took the GRE to potentially get my PHD and had to miss the St. Patrick's Day party she was hosting: "Well, that's very disappointing. Your father is going to be very hurt. (Click)." (A party where I'll be treated like your hired help? How could I possibly miss that!).

When she invited her Starbucks barista to said St. Patrick's Day party, years later, with clear intentions of match-making him with my sister after threatening to do so multiple times and my sister begging her to please not to: "Girls, meet Joseph. He's a hard-working, good-looking single guy. I'll let you guys take it from here." *Side talk to me:* "Be nice and include him, don't do your usual cliquey stuff." (Spent an hour in the bathroom with my sister balling her eyes out).

When a guy planned a date with my sister on a Sunday and then died by suicide the night before: "You know, she walked in the house and just broke down, like tears I've never seen, and all I kept thinking was: I don't need this trash in my house!"

( ).

Anytime I've ever gone to dinner at her house:
Upon arrival: "Oh, you're here already!" (I'll leave. Or you could?)
Upon departure: "Well, come back sometime, we <u>never</u> get to see you." (I'm literally here right now).

When I went to San Francisco: "Your father and I thought you were going to start smoking again." (I can always count on you to expect the best!).

After I gained a few (needed) pounds after quitting smoking: I've always known you to be very tiny, it'll come right off. (Oh, I'm just allergic to you actually, I swell up a bit when you're nearby).

When I needed a ride to the train station to get to my college internship and my dad had left for work so I had to ask her for a ride, the first and last time, and I'd only known her less than a year: (sounding like someone asked her to put pins in her eyes) "Ugh, alright already, I'm coming down, Jesus Christ. Let's go. Get in the car, I've had enough of all this. Can I ever just sleep in?" (I politely told her no, thank you and missed my internship—and also mentioned that she was not my parent).

When I bought a new SUV: "My, my, this is a FAMILY CAR!" (I was single).

Talking about my grandmother after she died: "She had a mental illness. It seems like everyone in that family does, it must be in the blood." (That's...my...blood. And your husband's.)

At the luncheon after my grandmother's funeral: (starts singing and dancing through the tables) "C'mon guys, let's get this party started! Get those hands in the air!" (It's time to go. Grandma would not like this).

154

Standing over my grandmother's grave, on the day of her burial service, mad at me for whatever perceived hurt: (while turning her back) "Oh, hi." (Noted).

The day my body conscious sister wore shorts at the lake house: (runs up to her urgently): "Your butt is HANGING out of those shorts, please cover up!" (Spent an hour in the bathroom with my sister balling her eyes out).

When I decided to take a road trip across the country: "I'm just worried about safety. You're not meeting up with men in these hotel rooms? This all seems so dangerous." (I know this is going to come as a shock, but I'm not as dumb as you think I am).

After I spent months volunteering with orphans in Peru: "I told your father not to let you go to South America." (Thank you for your continued support. Really means the world).

Whenever I say anything that doesn't align with her holier than thou values: "Well, we don't agree with your decisions but there's nothing we can say." (Same. Here.)

When I lent my grandmother "The Time Traveller's Wife" because I loved it and thought it was a really good book: "I cannot believe you gave that to your grandmother! The sex scene!" (Yeah, she's a grown woman and that was like two pages out of hundreds).

When I lost my virginity: "You're just so much more advanced in that area than I was." (By waiting until I was a legal adult and using protection with my boyfriend?)

On my 18th birthday: "I've always said you're never fully an adult until you're 25." (Cool, cool, cool).

On my 25th birthday: "I've always said you're never fully an adult until you're 35." (Has anyone ever told you to just...shush?)

A week after my 35th birthday after I received a gift of XL leggings: "Yeah well happy birthday or whatever, sorry for the delay, the day just got away from me. Did the pants fit?" (I don't know, we'll have to ask whoever buys them from Goodwill. The next year, I genuinely received a tin of expired cookies for my birthday).

On spending time with my own father: "You guys had all your dad's attention, it's our time now." (That sounds really healthy!)

When she hung a portrait of only my dad and their son over the fireplace: "This was just the one thing I wanted and I've given up so much for you guys." (Like, what, exactly? You've cut us out of the picture, literally).

After my little brother picked me as his confirmation sponsor: "Clearly not for religious reasons." (Thank God).

When I brought up anything from the past or how I'd known my father for nearly two decades before she even met him:

Silence. Walks away. Grimace. (Smug smile).
On being a stepmother:

"Don't marry a man with kids. It's too much."

(Oh don't worry, I'll never be like you).

156

11

IRELAND: BLOOD

(a world without borders)

I honor your path.
I drink from your well.
I bring an unprotected heart to our meeting place.
I hold no cherished outcome.
I will not negotiate by withholding.
I am not subject to disappointment.

- Celtic Vow of Friendship

St. Patrick's Day is a very big holiday for us Irish North Americans. Chicago dyes the river, everyone wears green, and drinks as if the world may end. I once hosted a baby shower on St. Patrick's Day, where we all wore green, drank beer out of baby bottles, and then headed out to join the parties, leaving the mom-to-be with her gifts and her choice of sober living. *So mature.*

Being a little bit Irish was really the only heritage I'd been handed and I was curious to see what that meant besides...drinking beer and wearing green. On both sides of my family, my ancestors lived in small farm huts (which I verified were in two different locations, otherwise I'd have some real DNA issues to sort out).

On my first trip to Ireland, I went to Westport, a town on the west coast because it was close to where my maternal ancestors came from. I went with my sister and we treated our mom to join us.

I worked really hard to maintain a relationship with her, even taking on debt so she could come to Ireland with us, in hopes of repairing the past. I'd circle back, over and over, trying to make things better. This trip was one (of many) attempts.

On our very first day, we decided to visit Croagh Patrick, the holy mountain where St. Patrick, the patron saint of immigrants, was buried. This was also where he supposedly banished all the snakes from Ireland too. Really, this was symbolic for banishing the goddess in the name of Christianity, since the serpent was a symbol of the feminine. *But they certainly don't teach ya that at Catholic school!*

I later found out Croagh Patrick was a sacred, ancient place for rituals dating back to 3,000 B.C. It's most famous for "Reek Sunday" a day in July when thousands of people climb the mountain at night, sometimes even barefoot, as a religious pilgrimage.
On our way there, we had a very nice cab driver. She was so cheery and chatty and friendly—basically, so Irish. She suggested:

If ya made it all the way here, ya might as well climb to the top. You'll just need a wee bit of water and a snack, and you'll be all set now, ya dears. It'll only take ya maybe two hours to get up the mountain and about half the time to get down. And it's worth it, don't you know. Wait til ya see the view. It's not too hard, people of all ages are doing it, all the time, all the time. Give it a go, I promise ya won't regret it.

We started up the trail and after eight minutes, my sister turned back to wait at the bottom. She was not what one would call a "hiker." My mom and I kept going, but as the drop-offs at the edge of the trail started getting more real, she turned back. Since I never knew when to quit, I kept going.

I quickly realized a few things:

1. I was the only person by myself on the trail. Everyone else was in a group.
2. I was the only non-native on the trail. Everyone else was an Irish local.
3. I was carrying a fucking purse. Everyone else had a backpack and a trekking pole.

As the trail went on, it was increasingly beautiful and increasingly more steep and slippery. With every step forward, the stones would slide me half a step back. But as I looked around me, it was like all of Ireland was showing off. The lakes shimmered with golden light, the ocean was the deepest blue, and the fields were the most vibrant greens. Way prettier than the suburb my family had ended up in.

The path soon became completely filled with loose limestone and took on an incline of about 45 degrees. I'm not a mathematician, so that estimate could be inaccurate. This didn't pair well with my gym shoes, which were super cute but featured zero traction. I never realized it was possible to climb a mountain by falling on your arse the entire way up, but I am here to vouch that it was entirely a very doable possibility.

With every new bruise added to my lower body, I took in the scenery around me. It was the most beautiful place my soul had ever known. I felt it in every part of my being, especially my new bruises.

When I was about twenty minutes from the top, sheer panic set in for a few seconds. I was slipping all over the place, my hands and legs were bleeding a bit, and I could not see the top. It felt like I had been accidently left behind in a beautiful, medieval setting of a fairy tale, but without any magical powers to get back home.
And that is when I remembered that thousands of people hiked this very same trail, every year, literally religiously, and sometimes even

barefoot. So I told fear to knock it off and focused on moving forward. Pretty soon, I could see the top.

Reaching the top of a mountain is one of the most uplifting and freeing feelings in the world. It was one of those moments in my life when I didn't want to even speak, and luckily, I was alone, so there was no one I could talk to, even if I wanted to. I didn't want any noise to interrupt what was happening up there, so close to the sky.

I took my shoes off, sat on a rock, and planted my feet on the ground. I looked out over the deep blue ocean, the little islands, the rolling green hills, the silver lakes, the wispy clouds and it was blue and green and white, all blended together in the most wonderful way. I felt something I hadn't felt in a really long time. Full of awe and wonder.

I thought about how my life—this life I was living, where I was climbing mountains—was only possible because of the people who came before me. The people who came from this very land. All those people in my past who made sacrifices, who worked hard, who dreamt of a better life, who poured their blood, sweat, and tears into just surviving, who got on a BOAT and left the rest of their family behind. I felt so at home there, overlooking Ireland. It was like my heart recognized the heartbeat of that land.

I thought about why my family would ever leave a place like this. And then I remembered it was because they had to leave. Because they couldn't survive there anymore.

And isn't it that way for many families? They have no other choice than to leave their home, because if they don't, they won't survive. They need food or money or love or freedom or safety or something so badly that they are brave enough to give up the world they know to venture into a new one. Or, worse, they weren't given a choice at all. They were forced to leave. Or kidnapped.

So now, all these families, everywhere around the world, left the land they came from. It's like the past few centuries have been a time of great dislocation for the world. And maybe it didn't seem so beautiful at the time, but there had to be a reason why so many people were scattered from the land of their family. And why some stayed.

And, now, the world was all mixed up. We're all mixed together and we all have lands to call home and our colors are blending to create something even more beautiful. So maybe we all had to leave our homes so we can all head in the same direction together. Maybe we are getting rid of the things that divide us and starting to live in a world that has no borders, where all the world will be home for everyone, no matter where you are. Or maybe I'm just a very wishful thinker.

Because when you look at the earth from the moon, you don't see political parties or walls or countries or borders. You see a shining globe with clouds and land and water. And you know that billions of beings are living on that globe. And when you sit on the top of a mountain, even the slightly elevated viewpoint makes you see that we're all just tiny pieces of something so much bigger than we can ever fully know.

I sat on that rock on the top of that mountain and I thought about all the beauty in this life, and how lucky I was to be sitting there, at that moment. My life was built on the dreams of my ancestors. Their dream of living a life with more abundance and more freedom.

If two Irish families hadn't run out of potatoes, if Ellis Island hadn't welcomed my great-grandparents, if my grandmothers hadn't met my grandpas at dances, and if my parents hadn't wanted to write for their school newspaper, I wouldn't be there.

Without all the twists and turns of fate, without the stars aligning, I wouldn't be on that mountain—an Irish descendant who was lucky enough to have the freedom to travel.

And there I was, thinking about all of these things, and it's all because of them. The people who lived here before me.

I thought about all the different mountains I've climbed in my life:

when my family imploded

when I felt alone and wasn't on the same page as my friends

when my grandpas died

when I went to peru and costa rica

when my grandma died

when my heart was broken

And all the mountains my ancestors, and in particular, my grandparents had to climb too.

Two weeks after I'd returned from Peru, I sat in a specialist's office and watched my grandmother hear:

We're sorry, but you have stage IV cancer. We don't recommend treatment. And we can't predict how long you have left.

My grandma took her new diagnosis with grace. She sat in that chair and said: *Okay, well, what shall we do next?* She always went to California to stay with my aunt each winter so after Christmas, she got on the plane to go on her trip. And we all hoped for the best.

I went to visit her in San Francisco for a weekend and realized: a. she wasn't coming home and b. she was dying sooner than later.

I called my mom and told her she needed to come out and see my grandma like yesterday. And I started realizing the weekend was going to come to an end and I was going to have to say goodbye to her, knowing it was the last time I'd ever see her.

Of course, my flight was super early, so we went to bed and I barely slept. When my alarm went off, I quietly got ready, wheeled my suitcase to the front door, and then slowly approached my grandmother's bed.

I gently shook her and said:

Issy. Issy. It's me, Caitlin. I'm leav....

And she shot straight up like she'd seen the devil. She started screaming and was so afraid and had no idea who I was. My aunt explained that she sometimes gets confused in her sleep and that it's ok and to just go.

So my final goodbye with my grandmother did not go as planned, it actually went worse than I could have ever imagined. I had to leave to the soundtrack of her wails and screams, pure terror in her voice. The flight home was a blur of an experience. I didn't even cry, I was so numb to how horrifically awful that last moment was. I actually laughed a lot, because why would the world do that?! Three weeks later, she died.

When I got home, I went through all my boxes of memories and found a card she'd given me:

Dear Caitlin,
I believe in magic...
in fairy princesses

and dreams that really do come true.
It isn't any wonder
that a thousand years from now,
somewhere, somehow I'll still be loving you.
Love you always!

Love,
Issy + Pa

I also found a card I'd made for her, the very first time she ever got sick:

Dear Issy,

I hope you get well <u>very very very</u> soon! We will visit you at the hospital and at your condo. I promise to help make you food. I hope you like Spagghettio's, macaroni and cheese, and Little Caeser's pizza because I really am not a good cook, but when I went to the grocery store with my mom I did save you an extra can of Spaghettios. Well, I love you.

xxxooo

Love,
Caitlin

On the top of the mountain in Ireland, I had a little conversation with my grandmother:

Thank you for this trip. Thank you for this mountain and thank you for this time I get to have alone at the top. Except I know I am not really here alone. I know that somehow, someway you'll still be loving me and I just want you to know that somehow, someway I'll still be loving you too.

164

The Druids of Ireland believed that nothing was ever lost. They didn't believe in death—they believed in a change of condition, a passage into another existence, hidden from us by the thinnest of walls. And that veil is thinner at the top of a mountain.

I sat in silence for a while after that and breathed in the beauty. My heart started to feel so full that it could burst. Once I knew I'd soaked up enough, I started back down the mountain.

The descent was no easier than the climb. In many ways, it was almost harder. It took me nearly six hours to get up and down the mountain, which was about triple the estimate from our cutesie cab lady. A quick Google search that night gave me the real answer:

Is it hard to climb Croagh Patrick?

"Difficult to climb": One of the oldest religious sites in Ireland, the mountain is very difficult to climb as there is a small rivulet running down the hill so the surface is very slippery and there are big stones everywhere.

I think that lady underestimated on purpose, because I never would have done it if I'd known how long it would really take or how difficult it was going to be. Which was oddly comparable to lots of other things in life, I guess. Sometimes it's better not to know how much time it will take for certain things.

A few months after the trip, I read a book about Croagh Patrick and learned about the Buddhist questing practice called nyubu, which means to go into the mountains in order to understand oneself and to remake one's connections to the gods. This was the advice from the book, *Croagh Patrick: Ireland's Holy Mountain*:

It is good to take to the mountain when we don't know what else to do. When we are drawn to quests we know little about, this makes life and develops soul. Where can we find this process that will free us? On the mountain. To lift the veils makes one strong enough to tolerate what life is about; to see into patterns of events, people, and things; to learn not to take the first impression so deadly seriously, but to look behind and behind.

I realized that enlightenment does not necessarily happen at the top of the mountain. Maybe it's about what we learn up there, and how we take it back home with us. If we're willing to bring those lessons back down to the ground and into our everyday life. It's about returning home and little by little, putting to work what we learned along the way.

The night before my grandmother passed away, I had a very vivid dream with her. She was sitting in a rocking chair and she pulled me on her lap and I was a little kid again. She held me and she told me it's all going to be okay.

It's not so much what she said in the dream, but it was the feeling that stuck with me when I woke up. It was this pure, deep sense of love and peace, and I felt it through to my core.

I spent weeks googling "Can a dying person visit you in a dream?" after that because it felt so real and unlike anything I'd ever experienced before. I knew she was going to die that day when I woke up. And she did.

A little while after my grandmother's funeral, I made an excuse to go to her place. She lived in a small retirement community in a suburb nearby, and I loved her place because it was filled with her and my grandpa. All of their things and their memories. It was their space in this world.

It was before we moved all her stuff out, so it was all just piled up, looking like she was about to move, but really she wasn't moving anywhere. Her body died and in a shocking plot twist, she did not take any of her stuff with her. I went into her place thinking:

Okay, I can do this. I'll go in, I'll get that random thing, and I'll leave, and I won't cry and I'll be strong and I'll just do this because I can and I'm old enough to handle it.

Within 20 seconds, I was sitting in her favorite reading chair, surrounded by piles of her books and boxes, crying my bloody eyes out.

I cried for her and I cried for me and I cried for my family and I cried for all the people who have ever lost someone who they love so much. Who they really, truly, unconditionally love. The kind of love that is really real, because it doesn't hurt, it's always been gentle and caring and supportive. The kind of love where someone thinks only the sun can shine out of your face. I cried because I knew I would have to keep going, without her kind of love calling to check in or sitting next to me on Sundays anymore. I cried for knowing that I would have more love in my life and that she wouldn't be there to see it with her eyes.

But I also knew, without a doubt, that she was still with me—on Sundays, on good days, and on bad days. That even if I can't see her with my eyes anymore, I can feel her in my heart. And she's working whatever magic she can to give me what I need when I need it.

One of my favorite quotes is from Donald Rumsfeld, a former politician, ironically. He said:

There are known knowns. These are things we know that we know. There are known unknowns. That is to say, there are things that we know we don't know. But there are also unknown unknowns. There are things we don't know we don't know.

On that mountain in Ireland, I knew I felt something very different, something new but also, ancient. Something we don't know we don't know. It's whatever the thing is that makes me know my grandmother is with me, even when her body is not. Whatever made me climb a mountain, even though I've worked out on average twice per year. Whatever is pulling us forward, reminding us that there's so many beautiful things waiting for us. Whatever keeps us all connected, the living and the dead.

I wrote my grandmother this letter, when we found out she was going to die. I didn't want her to go with any unknowns about what she meant to my siblings and I:

Dear Issy,

I wanted to write you this because I want you to know some things, especially after what you've been through the past few months. I am better at writing about this stuff than I am at talking about it so I hope you don't mind that I'm putting all this in a letter, but it's the best way I could share it with you.

I'm so sorry for everything you've been through. Life is unfair sometimes and it was so hard to watch you go through all of that and I can only imagine what it felt like to be the one going through it. But I want you to know that I admire your strength and poise - and I always have and always will.

I want you to know how IMPORTANT you are to me. I've wanted to tell you this many times before but it never seemed like a good time. After everything you've been through, I figured now is as good of a time as any!

I am so grateful to have you in my life and I don't think I can ever fully express my gratitude in words. When I look at the years I've been on this planet, there are only a handful of things that have remained constant.

One of those constants that I am extremely grateful for - and which has always been the same - is you & Pa. Some of my very first memories are of doing fun things with you and Pa - going to Santa's Village or coming to visit you in Northbrook or going to tea at the Walnut Room. I remember when I wanted a new bike so bad and that Christmas, Pa told me to follow him to the car and he pulled a brand new bicycle out of the trunk. I loved sleeping over at your condo because I always got to eat Spagghettio's in the wooden bowls and have NesQuik chocolate milk. You always brought me Chiclets because they were my favorite. We went to Cubs games and plays at Drury Lane and did so many fun, memorable things when I was little. Thank you for always spoiling me and buying me pretty dresses and red coats. I've always genuinely enjoyed spending time with you and Pa, ever since I could remember. And all your kind actions taught me something very important - how to be loving.

But you & Pa weren't just there for the happy times. What happened with my family was really hard for me when I was younger. And I will never forget that you & Pa were there with us almost every single day throughout that time. I can say this now, because I'm older and have a clearer understanding of what happened, but you & Pa really stepped in during that hard time in our lives. I will never, ever forget that and I will always be grateful for all you did. My mom didn't have to worry about going to work because she knew you guys would help her. You & Pa took me to Piven Theater School and drove back and forth twice a week to take me there. I loved going to Homer's and eating their fries and chatting with you guys. It was a really hard time at home and I was confused and scared, and mostly just sad. But luckily, God blessed me with two of the most amazing grandparents in the world - Issy and Pa. You and Pa helped us when we really needed it the most and you did what you could to make things better. I will never, ever forget that.

You and Pa are, and always will be, constants in my life. I've always known you guys are there, and I can always depend on you, no matter what. I can't tell you how comforting it is to have such a never-wavering presence of love in my life.

I have always known and will forever know that your love and support for me is absolutely unconditional and you will always be there for me no matter what. That means so much to me and having you and Pa in my life has taught me how simple things can have a big impact - because all the simple acts of kindness you've done for me have had the biggest impact on my life and who I am.

So I wanted to say THANK YOU. Because you mean more to me than you'll ever know, Issy. I am so grateful for your support, love, and understanding. I hope the next few weeks are relaxing and peaceful and you can get some well-deserved rest. As a fellow Scorpio, I want to say that I hope you always do what you want. Please know that you have a loving granddaughter (and many more!) that will support you no matter what. I love you very much Issy and I would give anything for you to be comfortable and happy. Thank you for everything you've always done for me and for all you've taught me through the years.

I know the past few months have been really hard - and I know that Pa is watching your every move and protecting you and all of us. And that brings me great comfort every day and I hope it does the same for you :)

I'm excited for you to return home refreshed and I will miss you while you're away, but you'll never be far from my thoughts.
Love,
Caitlin

My great-great grandma, great-great uncle, and great-aunt, at their
home in Bunnyconnellan, near Westport, Ireland | A long time ago
~early 1900's

12
SOUTH SIDE: AS
(faith)

The light shines in the darkness,
and the darkness has not overcome it.

- John 1:1-5

Many great things have been born in Chicago. It's the birthplace of social work, thanks to Jane Addams and her Hull House. Mother Cabrini founded hospitals, houses for the poor, and orphanages there.

But Chicago's dirty little secret was...segregation. Just kidding, it's not a secret at all—it's blatantly obvious! There was a clear, defining gap between the neighborhoods and often the races in the city, specifically between the North and the South and some of the West. The spoken and unspoken dividing lines felt oddly reminiscent of...the Civil War Era?

Somehow I ended up floating between these divided worlds for a few years. First, I was connected with a very wealthy woman from the North side. I met with Mimi in her basement and she told me she felt drawn to help Black mothers on Chicago's South side.

My gut takeaway after our initial meeting was that she would probably be high maintenance to work for (I was right), but that she also was doing something really unique and very personal (I was also right).

Mimi's jewelry, clothing, purses and shoes were worth more than all my assets combined. I'd go to her 4-story home in Lincoln Park, one of the ritziest neighborhoods in the city, and her maid always let me in. The interior designer would often be there rehabbing a room that already looked beautiful, testing out new velvet wallpaper and gluing diamonds to the ceiling. Even though on the outside, Mimi appeared to be everything I was so...not into—on the inside, she had a heart of gold, which goes to prove that you should never judge a book (or person) by its cover.

Mimi's idea was to work with mothers in Chicago's most underserved neighborhoods, Englewood, Woodlawn and Auburn Gresham—the places we hear about on the news with a total number of gunshots and drive-by shootings.

At a young age, I stopped watching the Chicago news, specifically when the story of Girl X came out. She was a 9-year-old girl who had a sleepover at her best friend's apartment in Cabrini Green, a Chicago housing project on the North side, and the next morning, was kidnapped, raped and left for dead. She lived in a coma for weeks and was living the rest of her life blind, mute and wheelchair-bound. Cabrini Green was torn down years later and replaced by a Target. But I just remember watching this story unfold, when I was the same age as her, and deciding the news was worse than any scary movie.

On my first day working for Mimi, I met Suki, her event planner, one of the sweetest, most kind-spirited humans ever. I found myself in a Lexus, driving to Englewood for the very first time with them both. Mimi started making conversation as we got on the highway:

It's so crazy how everyone thinks you have to go to another country to get involved. That's sexy and all, but what about in your own backyard? You don't need to go to South America, there's people right here to connect with.

Totally.

What did you do before this again?

Umm...

There was a transformation that happened when we drove south down I-90. Once we were past the skyline, I recognized the White Sox ballpark on the right...and then, it was like another planet.

The first thing I noticed was all the people walking around. Lots of people in certain areas were wearing certain colors, like all red or all blue. The cars were an interesting mix, with lots of old cars and a few brand new expensive cars blaring music. The buildings and homes mostly looked old and unkempt, as my European ancestors would say. Lots of boarded windows. It felt like a forgotten world in the midst of a growing community.

We picked up two moms, Deedra and La'tanya, from a school in Englewood. Even though they weren't getting paid, they went to their kids' school every day to volunteer and help out. I was immediately in awe of their dedication.

Mimi hosted weekly meetings for Deedra, La'tanya and a few other moms in a church basement, brought food for everyone and gave all the moms rides to and from the meetings. The church was on King Drive, a few blocks from the housing project Parkway Gardens, which was also on the "O Block"—a block known for having the most violence in Chicago.

I started going to Mimi's meetings with the moms every week and drove myself. I cannot say I felt totally comfortable driving there on my lonesome, just as I wouldn't in any place where the odds of violence are higher. This was because I'm afraid of guns and I felt the same way when I had to drive through Texas—just to be clear.

I eventually stopped telling a lot of people when I would go because they would say things like:

What are you doing in that neighborhood?
You shouldn't be going down there. It's not safe for you.
That's too dangerous for you.
I'm worried you'll get hurt.

Replace you with "white girl" and you'll see how deep racism runs. They never outright said what they were implying. But I knew what they meant and it made me see that fear and ignorance are often what keep people apart.

At first, the moms from the neighborhood had a WALL UP (*hmm...I wonder why?!*) They wouldn't say much, they didn't really trust Mimi, Suki or me, and it was basically just a free lunch for all of us, once a week.

The ice started to break the day I wore a dress for the first time. I actually had a date that night so that was the only reason I was remotely dressed up at all.

The women perked up right away when I walked in and started teasing me: *Look at you all dressed up! You're fancy!! Where do you think you're going?*

The truth was I had recently decided to try dating on an app for the first time. Maybe you've heard of it, it's kinda elite, but it's called Tinder?

I started dating the very first guy I matched with and actually met in person. His name was Ari, he was from Israel, sold diamonds for a living, and was very good-looking.

We had great chemistry from day one, and he even brought me to my first authentic Passover seder meal. All the Israeli women in the room glared at me when I walked in, clearly not happy to see their hottest guy friend with a new Gentile. I could understand why, I looked very Aryan. Between the scripture being read aloud, everyone was still speaking in Hebrew, even in casual conversation. Only one person at the table actually attempted to talk to me. It was one of the other Israeli guys at the seder:

Where are you from?

Palatine

PALESTINE?!?

No, no. Palatine, it's a suburb.

Dead stop to convo.

So, I was wearing a dress to meet up with Ari later, and the ladies all started calling me a "thot." I had no clue what it meant so I just played along and laughed too. *Hahaha...I'm a thot today!!* Then I got home and found out what a thot is (that hoe over there). I was glad I could make the ladies laugh, even if they were laughing at me, not with me. It *was* funny. And I did have a thot vibe that day.

With time and consistency, the group started to come together and bond. The moms opened up about what life was really like in their neighborhood.

Here's what I learned as I grew closer to these mothers:

They were strong.
They were resourceful.
They didn't need anyone to fix them.

176

They had more faith than anyone I knew.

They deserved to live in a neighborhood with the same resources as the other neighborhoods in the city.

The moms explained how their men—brothers, uncles, dads, sons— usually faced one of two fates: jail or violence. One of their brothers was arrested because the police planted a gun on him. The stories were heart-wrenching and twisted and filled with injustice.

The reputation was that their neighborhoods were a horrible, dangerous place and no one who doesn't have to go there should be there and it's where there's only drugs and gangs and violence and sadness.

The truth was the South Side was divided and oppressed because of racism and that thing called "White Flight." It's why there was a noticeable lack of color in the suburbs I grew up in. And what infuriated me the most was that most white people just didn't understand that, at all. I can say that because I'm white and it's sadly been proven true to me, through experience.

At the same time, what's also been proven true is that there were white women who were willing to take accountability for their role in history and do something to uplift women of color. I saw that in Mimi, in Suki, in my sister and cousins who volunteered to support events, and all the women who participated in the group. It was really beautiful to watch the dividing line start to melt away.

Here's the truth about what I experienced when I was in those neighborhoods: I joined a gang. Just kidding, *nothing bad ever happened*. Only WONDERFUL things happened!

For three years, I drove into and out of Auburn Gresham at least once a week, all by myself. People were nice to me. I formed new friendships. I got involved in a community that needed people to care. I met a group of mothers and tons of organizations who were rallying together and working hard everyday to make change in their community.

They weren't looking for a hand out from the outside, but they were looking to build renewal from their own resources—because they felt neglected and abandoned by the world around them and had learned to take matters into their own hands. In my eyes, all of those things were really fucking beautiful.

I went to Church with Latisha (because she kept begging me to come), and people were taking selfies and dancing and singing. They were all making fun of me because I couldn't dance and I was very awkward about it. At the church I went to as a kid, I was taught to sit the fuck down and be as silent as possible. It's hard to erase those years of conditioning from your body.

La'tanya and I had a talk once about the violence in her neighborhood. I honestly wanted to know—how does a human being handle this? After a long pause and a huge sigh, she said:

I'm numb. I had to become numb to it. When I was in high school, I was really in love. I loved my boyfriend so much and we spent all our time together. We weren't involved in any of this shit, we were smart and we were going to live a better life. And then one day he walked down the wrong block at the wrong time and he was shot and killed. At that moment, I went numb. I can't feel it anymore. My little cousins were just killed, and I acknowledge it, I attend their funerals, and then I carry on like it's whatever because I do not feel it anymore. I am numb to all of it.

I feel a fire and rage that burns, deep in my soul, when I hear people say ignorant things about Chicago's neighborhoods, especially the ones they've never even been to.

There were so many beautiful and kind and loving people and mothers and fathers who were working their asses off to create a better life for themselves and their community, despite a system that oppressed them.

Even though they lived in a city where the resources were clearly not evenly dispersed. Even though life had been unfair. They were still giving it their best.

My favorite project we worked on together was creating a Peace Mural. It's at 63rd and Wallace, across from the murder mansion from *The Devil in the White City*. It's on a wall underneath a train track which was also by a stop on the Underground Railroad. All our names are on a tile in the mural.

This public piece of art was created over a few weekends, with each tile placed by volunteers and community members. We had music playing and snacks and everyone did their part to create it. The words: LOVE, UNITY, PEACE, and HOPE are permanently embedded on this wall, right between Englewood and Woodlawn. It was a clear sign that: a. people cared; b. good things were coming there; and c. it marked the place where the two neighborhoods met with something positive.

The intention behind everything Mimi and this group was doing came from something she'd read about the original Mother's Day, which surprisingly, was not created only to buy Hallmark cards and flowers.

It was actually a day to bring all mothers together to stand for peace during a time of war and great division in the country. Started by Julia Ward Howe, an abolitionist back in 1870, she worked to establish a Mother's Peace Day—to celebrate the eradication of war. She wrote a Mother's Day Proclamation, that's really good and also quite lengthy, but this was the best bit:

From the bosom of the devastated earth a voice goes up with our own. It says, "Disarm, disarm! The sword is not the balance of justice." Blood does not wipe out dishonor nor violence indicate possession.

Mimi and the moms I met on the South Side of Chicago were following in this lady's footsteps and living out her legacy. The moms faced a war on their streets and so, they gathered together to end the violence and work for peace.

And even though Mimi wasn't low maintenance, she was right about one thing: I didn't need to go so far away to be a part of positive change in the world. None of us do. The opportunity is usually right where we are, if we take the time to look around and cross the unspoken borders around us.

Peace Mural, 63rd and Wallace, Chicago, Illinois| September 2014.

13

BALI: MY SWEET LORD

(unconditional love)

A woman has to be outside of culture to find out who she is.
- *Martha Beck*

San Francisco was the number one place I'd wanted to live in the world, mainly because every time I'd ever been there, my aunt spoiled me rotten.

When I was thinking about moving out of Chicago, my aunt said: *Why don't you come here? There's an open loft down the hall from me that you can stay in, totally rent-free!*

I thought: *Hmmm. An entire loft, empty and waiting for me in San Francisco, the city with the most expensive rent in the country? It does sound a little too good to be true...but I'll take it!*

It was (a little) too good to be true. In this case, there was one critical detail I learned about upon arrival: the light rail that was being installed on the street below via 24/7 construction, with a chorus of jackhammers kicking in around 3am. That was why no one was renting the loft. Non-stop construction.

Thus began what ended up being a very sleepless few weeks of my life. The owner of the loft I was staying in would randomly "visit"— seemingly out of thin air. He lived in Texas but owned a pet store in SF—and was kind enough to let me stay in his vacant loft. But he'd pop back in and stay for a few nights, leaving me and my dog to find somewhere else to live whenever he showed up. *Oh, you're back? Okay cool let me just find a tent to live in.*

I'd hang out with my aunt's friends who were all so kind—and they'd spend the evening listing off everything I needed to do to start my new life in that city: *Work there! Move here! Live with this person! No that person! Do this, do that, do this, do that!*

I'd literally look in the mirror at night and think: *How did this happen? I just LEFT a city where everyone was telling me what to do. And it's happening...again!!!*

It did not feel like a step forward. If anything, I was regressing.

The main redeeming moment of this time was when I met Joy, a spiritual mentor and psychic, in San Rafael. Krissy, another resident of the loft building, asked if I wanted to go get a spiritual reading with her and go to Target in Marin. My answer was: *Yes, please!*

I'd always been drawn to psychics, knowing some can be great and some can also be a total sham. I'd had a psychic tell me how my best friend was pregnant (and I was the only friend who knew, so it was a real doozy when she picked up on that!). I'd also had a psychic tell me that I was cursed and if I just went downstairs to an ATM and withdrew $247, she would cure me. *Thank you, but I'm good with my demons.*

Really, we all have psychic abilities, it's just sometimes easier to go sit in front of a woman and ask her to tell you what you already know, in some part of your energetic layers. And that's because we usually shut down our own intuitive "gifts" between the ages of five and seven. Because that's when schooling starts.

I can literally remember sitting in a classroom being tested for kindergarten (to make sure I was ready). The teacher asked me to close my eyes and imagine—and I looked at her and said:

I don't need to close my eyes. I imagine with my eyes open.

(laughing) No, you need to close your eyes.

No, I don't.

Well, just close them for me and imagine…

From there, I realized that being able to imagine and see things with my eyes open wasn't the norm. So there I was, as a grown ass woman, venturing across the bay to meet Joy, so she could tell me what the heck was going on with my life because I'd been trained (and conditioned) to keep my eyes closed.

Joy's office was in a residential neighborhood in San Rafael and I immediately felt comfortable in her presence. She was so kind and loving. She helped me see that I had "infinite possibilities"—a.k.a. I was absolutely not stuck living in that loft. And that yes, my trip to Bali would be a magical, wonderful experience for me. I guess I could have predicted that too.

I'd made plans to go to Bali last minute. I could tell my aunt was not happy to hear I'd both be arriving and leaving right away, but it was an opportunity I couldn't turn down. In exchange for doing copywriting work, if I could pay for my flight, a yoga teacher was giving me a space at her yoga retreat in Bali. Excuse me, her yoga TEACHER training retreat in Bali. A 200-hour training experience. And I'd taken approximately five yoga classes before, but I was up for the challenge if it meant traveling to Bali.

The day before I left, my aunt and I went to church and shockingly, I had a big breakthrough there.

Growing up, I went to mass every Sunday with my family. But I didn't totally love it, mostly because the church was a place I went to repress laughter and get punished. Honestly, I've never laughed harder than I have in a church. At funerals, I used to be in hysterics.

Because my body either needs to laugh or cry when facing loss—and for some reason, in the presence of death, my kid body consistently chose laughter. It was the only way for me to process all the heavy emotions in the room.

Even on a regular Sunday, sitting in a pew next to my brother for an hour while everyone was forced to be quiet, barely move and softly sing songs was truly a form of cruel punishment. It was so stuffy and unnatural and my only instinct was to burst into laughter. If my brother and I made eye contact, forget about it. Someone was going home grounded. No one could make me laugh more than him and all it took was one moment of eye contact or one funny gesture, and I'd lose it. We both came unglued the day there was a reenactment of Jesus being stripped and whipped—a not-so-funny scene but played by a 12 year old dressed only in a loincloth. We could barely breathe.

But on that Sunday in San Francisco, my aunt took me to Glide in the Tenderloin, the neighborhood where all the prostitutes and drug dealers and all the people suffering from marginalization live.

When I walked into the church, I looked around and saw all different kinds of people gathering together by choice. Like from all income levels, all skin colors, and everyone was there, together, to celebrate. There was lots of togetherness and hugging happening. I felt like I was being converted—and I wasn't fighting it.

The speaker that day was a man who was a black gay veteran and a recovering alcoholic. He sobered up after joining Glide—and also found out he had HIV and terminal cancer that same year. He stood on the pulpit and told his story.

He started crying when he talked about the new apartment the people at Glide had helped him find. And this second lease on life that he had and how grateful he was to just be there, alive, telling everyone his story. I sat there in total awe. He was one of the most beautiful people I'd ever witnessed.

He spoke about how he wasn't always accepted places. About how when he told his father he was gay, his own dad disowned him. And how that hurt him so deeply, and drove him to drink for years and years. His pain was real and it was raw and it was still very much with him.

He said he found a new way to approach the situation. He shared this quote:

He drew a circle that shut me out—
Heretic, a rebel, a thing to flout.
But Love and I had the wit to win.
We drew a circle that took him in!
-Edwin Markham

I'm not kidding when I say I felt the magic of love pour over me as he said those words. This was what unconditional love really looked like. I'd always thought love being unconditional meant I had to suffer, like I had to accept all the conditions and still give, because that's the way it was.

But I realized it's more than that. It's about finding peace in your own heart, regardless of what anyone else says or thinks about you. And loving them anyway, not returning hate with more hate.

His experience and his message stuck on me for days (probably weeks) afterwards.

I realized that he had taken his pain and turned it into something beautiful. That his hurt led to more heart.

Some of my greatest gifts have come from my most painful experiences:

The Hurt	that led to →	the Heart:
Heartbreak		Traveling the World
Parents divorce		Deep sense of empathy
Death of my grandmother		Spiritual connection
Issues in my family		Showing up for others
Addiction		Owning my life
Anxiety & depression		Love ♡

I have to draw a circle that includes not only the people I love, but the people who have hurt me too. The people who have lied to me, who have been selfish, who have not cared about my best interest. I can still put them in my circle. But that didn't mean I had to subject myself to mistreatment either. It's possible to love someone even from afar. Because sometimes protecting your heart is the most loving thing to do...for you. I saw that love has to be both unconditional for yourself and others. And if everyone practices that, with themselves and the people around them, we will save this place.

After this beautiful, transformative church service, my aunt and I were walking home in the sunshine and I felt okay about life again, forgetting about my many sleepless nights listening to a jackhammer. My aunt asked if I wanted to really experience something new?

We walked through the Folsom Street Fair, not twenty minutes after leaving the church. This was an annual BDSM festival. And BDSM, in case you don't know, is an acronym for a wide array of erotic practices and roleplaying, mostly involving leather along with dominance and submission. I wasn't fully aware of what that means, but boy, did I learn!

I played it cool at first and smiled and waved at all the men in chaps. Most of them weren't interested in me anyway. Then the crowd got tighter. I saw a woman on all fours being walked on a leash. That's when I glued myself to my aunt's back. I'm all for sex positivity and I have zero judgment for what anyone wants to do in the bedroom, as long as there are no real animals involved and there is mutual consent. But being in a sex fest, unwillingly, was like soul rape.

My eyes cannot unsee what they saw.

Needless to say, I was ready to get the fuck out of the States. I boarded my twenty-six hour flight the next day to the other side of the world, just as the first presidential debates were kicking off for the 2016 election.

I started finally reading all the information about that yoga retreat. I learned there would be a vow of silence for the first half of every day. Might be tough but I could (maybe) handle that. That we would be practicing yoga for six to eight hours a day (uh oh) and I would become a certified teacher after three weeks (over my head).

And then I landed in Bali. And it was so, so beautiful. And magical. And tropical. And colorful. And peaceful. And it was everything I could have ever hoped for and more. It was warm and luscious and so pretty and there were butterflies and flowers and rainbows and I'm pretty sure unicorns were there too and magic floating in the air.

From the moment I stepped off the plane, I felt like I had traveled to Mother Earth's belly, where she was going to keep me safe and warm, and nurture me back to health—mind, body, and soul.

I signed on to Facebook and saw updates in the private retreat group. Women who had just met (the retreat hadn't started yet) taking selfies together with the caption: *Finally found my family!* Uh oh. This retreat group felt like the sorority I'd joined and immediately quit. Not my bag.

I thought about spending my time there in a hut, forcing myself into silence and crying and listening to everyone's story. And while there was a time and a place for that, I just couldn't do it. I'd invested enough in therapy already. This place was too beautiful not to be deeply enjoyed. I knew I'd just be staring out into the rice fields, wishing for my freedom to be able to explore this island.

So, I ditched the yoga retreat.

I'd gotten myself to Bali and I didn't have any rent to pay, so I was able to afford a relatively cheap but safe hotel room—and a $10 massage most days.

Oddly, the zen yoga teacher turned vicious quite quickly, letting me know that "karma would catch up with me one day" when I tried to explain that my heart wasn't up for this group experience. She wasn't losing any money in my absence and it made me realize I'd made the right choice. *NA-MA-STE TO YOU TOO!*

I let myself just fucking relax for once in my life. I let myself not be perfect. I let myself stop achieving. I let myself live. I let myself sleep. I let myself eat. I let myself enjoy having no to do list. I let myself write. I let myself be. I had nothing to prove to anyone anymore. For the first time in my life, I made a decision 10000% based on love for myself—nothing else.

There was still a voice inside me that said things like:

Who do you think you are to deserve this? You're so spoiled.
You should be working more. You should be figuring out your next steps.
You're a failure for quitting. You could have become a yoga teacher!!
What are you even doing with your life?

But I woke up every day and practiced telling those voices to, basically, shut the fuck up.

All my life, I'd been striving and pushing and carrying around stress and loss, and maybe it was time to cut myself a break for a goddamn hot minute. That if I wanted to become a yoga teacher, I would become a fucking yoga teacher—and this moment in time was not defining my ultimate purpose in life.

And let's be honest, I probably needed to actually do yoga more than five times before I considered teaching it! That maybe I needed the retreat to get me there because I wouldn't have done it just for myself. That by saying no to that opportunity, I was actually saying yes to myself. And that what I was doing with my life was LIVING it how I wanted to live it and ENJOYING it.

I spent my days in Bali basically in silence, which was ironic, because that's exactly what I wanted to avoid at the yoga retreat. Staring at a rice field and listening to the monkeys. Watching butterflies fly between flowers. Admiring temples and climbing into ancient sacred places, a now fervent passion of mine. I went for walks, I soaked up the sun, I got massages, I wrote and wrote and wrote and read and read and read. And while I did all these things, while I let myself just rest, I felt Bali healing me up with her love, love, love.

Of course, I wanted to visit one of Bali's famous Master Healers while I was there. I signed up and had a cab driver take me to a random house where I was going to meet a group and then head to the Healer's house.

Our group leader was a French woman named Marie, who appeared out of nowhere. She was wearing a sarong and a turban and instructed all seven of us to get into one van with only five seats. I spent the ride to the Healer bent in half, basically sitting on a (very nice) stranger, now close friend.

Once we reached the Healer's home, we had to be reverent. I was whispering to an Australian girl and a European couple hissed at us to be quiet. We were all being really stereotypical (chatty American + Australian, salty Europeans).

We each put on a sarong, and sat under this hut—waiting to be seen. The Healer was an old Balinese man, who appeared to maybe be blind, and spoke in grunts and faded, one-word English. Marie the French guide helped translate.

Each person took their turn approaching and sitting at his feet. The Healer would first feel your scalp, sticking his fingers everywhere, including inside ears, if needed. *Does he wash his hands between patients? No, okay then.*

Based on the feel of the head, he would determine any ailments or need for healing. Once he knew what needed work, then it was time to lay down on the straw mat while he performed his healing methods with hand gestures and chants. I am no stranger to alternative healing and hippie shit, so all of this was totally up my alley.

I was quite nervous to be diagnosed in front of a group of people, however.

As the Healer worked, Marie would explain to the person being healed what the Healer was doing. Since we were all sitting in silence three feet away, we could hear everything being said. Things got personal, real quick. I found out intimate secrets about all the people I was with who had just been strangers less than an hour ago, including what that European couple was so angry about (infertility issues). Tears were shed. Things were getting emo. I was one of the last people in our group to go, which was a blessing because it made me less anxious. The Healer felt my head and I was healthy overall, but my mind worked too fast and caused worry. Pretty spot-on diagnosis.

I got down on the mat and he got to work a bit more. As he started diagnosing me, the next group of twenty tourists sat down, in and around the hut. With double the audience now, I could feel something happening. He muttered and muttered—and everyone was waiting to hear what his final assessment would be. Finally, he spoke. And Marie, the woman in a turban, translated:

He says you must avoid tuna. It is bad for your body. It will cause problems for your woman parts. Other than that, you are well.

This was exactly the type of thing I did not want him to say in front of a group of people. First, I barely ever even ate tuna. And also, seriously?! That's what needs healing the MOST in my life? *Why did my life always have a punchline!?!?*

My time in beautiful Bali was spent in hours and hours of contemplation. I thought about my life, and how if I were to dig through the planet, all the people I loved would be there on the other side. How the world was so huge and so small at the same time.

The way of life in Bali was so relaxed. Nothing was urgent. Everything was slow. Back home, life was mainly the exact opposite. I would rush around and there were deadlines and notifications and emails and appointments and meetings. Sometimes it felt like taking a break from all that was seen as a sign of weakness. Like if I didn't keep up with the fast pace, there was something wrong with me. I wasn't successful enough. I wasn't enough.

I started to see that I'd always defined myself by what I do—so who am I when I'm not producing? When I'm not trying to help everyone around me? Maybe I don't have to be defined by what I do? Maybe I'm enough without "doing" anything at all?

Being in Bali made me realize that I am enough. That there is nothing I have to do or be, other than to be myself and follow my heart, and that I don't have to prove myself to anyone but myself. That there was a different side of the world and a different way to look at life. And a more slow, natural rhythm that I can sync both myself and my menstrual cycle up with. And it made me feel more balanced.

Which is something I guess I hadn't felt in a long time. I always felt these pulls in my life, mostly to side with mom or side with dad. I clearly remember when this battle began for me. I was folding laundry in the family room, and my parents were in a heated discussion. It started growing more tense and I was standing in between them.

One of them said: *Well, what do you think?* And at that moment, I felt a shift in my whole universe. My world was not going to be the same. I was going to spend a good deal of my time dealing with the struggle of trying to choose between mom and dad, figuring out how to make them both happy—and always filtering what I think, so it didn't hurt anyone. And in my adult life, I'd recreated these patterns, always putting myself in the position to please other people, before myself. And it was exhausting. I was exhausted.

Bali breathed some more life back into me.

Of course, I had wanted to come to Bali and fall in love. Trust me, I'd read and seen *Eat Pray Love* enough times to know that my subconscious had an ulterior motive. It was like I was telling myself: *I'll just go there to be alone* (wink, wink, nudge, nudge). But I really couldn't wait to give an update like this to everyone back home: *Hi guys, this is Chad and we're in love now. So wild how fate just brought me together with my soul mate in this totally tropical location! We live here now. Bye!*

But once I was on the island, I somehow entered this foreign state of mind: I wanted to be alone. Dare I say, I liked it. I liked being with myself. And I always had, but now, it was different. I was giving myself something I'd been searching for from others, desperately: unconditional love.

I stopped seeking approval from outside sources. I didn't need anyone else to tell me it was okay. I gave myself permission and I wanted to be with just me. And I did have to go to the other side of the world to give myself that space. I needed to be out of touch and away.

I had to unplug and be isolated and basically forced to see that I do have true love in my life, with or without someone else by my side.

I was learning to trust my own path, even if no one else does. And to love myself, even when I make mistakes. If I can do that, then someone else's love was a bonus.

My first solo trip had been about helping others, reaching out to the most vulnerable people I could think of and volunteering. Bali was like a volunteer trip for myself. I was taking the time to help me, instead of everyone else around me. Even though I ditched the retreat, it turned out to be a very spiritual vacation.

When I got back to California, shit hit the fan. The guy who owned the loft I was staying in, kept coming back.

When he came back to town (again), I rented a car and went up to Marin. I drove through the forest with big trees and just soaked in all that beauty and thought about how I would love to just keep on driving and exploring but I didn't feel like I could because of all the excuses for why I couldn't. *Nope, you need to find a place to LIVE, you need to SETTLE, etc.*

I wasn't sure if I should stay in California and try to head south (and officially shatter my aunt's heart) or what I should do. I knew I wasn't where I was supposed to be, but I wasn't sure where to go next.

My fate was sealed on November 8, 2016, just two weeks after I'd gotten back from Bali. I sat in a closet, on a mattress I'd pulled in to avoid the construction noises, and watched the election results roll in. I stayed up all night until they finally made the call.

I sat in this dark room on the floor by myself as I watched the U.S. go to hell in a handbasket. It felt like a shock to my privileged system.

I knew I needed to go home, even though I felt like a big fat failure for calling it quits in California. If I was going to chase my dreams, I was going to fail at some point. And usually, that failure dumped me right where I was supposed to be. Turns out, I was supposed to go home and if I'd known why, I probably would have been too scared to do it.

Mother Earth showing off in beautiful Bali, pouring manna water
from the heavens.
October 2016.

14
NURSING HOME: (SITTIN ON') THE DOCK OF THE BAY

(grace)

Grief is praise, because it is the natural way love honors
what it misses.

-Martin Prechtal

I always knew I didn't want to live in my hometown forever, even
though most of my family lived there (or nearby). It was built to
support families, and it was a safe, stable place for those families to
grow.

There's something to be said for having roots, for being established,
known, secure and stable. If I mentioned my last name to, say, a
local police officer, there was a good chance he might know one of
my aunts, uncles, or (god forbid) my dad.

My main issue with living in the suburbs was it just felt so goddamn
vanilla.

Every year felt like Groundhog Day, going to the same places on the
same holidays with the same people and the same bars and the
same restaurants. I'd look around and everyone else was LOVING it
and I'd think to myself: *Anyone else choking on the air around
here?! Is it just me?!*

Where I'm from, it felt like going to an ice cream counter and
asking:

What flavor do you have?

Vanilla.

Any chocolate?

No. Only vanilla.

Anything with sprinkles?

What do you think?

Ok, I'll come back…

But every time I came back, there were never any more flavors. It was always just…vanilla. And for people who love vanilla, it's perfect. But I was interested in exploring other flavors.

My (other) grandmother, my Gram, understood why I felt that way, even though she lived in the suburbs for most of her life. But she got it. She made peace with living there, even grew to like it while raising her children and supporting her (doctor) husband.

But she never made me feel like I had to do that too. She never told me what to do, but I did get the sense that she wanted me to get out there and travel. Mostly because any time I told her I was going to Peru or wherever, she would light up and shower me with praise, reminding me that it doesn't matter what anyone else thinks. *It's your life, kid!*

It wasn't that I was her sweet granddaughter and she was my sweet grandmother. Honestly, only a handful of people ever called either of us "sweet." She was a stern rule maker and I was often a careless rule breaker—but she saw all the good, the bad and the ugly parts of me—and accepted me fully.

Her husband (my grandpa) had the same name as my dad. Growing up, this got tricky at places like the library and Blockbuster. I'd check out a library book on what I thought was my dad's account and then return it 17 months later, when my Gram would politely mention the fees she had to pay. I once lost a videotape I'd rented so I tried to put a different one in the Blockbuster cover and returned that—and of course, it just happened to be on my grandparent's account that day. She called me swiftly and I used my allowance to pay the fine. When I was in my 20s, I asked if I could bring just a "few friends" to her lakehouse—and the cops called her twice in the middle of the night. Their direct quote was: *We can hear the music reverberating across the lake.* She called me directly again that Monday and her opening words were: *I am not a happy grandma.* Gulp.

Even when I didn't get it right, she'd tell me that I messed up, but never stopped treating me with respect and kindness too. She made me feel like even though I made mistakes, I was still worthy of being loved.

She taught me how to swim. She'd put seaweed on my head and call me the Queen of the May. I once walked out of the kitchen holding a cupcake and I was stopped dead in my tracks by her finger, telling me to march back and get a plate, did I see the trail of crumbs?! She'd take me shopping at Woodfield Mall every Christmas to pick out a gift, even though she absolutely detested both shopping and shopping malls. She made amazing bread (from scratch) and delicious meals and we would drink a cup of tea afterward.

One of her proudest moments was sitting on her lake house lawn, surveying all the grandkids and aunts and uncles and various significant others we brought along for the ride, and asking us, with such pride: *Did ya ever think you'd have such a big family?*

The biggest silver lining of everything with my parents was we spent an enormous amount of time with our grandparents. My dad moved in with my Gram and Grandpa when my parents first separated and my mom's parents (Issy and Pa) babysat us nearly every day for years. They all became involved in our everyday lives, with everything from helping us with homework to feeding us to driving us to our friend's houses. I don't want to say they were like my parents, but they played a starring grand-parental role in my upbringing.

I'd watched three of my grandparents suffer towards the end of their life with everything from cancer to dementia. Either the mind or the body went first—and either way, it was brutal to witness.

My grandpa (Pa) was once discharged from a very long (multiple months) hospital stay on the condition he continued to take medication—but when we got to the pharmacy, the prescription wasn't ready. It hadn't even been called in. Someone "forgot."

My poor, suffering grandfather was still in pain and was sitting in the backseat of the car, desperate to just get home, and I couldn't believe that after everything he'd been through, the medicine he needed to stay alive WAS NOT AVAILABLE!!!

Hell hath no fury like a granddaughter scorned. I said in my sweetest, most calm voice that I would take care of it and there was nothing to worry about.

I dropped him and my grandmother back home—and proceeded to drive like a banshee, back to the hospital where I marched up to the nurse's station—and let's just say, my grandfather was swallowing his next pill within 15 minutes.

After he died, I went with Issy to his grave for the first time because old people like traditions like that and even though it was hard, she wanted to go, so we did.

And when we arrived, his grave marker was at the foot of his grave. My grandmother was so upset to not only visit her husband's grave for the first time, but to have it be messed up, like a cruel prank. This made us, the living, feel like a bunch of nitwits who couldn't even honor him properly. I called the cemetery promptly that afternoon and the marker was fixed by nightfall. I was fiercely protective of my grandparents and would stop at no lengths to care for them, as they had always done that for me.

I used to be obsessed with this Death Cab for Cutie song called *What Sarah Said*. When I saw them play it live, with an orchestra might I add, I cried. My sister rolled her eyes:

Omg are you seriously crying right now?

But this is what got me. The last two lines:

That love is watching someone die,
So who's gonna watch you die?

There's nothing more intimate in this world than birth and death. I'd reached an age where my friends were becoming mothers to one, two, three children. While they were spending time in the birthing stage of life in the suburbs, I found myself back there too, but spending time on the other end of life.

Ironically, or maybe not so ironically, on the same weekend that the largest surge of feminine power in modern history came together, one of the strongest women I've ever known met her demise. Literally two days before the history-making Women's March, my last remaining grandparent, my Gram, had a stroke.

She was playing bridge with her friends and they called 911 because she was acting real out of it. The hospital said it was a stroke and she had to move to a rehab facility, then a nursing home. She went from swimming every morning to being in a wheelchair, not remembering anything from thirty seconds ago.

She honestly couldn't have picked a better time. She had no idea what was going on anymore, so she left this world without any clue about how poorly current events were going. *Genius.*

Everything else in my life became secondary to Gram. I wouldn't (couldn't) move forward until I knew she was okay. As fate would have it, when I got back from San Francisco, I was staying with my mom while I debated where to live—and I was just five minutes away from my Gram's nursing home. I ended up exactly where I was supposed to be, for the moment.

I'd take her to get her hair done or I'd paint her nails or we'd wheel down to the cafe and have a cup of tea. These little rituals became important, they were like an anchor during a time when she didn't know what the hell was going on and neither did the rest of us. We were all just waiting to see.

She was very confused, mainly because she couldn't remember what happened sixty seconds ago. She had no idea that she had a stroke, that she was in a nursing home, or that she couldn't walk. All she wanted to know was: *What day is it, what time is it, and what am I supposed to be doing?!* Mostly because she'd spent her whole life adhering to a schedule and always doing, doing, doing. She'd ask the same questions, over and over again. I basically had a monologue I'd repeat, sometimes one hundred times in one visit:

You're at the retirement village, but in the apartment part, like where your friend Mrs. Mayer lives.* Do you remember her place? You still have your townhouse but you're living here for now. Don't

worry about swimming, you don't have to go today.** Your
schedule is up on the wall. See, you have breakfast at 9am, then
exercise with the physical therapist, then lunch, then you get to take
a rest (the best part of the day!), and you'll have a visit*** when you
wake up around 3pm and then, you'll go to dinner and you can
watch the news before bed. I'm not sure who is visiting today, you
have so many people that love you!

*This was a lie, she was on a locked entry floor for the memory-
impaired.
**Another lie, she would never see a pool again.
***The plus side of having six children and tons of grandchildren
was you will always have a lot of visitors, wherever you are.

Most days, she went along with this charade. But other days, she'd
just shake her head and say: *Oh, this is the pits.* And she was right.
It was the pits, for her and for everyone that loved her. No one
wanted to see her suffer.

On one particularly rough day, I called my brother freaking out in
tears, saying we had to move her back home, she was confused and
at least she would recognize where she was if it was a familiar place
and WHY WAS THIS HAPPENING TO HER?!?!?!?! WE HAVE TO
DO SOMETHING! WHY ARE OLD PEOPLE PUT IN WARDS AND
TUCKED AWAY FROM THE WORLD?!?!?!

And he said: *You are grieving, calm down, she is in the best place
she can be.* The truth was: It wasn't really about where she lived. I
just desperately wanted to do anything to take away her suffering.

I went every day to see her, religiously. Then I started to go every
other day because I wanted her to be able to rest and I knew I had
to let go. That I wasn't going to stop her from dying just by having
perfect attendance at her bedside. The world doesn't work that way,
unfortunately.

Even though she was kinda gone, she was still kinda there too—and I really looked at this as my opportunity to be there for her the way she had been there for me. So for that reason, I was happy to be where I was.

But my life was in limbo. I felt an increased sense of anxiety over those months, but I think that's only normal given:
1. The transition of power in my country at the time (to put it lightly)
2. I didn't even know where I wanted to live.
3. I was living back in my childhood home. Yikes.
4. I started a business and even though I was successful, my imposter syndrome wouldn't let me even officially call it a business. *Who me? This is just a hobby!*
5. My grandma was dying—and I was sad.

What was really going on for me was a crisis of empathy. When we talk about grief, it's always about the loss we feel when a loved one dies. But there's a stage that comes before that, when we see the person suffer as they go. I'd become overwhelmed with empathy for my grandmother, grieving the loss of this life for her and with her. And it was like a rollercoaster, because as I watched her fade, she was still very much there too.

Even though she didn't know what was happening in the present, sometimes, it was like Gram would snap back to her old self and we would have our deep conversations about life. She told me she'd had a good long life. I told her I prayed to Grandpa, her husband, and that he's watching over her and I think he hears me. And she would smile and tell me he was sometimes hard of hearing. He used to say: *I hear what I want to!*

She talked about how she taught her kids to read and she went through each kid - from my dad to her youngest, all six of them— and imitated how they each reacted to reading. *And this one would do it, and this one would say: Do I gotta?* She said girls weren't supposed to learn past high school in her day—but her parents let her, as long as she paid for it herself.

We talked at length about spirituality. And she really lit up when we talked about meditation. She learned about it in high school and took a class and it's one of the best things she ever did. She would meditate in the morning, in the afternoon, and at night before bed. She picked a time and no matter what she was doing, she would stop and meditate. She said it worked wonders and that she didn't tell a lot of people about it. She told her mom and her mom said: *That's fine but keep it to yourself.*

She said she loved to read and she learned in 5th grade to not share her opinion in class—because at first she would always raise her hand and voice her opinion, but she quickly learned it was always very different than what others thought. So, her teacher asked why she wasn't participating anymore and she said she'd cross her heart and not tell anyone. So Gram told her the truth that it was because her opinions were different and the teacher said: *Okay, you don't have to talk in class anymore but come meet with me and we'll discuss it.* I told her she was so lucky to have such a good teacher. She agreed.

One evening, after a particularly nice dinner chat, I wheeled her back to her room for bedtime. We had to wait for the nurse to help her get ready for bed—and Gram asked why, because she forgot she was in a wheelchair. And I said it's the rules and I try to follow them now that I'm older and her reply was: *Make your own.*

A few days before my Gram died, I knew it was going to happen soon. She was in bed a lot and was not eating very much. I fed her some chocolate ice cream and she would perk up a little. It felt like cheating to feed her sugar—but we only live once and she liked it.

Most days leading up to her last ones were not so easy. She asked me in whispers what was happening and I fluffed the answers. *You're just tired. It's okay, this is the time for you to rest.* Until I came across a YouTube video that was entitled: The 5 Things You Must Say to the Dying. I listened to them all and thought: check, check, check, check....oh, fuck.

The last one was: *Be honest and tell them they are dying.* I messed that up. Maybe someone else in the family told her, but I kept telling her it was okay and to just take a nap. Probably because I couldn't admit it out loud yet. I got in my car and went back to her bed.

She was asleep and I just talked to her for a little. I said thank you for everything and for teaching me so much and I have to be honest because you keep asking me what's going on and the truth is you're dying and it's ok because Grandpa is waiting for you so it's ok to go with him and I promise we'll all be ok and I'll help take care of everyone, including myself, so it's ok to let go now.

She kinda moved her feet a little and her breathing changed. I told her that her life had so much meaning and look at how much beauty she and my grandpa created. All these people who are going to do amazing things in this world and it's all because of her. That every little thing she did created the world for us to live in and that she'll keep going on and on in all of us for years and years to come. That I love her very much, so much, and I'm so thankful for everything and that it's ok to go.

The next morning, I got a text from my dad:

Grandma is rapidly declining. It's going to be any time now.

I felt weirdly guilty in my head. Like: *I think I gave her permission to die last night?*

That morning, my brother and I went together to see her and she was real out of it. I tried to be peppy and make the situation lighter, but there was no getting around the obvious: death was near. She didn't talk much and the last thing I ever heard her say was:

See you later, Alligator

It's what she used to say to us when we were little. Three days later, I woke up and got ready. I went to visit her for a bit, and my dad and uncle and my aunt were already there and everyone else was on their way, after spending the weekend on death watch. The hospice nurse said it's going to be any minute now. I gave Gram one last kiss on the forehead and left with my Dad.

We were heading to St. Thomas, the church I grew up going to and where I went to grade school, the community we used to be a part of, until the divorce and things got weird all around and we became *that* family.

We were going to a baptism for my youngest niece—and I was becoming her godmother.

When we got to the entrance of the church, my sister and I found a brick with my grandparents name on it, one they bought so many years ago to support our school (and us). And my dad walked up and I could see it in his face. He said she'd just died. We posed for pictures with my little baby niece—my brother and I trying to smile for her after just hearing our dear grandmother died.

We went inside to baptize my niece, with my entire (immediate) family all together again in this church—and the whole ceremony was about the circle of life, about being born and death and rebirth. Caroline Myss defined a baptism as the full acceptance of the life one has been given to live. I think that can happen in a ceremony in a church as a baby, or just whenever one finally decides to do that.

When I think about where my grandmother would want me to be when she died, I realized she'd want my whole family to be together, to be celebrating another special moment in life and she'd want me to focus on where I'm at and what's next, not what's happened in the past. On being a leader to the little goddaughter in my lap.

After the baptism, I drove to my mom's house to meet movers—because I'd finally made a decision to stick around Illinois for a while, not knowing how long my grandmother had left. I moved into a new apartment in Evanston that day.

I was really, really sad for the next year, if I'm honest. And the true real reason was I didn't feel like I was just losing Gram, it felt like the closing of a very happy chapter in my life—the one with my grandparents. They had been like my rock, my stability, my undying sense of support—and now, they were all on the other side of life.

I'd been through this grief before. Right before Issy died, when I visited her for the last time in San Francisco, every few hours, I'd get overwhelmed by everything, mainly realizing my dear beloved grandmother was dying, that she wasn't coming home, and that this was my last weekend with her. I'd take breaks and walk.

I'd sit by the dock of the bay and literally listen to *(Sittin' On) The Dock of the Bay* while balling my eyes out. The song oddly made me feel closer to my grandma and reminded me of where she must have been at that point in her life (the end of it), miles from home and knowing there's not much else she can do. But I also felt like: How had this city, this place I'd always run to for fun and comfort, now become the place of my greatest loss? How could my grandmother die there?

I bargained with the universe to please make things easier. I knew better than to ask for her to stay alive, but I just wanted her to skip the suffering part. I was losing my grandmother to death and I was also losing who I used to be because I was not the same person anymore.

What I didn't realize in the moment, but what became crystal clear later, was that this was actually good grief. I was so sad because I loved my grandmother so. What a beautiful thing to be blessed with, a relationship like that. And this loss was pushing me into a new life, whether I agreed to it or not.

And it turns out sitting by the dock of the bay, in San Francisco, was exactly where I needed to be then. Because San Francisco was a city that had been there for me, had nurtured me through hard times and life's toughest transitions. I was there when my dad had to move out, and it was there for me as my grandma was dying.

It takes courage to love when we know there will always be an expiration date in this physical world. But there's something that makes us do it anyway.

For a while after both my grandmothers had passed, I questioned what was the point of all this, even though it all seemed incredibly fated. Like we had made an agreement, way before time, that they'd help me and I'd help them. And that by being so close to them, that it would open me up to a whole new way of looking at the world, where maybe life doesn't just end at death. Maybe some people are put so close to our hearts, so deeply in them, that we cannot see where they go but we feel it. Our hearts might break into one million pieces—but the love is still there. And we still feel them here. Even though they are "gone."

That lesson was literally on a piece of paper, waiting for me. Once it became clear my Gram was never going back to her house, Emmy and I went over to her place one night to pick what we wanted from her stuff, as everyone else did all the hard work, to clear and sell her home. Honestly, my sister and I were both dreading it because it felt weird to take her things when she was not even dead yet, she was very much still alive at the time and only a block away. It was upsetting to see her house not "put together" anymore because she'd been so tidy—and it felt weird to see all her things no longer in their "place."

Her bookshelves were all out of order and my first reaction was: *Shit, we're gonna be in big trouble*—because she was seriously militant with her books. She'd bring us down to her basement and let us each pick one off the shelves and we'd check them out from her, like a library. She kept a record on index cards. I honestly never returned a library book on time, but I always at least attempted to return grandma's books on time.

As I was picking up a few books I wanted, one fell on the floor in front of me and a piece of paper was hanging out of it. It was a poem that had been printed in a magazine and my grandpa had ripped it out and written "Poetry" at the top and stuck it in a book, where it stayed until that moment. The poem was titled "How Do I Love Thee?" and written by Elizabeth Barrett Browning. The last line was:

I shall but love thee better after death.

It felt like a very clear message from my grandparents that just because they had to go, didn't mean their love did too. And I guess, after they all died, I was finally coming to live in a very real version of the world...where my grandma can be trapped in a mind that can't remember and also smile and share a cup of tea with me. Where my grandpa can serve his whole life curing other people and end up forgetting how to swallow. Where my grandparents can be so loving and caring and yet, still suffer in the end. Where all this pain lives right next door to all the beauty. And the only way to have one is to also have the other.

210

Watching them suffer and still be kind, still split their donut in half to give me a bite, still sit up in her chair when anyone came to see her, still hold my hand until the end—that was truly a lesson in grace.

Want to know what grace is? This is what my grandparents showed me:

It's watching your brother die in a pool, but still waking up to swim every morning.

It's raising six children while working as a nurse, with little to no help from anyone but your husband.

It's showing up each and every day to care for your grandchildren and never flinching in being a rock-solid foundation for them.

It's working for decades and saving every penny you can so your kids and their kids have the opportunity you didn't get to go to college.

It's the meals and the dishes and oh dear god, the laundry and the books and the Christmases and all the heartache and all the best moments of leading a big family.

It's watching your husband fade away and the life you built together. And realizing after all that, there's still more life left to live.

It's filling your days with bridge and book clubs and college classes, still eager to learn.
It's seizing every day and creating a life for yourself, even in circumstances you don't love.

It's having a stroke and losing your ability to walk and to remember, but still telling everyone you're getting better and better.

It's being told you're going to die, but going to California anyway.

And it's sitting in a wheelchair, having a cup of tea with your granddaughter as you smile and exchange niceties, even as you, yourself, are dying and you don't know how many more days, hours, minutes are left.

But you do it anyway, with a smile. You sip your tea and you still do your best to enjoy what life has given you. You know there's a sunrise and a sunset, a baptism and a death, birth and life, all at once.

When things are low in life, there is a power that brings them back up. That's what grace is.

Gram, enjoying her favorite things
circa 1965

15

ICELAND + FAROE ISLANDS: SIGNALS

(forgiveness)

It doesn't happen all at once,' said the Skin Horse. 'You become. It takes a long time. That's why it doesn't happen often to people who break easily, or have sharp edges, or who have to be carefully kept.
Generally, by the time you are Real, most of your hair has been loved off, and your eyes drop out and you get loose in the joints and very shabby. But these things don't matter at all, because once you are Real you can't be ugly, except to people who don't understand.
— *Margery Williams Bianco*

Like most Millenials, I spent a good deal of my time in bed on my phone, fantasizing about my next move in life. I stopped scrolling one day when I came across this beautiful picture of a windy road, going down a hill on an island with a foggy sunrise.

THAT! That is where I needed to go next. And in under two minutes of some aggressive stalking, I figured out where that place was.

It was the first trip I'd taken after my Gram passed—and I convinced my sister to come for part of the journey.

Although I always felt like I needed to get out of Illinois, I really needed to then. For the months following my Gram's passing, I felt like I was barely keeping my head above water in an ocean of grief. I'd grown so close to her and now, she was at peace and I was left, finally able to process what had happened. It was like my Gram's passing unlocked the tears I hadn't cried my whole entire life, the part of me that just wanted my mommy.

Of course, my mom and I had (another) terrible falling out. Exactly one year after being in the hospital with my Gram, I was at the exact same one, this time with my mom.

In the fall, she was told she had some polyps in her colon, so we spent Christmas not knowing if she had the c-word or not. Or at least, that's what she told my siblings and I. I took her to her procedure in January, which she told me was colon surgery—only to find out that it was actually a routine colonoscopy and they removed everything and all was well.

As she came out from being put under, she confessed how she'd watched YouTube videos of colonoscopies that had scared her—and that's why she was so worried.

I was fucking furious. I knew she liked drama, but I never in a million years imagined she would exaggerate about her health. But I held it in because I knew she was probably just scared of her own mortality and everyone deals with it in different ways.

Until, she, once again, lied to my face about something else—and even though I knew what would happen, I called her on it and said:

You know, I actually know that's not the truth and it's hurtful that you'd lie about it.

I knew the likely reaction that would come. But I thought, because we were with my brother's kids, that she wouldn't be able to do her usual rage fit.

I was wrong.

She was holding my niece and started storming around my brother's house, raising her voice. I realized my worst nightmare was coming true: she was doing this in front of the children.

One thing I'd always promised myself, from the day I was eleven years old, was that if I had kids, they would not be exposed to any of this. And if my parents wanted to see their grandchildren, they needed to suck it up and behave better in front of them and be kind.

That was my line and it wasn't to be crossed. And even though I didn't have my own kids, I felt the same way about my brother's kids. I did not want them to see adults behaving like that, ever.

So, I got the two oldest ones to follow me to the basement, pretending everything was fine as my mom was screaming from upstairs. I put on a movie for them and I said: *Nana is going to stay with you now. I love you*—as if everything was totally normal. My mom came down and continued to scream and I looked her dead in the eye, and slowly and calmly said: *Stop it.*

Then I gave the littlest one, who she was holding, a kiss and walked out. I texted my mom afterwards and told her that what she just did was not okay and that she needs to get help. It was something I'd wanted to say to her my entire life, but never had the courage to say it when she was just doing this to me. But when she did it in front of those kids, I reached my limit.

A few days went by and I didn't hear anything from her. I cooled down and knew how things went. I knew she would never admit to what happened, that she would pretend it, in fact, never happened, and that I would have to be the one to apologize. I knew this cycle all too well.

But I called and left her messages and....got no reply. She was icing me out, cutting me off. And as much as I thought I'd be angry, it made me desperately sad. I called her and texted her weekly—and got nothing. Nada. It took me a long time and so many attempts to reach the point where I stopped trying.

So, the trip to Iceland with my sister was perfect timing—and also, slightly awkward when my mom was texting her, but not even speaking to me. Luckily, we were both so used to the total dysfunction that we were able to compartmentalize that experience and enjoy our time together in another country.

It wasn't the most joyful period of my life—and I was in need of a change of scenery, to say the least. And so, I went to Iceland with my sister, with only one actual bag and about 30 tons of emotional baggage I was in the midst of processing.

We came in real hot and started roaming the streets of Reykjavík at sunrise. I let Emmy lead the way, even though I knew she had no fucking clue where she was going, but she was so overcaffeinated and excited—it was cute. We went straight to the top of the Cathedral and saw the panoramic views of the city—and then ran away from a cat that we felt was chasing us in the streets (a.k.a. we needed a nap).

After a sister siesta, we went to the local bathhouse, where neither of us were prepared to shower in the nude with strangers or each other. When we got outside to the hot tub and pool area, we squealed and ran into the water, complaining about how cold it was outside and instantly signaling to everyone else that we were not from the area.

It was only locals in the jacuzzi with us—and they asked: Are you from Britain? I nodded and smiled and whispered to my sister to not say a word, because—what a compliment! I'd rather be misidentified as a snobby Brit than a loud American any day.

We packed in the activities after that, starting with a bus tour of the South Coast. We were the last ones on the bus so we had separate seats. I sat in the middle of a group visiting from Florida and we were definitely on opposite ends of the political spectrum—and we all knew it. But since we were not currently in our country, we were mutually kind to one another, as if the heated division and all the madness going on back home didn't exist anymore. I consistently repeated to myself this Bible quote (Matthew 7:1) I'd picked up in grade school: *Judge not lest ye be judged.*

At each stop, my sister and I would reunite and we got to see a glacier (where I peer pressured her into walking down an icy trail) and a beach in a small town and two waterfalls. It was sunny and beautiful—and when we arrived at the first waterfall, there was a RAINBOW over it.

Life felt magical again.

We went to an English Pub, for my sister, and an American bar, which I'd previously scoffed at and later patronized because I was craving a cheeseburger. *When in Reykjavík!*

As we were sitting at the American bar, we decided to download a dating app "just to see." And within half an hour, I'd made "arrangements" to have a random guy come meet my sister and we were both laughing and thinking this would be so funny.

In the meantime, I pulled my head out of Emmy's phone and looked to my right and saw a futbol match playing on a big screen—and a cute guy sitting right next to me? When did this happen? All I needed to say was: *Um, excuse me, but what teams are those? The ones like playing soccer?* He had glasses and an accent—and I was instantly into him.

And then, my sister's "new friend" joined us. Somehow, we'd accidentally created what almost felt like a double-date situation in less than an hour at the American Bar, of all places. It felt like a scene from *Love Actually*—and I was weirdly okay with that.

My four-eyed crush was a little weirded out that this random guy seemed to be joining our table. I told him about the Tinder situation and he admitted that's how he met his girlfriend. My sister gave him the stink eye and I tried to kick her under the table and communicate to her with my eyes:

It's okay that he has a girlfriend, sister, all we've done is innocently chat and I would want him to be happy and he didn't even know about me until like twenty minutes ago. He's being honest!

Maybe it was the multiple beers, but it was so refreshing to sit and talk with someone and have a genuine laugh. Oh my god, it was so refreshing. I'd put myself on a hiatus from all men (and man-boys) because I knew I had to get my shit together. And meeting him made me realize I was (maybe) ready-ish again.

Eventually, he left because it was a Monday and he had to work and oh yeah, he had a girlfriend. But my sister's date stuck around, even after she met (another) new Icelandic boyfriend. The night ended with us fighting, because that's what two sisters in a foreign country who have been together for three days do, sometimes, especially with alcohol involved. But we also swore that we'd never speak of it again, because that's also what sisters do (until one of you writes a book and documents it forever).

On our last day, we were wickedly hungover and tired, but we went to the Blue Lagoon, a.k.a. heaven on earth. It was like a communal bath with a face mask and everything. I seriously didn't want to leave. We bought a disposable water camera and took loads of selfies, where she looks adorable and I look like the *Where Are They Now?* photo of the middle Hanson brother. But it was magical to be in this beautiful outdoor bath with my little sissy in Iceland. Was that happiness I felt tugging at my heart again?!

She flew home the next day and I went onwards by myself to the Faroe Islands, a remote location in the Atlantic between Iceland and Scotland, as seen in *The Secret Life of Walter Mitty*. When I landed, I had a taxi pick me up to take me to the hotel. The weather changed every ten seconds on the islands, so within the first five minutes of the drive, it was sunny, snowy and sunny again. The driver was super kind and said he'd take me on a special route, so I would get the good views.

We started winding up the side of a mountain, and I could feel my anxiety start to peak it's little head up and say: *Um, I'm here and ready to rage whenever you need me. This is heights and um, you have not always been a fan of those. I'm ready when you are... I* quietly told it to please not interrupt this beautiful moment in time—and it actually listened.

As we came to the top of the mountain, the driver pulled over and told me to look out the left window. We were at the exact spot from the picture I'd seen, the one that inspired me to go there in the first place. It was a trippy moment, to say the least.

I spent the next few days unwinding, which meant hibernating and going for walks. I pulled up a chair and just stared out the window, watching the sky and the ravens fly around. It felt like a modern-day version of *Game of Thrones*—and I was sitting in a hotel version of Winterfell, well-fed and protected.

And just like in Bali, it's like I needed to get away, to be on my own, in a beautiful place, in order to make peace with the fact that I didn't currently have peace back home.

The drama with my mom had been going on for (most) of my life. But I think what made it all the more painful was that: a. she wasn't always this way and b. I knew she didn't even realize she was this way. Because when she'd snap out of it, she was kind and thoughtful and did really nice things for other people. And she did work really hard and she did the absolute best she could to give everything she could to my brother and my sister (and sometimes even, to me).

It felt like a crossroads in my life—a point where I could decide: do I want to carry on with her in my life or do I walk away? And what are the consequences of that decision?

And that's when I decided, in my heart, to do my very best to forgive her, for myself. Even though the rage inside me did not go away (not sure it ever will), another part of me started to grow. It was a more mature part, a part that could be a leader, a part that knew what the better choice was. Choosing my own peace.

During my alone time in the midst of the Atlantic Ocean, it felt like I was finally turning a corner. Mostly, I was learning I have to bear the things I never thought I could bear—we all do. And accepting the truth about the relationship with my mom. And embracing the truth of the love I did receive—and the love I didn't.

And I know, in my heart, that one of the greatest privileges of my life was to have been so loved by my grandmothers. They always wanted what was best for me. And there's absolutely nothing I could do in this world that would make them doubt me for a minute. And that was a goddamn miracle.

I used to look at my grandmothers and think: *Would you speak up? Why are you taking it on the chin?* But then I learned. It's called wisdom. They knew when to let things be and when to say something. They knew when to fight and when to not invite trouble. So when they did speak up, it held tremendous power.

I knew that the only real and true way for me to honor them is by simply being myself. By loving myself the way they loved me. If we're lucky enough, we get someone in our lives who reflects just how special we are back to us.

I decided in the Faroe Islands, during my hours and hours of time staring out a window, that I had to do my very best to find the answers to why I was so incredibly devastated by the loss of my grandmother(s). And it was because all the grief I'd carried around for years, was now, coming to the surface to be healed.

I realized that there was nothing wrong with me for being in the throes of grief. It would have actually been totally weird if I responded to that sad time in my life by being totally happy? Of course, I had moments of joy, and they started to become less fleeting as time went on and I healed.

I was handed a life with so many beautiful things along with a side of emotional trauma, as we all are. It's my responsibility to heal it and move forward. And sometimes, the only way to do that is to stare at the sky for a while on a random island. And to think about how I can make my life better. To know I have the power to change the rules. That's one thing my grandmothers taught me.

On my last day in the Faroes, I was nervous. Probably because my flight time kept getting changed with the crazy weather—first it was delayed three hours, then it was suddenly an hour earlier than the original time. I kept refreshing my phone and thinking: *What the fuck? Am I going to make it off these islands, like ever?*

The shuttle driver pulled up and she was the cutest. I sat in the front seat next to her—and we laughed about our shared love for the show *Rita*. She told me how she'd lived on the islands her whole life and how she knits and that I have to come back in the summer. Her bright blue eyes reminded me of my grandmothers and I felt calm. And happy, again.

She dropped me off at the tiny little airport and I waved goodbye. I checked my bag and went to buy a little pastry—and when I turned around, she was standing by a little table and waving at me.

I had some time to burn so I figured I'd come and keep you company.

We sat and chatted as I ate my pastry and she showed me pictures of island life. I don't think she realized how meaningful that gesture was for me, especially at that time. I missed sitting with my grandmothers and talking to them. So having this random, kind motherly woman sit and spend time with me was truly a treat.

I got on the plane and landed back in Iceland. I had one more night and I knew exactly where I needed to be.

I sat and soaked and watched the sunset in the Blue Lagoon. I wanted to freeze time. It was so peaceful and warm and cozy and pretty and the sun was shining and I never wanted to leave. I was totally alone and yet, I was extremely happy.

I grew up with this idea that romantic love was the only source of love worth seeking in life—but I realized, after my own trial and error, that I could get love from so many places.

And it's absolutely wonderful when it's true love between two people, it's really the most beautiful thing in the world. But there's so many people who desperately want to be in love so badly, that they'll fake it. A life of pretending does not a life of true joy make. I found more joy in one night alone in a lagoon than I had in years of trying to "make it work" with someone else. In this cold icy country, my heart was starting to thaw and open back up, a little more.

When I got back home, in the middle of the night while scrolling in bed again, I came across a post about a woman who was starting a business writing letters to strangers. I completely forgot I ever submitted my address, until I checked the mail one day and received this letter:

Dear Caitlin,

You are brave for having the courage to put yourself first. To recognize your needs, your dreams, your passions for this life of yours.

You matter, your voice matters, and you can share your vision of the world with others. Don't pressure yourself, you don't have to do all this on your own. You are worthy of love and I know you have a support system.

Keep shining, the world needs your light.

Sending <3 from France,
Charlotte

Soaking up a slice of heaven with my sister | Blue Lagoon, Iceland
2018

16

FOOD PANTRY: DOWNTOWN

(charity)

Don't judge a man
until you've walked two moons in his moccasins.

- Sharon Creech

When I found myself back in Chicago after Peru, the city I left, I also quickly found myself back on a therapist's couch. Regularly. We had a lot of material to work with, but eventually, we moved past age 14 to talk about bits of my adult life.

Tell me more about your time in India and Peru.

Well, when I went to India it was the first time I saw poverty like that. And it was overwhelming. I knew I had to do something. So, I went to Peru. And I did something, but it's still all there. It's all still everywhere. And I think about it alot.

What do you think about?

Just the disparity of life. That people have to live that way. And that there's nothing I can do to change it. It's too big to ever fix.

Does it feel like you don't have a choice?

(crying) Yes. I just don't understand why the world is this way and why some people have to suffer so much.

How does that make you feel?

Guilty. Like I need to do something to fix it all, but then I know I can't so I feel helpless.

Maybe think about this. Do you feel like it's your responsibility to...take care of everyone?

How do you know everything about me?!!!

My therapist could read me like a psychology textbook. She always knew how to get to the root of things, almost in an annoying way.

When she touched on the raw nerve that was general poverty in the world, she tried to tell me that it's something I must learn to live with, which is true, in some ways.

But my sense of empathy was not something I could turn off. I felt it, deeply, and I couldn't just ignore it. So I nodded and listened to her advice while also telling myself she was clearly comparing people living in poverty to Preston, which was very unfair to them.

After Peru, I swore that I was going to live my life differently. I was so over shopping and material possessions, I was going to live a minimal, frugal existence out of humble respect for all the people suffering around the world. I wanted to live my life like a renegade saint—a one woman effort that would save the world. So I found a job at a food pantry.

It was a drastically different work environment than the ad agency, to say the least. I went from modern glass-walled conference rooms and free happy hours to working from a kid's chair in a Sunday school room in the basement of a church.

I was in charge of serving a hot lunch and figuring out what else people needed outside of food, from finding a job to getting food stamps and medical benefits to seeking mental health care to *literally anything.*

The common denominator between every person that came through the door was they were in a vulnerable position. They may have been considered "poor" based on their bank account or lack thereof, but they were some of the most radiant people I'd ever met.

I was desperately trying to solve anything I could in a world I felt I owed something. I knew I'd been given so much, now it was time to take all that and do some good with it. And by good, I mean have zero boundaries and try to help anyone and everyone, whether I was qualified to or not.

I made new friends. Like an older lady named Luciana. She was my pantry grandma and always gave me the biggest hug every time I saw her. She brought me little gifts.

Rocky was an ex-gang member who would draw art of and for me—and desperately tried to take me on a date to a Cubs game.

Maria was living with an abusive boyfriend but couldn't find work to move out and get her own place.

Cherie was so busy taking care of her kids and grandkids while living with all sorts of cancer.

Ama was an immigrant single mother with four kids and no work living in a foreclosed apartment.

Don was a vet who lived in a hut he built himself under a viaduct and was about to have major spinal surgery.

I had a soft spot for Joe, a middle-aged Irish American dude with big blue eyes who wore a cut-off tee most days, regardless of weather.

He drew a tattoo on his arm and carried around business cards with the same self-designed logo: his name in the middle of the Chicago flag. I liked his creativity.

I'd sit down with him and we'd talk about his resume, which would always end in him crying and me soothing him. He was so ashamed of his drinking and his unemployment, and even more ashamed that he had to ask me for help. He'd bring me recommendation letters from his past and eventually, I had a full file with all his stuff, most of which couldn't be used for anything, but I never had the heart to tell him that.

I really believed Joe could do it. I saw the will in his eyes. I knew his heart was in the right place. He tried to quit drinking and in the process, he started having seizures. A guy picked a fight with him one day at the pantry and they both got kicked out. Joe was one of the most non-violent humans I'd ever met, he wouldn't hurt a fly. But the guy who picked the fight was notorious for starting shit, all the time. Joe tried to come back and our security guy called the police. Joe begged to talk to me, but my boss wouldn't let me go outside.

I knew in my gut that this was wrong. I knew Joe wasn't the cause of this fight and the guy who was taunting him was a real asshole. I wanted to go outside. But I didn't.

The next week Joe's friends came into the pantry and I knew right away that something was actually wrong. They told me Joe had drank too much one night and never woke up. I kept it together until I got home—and then I cried for hours in the bathtub.

I went to his wake with two of his friends. I brought the file with all the glowing letters about what a great guy Joe had been and I gave it to his mom. His siblings and parents were there. There is nothing worse than watching a parent outlive their child, even when their kid is now 40+ years old. The room felt very heavy.

The experience was stuck on me. I knew I'd made a big mistake.

I couldn't keep Joe from drinking, I couldn't make him not die, but I could have fought harder to make sure he didn't lose his one safe place. I could have stuck up for him to my boss and to the cops.

But I didn't. Because I knew they'd just dismiss me as being overly emotional, a too-attached woman with no boundaries (and they would have been mostly correct, but that didn't make me wrong).

I knew that for Joe losing access to the place he was coming to get help was a big catalyst in his falling apart. He literally just faded away after that, in the matter of a week.

Joe had a good heart. But he had a disease and he couldn't fight it alone. Just like everyone else at the pantry, he needed community.

What I saw in all these people who had hit a rough patch in life was that they didn't have a safety net to fall back on. They had nowhere else to turn so they were stuck.

And they were trapped by the labels. Homeless. Victim. Immigrant. Disadvantaged.

All of these words were so negative. What I saw were beautiful people who were struggling to survive. What all of these people wanted most was to belong and to matter. To find a place to fit in.

The pantry gave them that. It was a place they could come every week to connect, have a meal, talk about their problems, and get help. These people were being pushed to the sides in society. And true charity was about inviting them to the table, including them.

That's what Jesus was all about —inviting everyone to the table to break bread, especially the immigrants.

Every person I met, no matter what crap life threw their way, they wanted a better life. They wanted to get out of the place they were in. They were all just doing the best they could with the circumstances they had.

As I poured myself into helping others, my needs came second (or 17th) to whatever else was going on. I learned to become a selfless servant because this was the new way I could get love!

If I gave, if I was the girl making sacrifices and working with the poor, then I was praised for my good deeds. If I gave enough, I would be loved. By trying so hard to fix the world, I realized that it was the perfect way to avoid working on myself. If I focused on everyone else and their problems, I could keep brushing my own issues under the rug.

Most sensitive people will turn to addiction to help ease their pain (even though it's really causing more of it). I turned to a cigarette when I needed a crutch to get through life—something to help alleviate my stress in the present moment.

I tried to quit smoking probably a dozen times before I actually did. Smoking made me feel like I was in control of myself and my life. The truth was..I was not. I was being controlled by cigarettes. Everywhere I went and anything I did, my first and only thought would be: When's my next cig? It was almost like a game. A really fucked-up game.

After trying the patch, gum, and 3 sessions with a hypnotist, I decided it was on me—I needed to just go cold turkey. I picked a day, I went out with my friends the night before, and I smoked to my heart's content. The next day I stopped.

We point at the people we call "addicts" and say: *You're the problem. You need to learn to live without that thing that makes you feel better.* But maybe we don't know how to live in this world without something to numb us? Even though feeling better in the moment might kill us in the end. Truthfully, I get that.

The pantry (and quitting smoking) both made me question: What does it really mean to be poor? To be an addict? Is it really a lack of money or self-control? Or is it a lack of something else?

I think the biggest problem in our world, when it comes to addiction and most other things, is a lack of sensitivity and a lack of connection.

We've had to learn to become okay with and used to the tragedies that happen. We have to learn how to walk past a person sleeping in the street, how to look the other way when someone is suffering in the open, how to enter public spaces knowing anyone could be carrying a gun, ready to run if they open fire—and that's just not the natural human way. We aren't built to operate like that.

We've been taught to turn down our sensitivity to live in this world. And some of us are only able to do that with the help of substances or medication or anything that will just ease the rawness of life. But what we actually need is more sensitivity in the world—and many of the people with the most of it can be found at your local food pantry, both giving and receiving. And that is not a sexual innuendo.

There's a big ginormous gap between the rich and the poor; between the haves and the have nots; between 99% and the 1%.

Two very wise men (named Bob Dylan and Jesus) once sang and said, *"The first one now will later be last..."*

I translate this to mean: There is a new way things are going to be done. Where we won't value people based on their wealth in dollars, but in their intrinsic wealth in spirit. The people we label "poor" are often so much richer than the rest of us because they have had to endure and live through things that have smoothed and shaped their character into something beautiful, like a polished diamond.

There is absolutely nothing wrong with having money—it's a necessity in this game of life we're in. Having money is the opposite of a problem. There is a problem with having money and hoarding it, greedily. 99% of humans are not like this.

This disparity that I cried about to my therapist is happening all over the world. There are groups of people who are more privileged than others. It's been this way for a long time, but not for all of time.

Here's what I realized from the food pantry: People can only experience this honor—the honor and privilege of existence—when they are able to exist freely in the world with all their basic needs met. Even my dog has that.

One day I was sitting in my church preschool office, squatting on a toddler's chair, and I had a flash of inspiration. I drew a stick figure and listed out these five basic needs that everyone has, no matter who you are:

1. Nourishment [Food. Air. Water]
2. Love [Community]
3. Security [Money]
4. Home [Shelter]
5. Health [Mind. Body. Spirit]

When even just one person doesn't have these needs met, we can feel it as a whole. Because like a flock of birds that somehow keep the same formation in the sky, we have a collective consciousness too, as human beings. I'm not a scientist or on LSD, but I do know this is true with all my heart. It's one of the things we don't know we don't know.

One day, food pantries will be extinct and will be replaced by something even better. If we can figure out how to send pictures of our faces with dog ears instantly to anyone anywhere, surely we can figure out how to feed, clothe, house, and welcome every human. Surely we can do that.

What I learned at the pantry is that we are linked together in ways we will never see with our eyeballs, but we feel it with our hearts. That's why when Joe died, it hurt my heart tremendously. I felt connected to him and even though he was just a random dude in a cut-off tee with a self-created logo and whiskey breath, I was invested in his well-being. When he hurt, I hurt. When someone else hurts, when someone else is lacking in one of these basic areas, the rest of us hurt too. It's what makes us human.

Art created by Rocky, a friend I made at the pantry. I'd say he nailed it | Chicago, Illinois 2015

Three

17

VIETNAM: BRACE

(play)

Stop worrying about
big deep things
such as to decide on a purpose and way of life,
a consistent approach to even some impossible end,
or even an unimagined end.
You must practice being stupid.
Dumb, unthinking, empty.
Then you will be able to do.

- letter from Sol LeWitt to Eva Hesse

I learned how to slow down the hard way. Like the really hard way. Life has to throw me a big curveball, something really uncomfortable (even painful) in order to get me to fucking take a breather. It has to whack me down at the knees for me to say: Okay, mercy.

For the first time in my life, I experienced health issues of my own and it took me about 37 doctor visits and countless hours of self-diagnosis using my WebMD degree to figure out what was going on. I found out I had a thyroid issue—and it turns out when your hormones get out of whack, it throws pretty much your whole body off. But since I didn't look "sick" and my symptoms were mostly painful for me but unnoticeable to others, it took me a while (a few years) to actually slow the fuck down and let my body heal, instead of continuing to shove my way forward, making everything worse.

On my quest to undo the physical manifestation of years of stress, I tried everything, including:

Reiki
Crystals
Flower essences
Homeopathy
Every supplement under the sun
Emotional Freedom Tapping (EFT)
Chakra balancing
A holistic psychiatrist
A "regular" psychiatrist
Therapy
A life coach
Acupuncture
Shiatsu massage
3 holistic doctors
300+ self-help books

If it exists, I tried it. And all of these things were much better than what I'd used before to "heal my life", which was: cigarettes, alcohol and a nice dose of weed. None of those things were bad in and of themselves (ok, cigs were very bad)—but when I was using them to fill a hole inside myself, there was something wrong with that. It wasn't the substances, it was my (lack of) intention with them.

Some of these healthier alternatives helped, others didn't, but I took a little something away from each of them.

Marie, the reiki healer, was so wonderful and I ended up getting trained in reiki by her. She was so funny, loving, kind and supportive, I'd always spend at least an extra hour just talking with her.

The holistic psychiatrist told me I was most likely gifted, but also that I was probably "twice exceptional" meaning I was both gifted (intelligent) and challenged (anxiety). *Um, thank you?*

Aurora the life coach helped me understand that I deserve to be treated with respect and the acupuncture made me cry. So did the Shiatsu massage. Apparently, I was carrying around a lot of sadness in my body and these treatments were releasing it.

The first holistic doctor gave me a package and told me to mail my "samples" to a lab. *Um, can't you do that here?*

The second one wanted me to insert a pellet of hormones into my hip and would not let it go, even after I said I wasn't interested like four times.

The third holistic doctor I went to was the charm. Dr. Walters worked out of a physical therapy office in a strip mall in the suburbs, and he was the most legit out of all the healers I'd seen. He'd been studying integrative medicine for decades and had worked in a hospital for most of his career. For someone who had always mocked strip malls, it was ironic that I was regularly going to one in order to be healed.

I went for my first appointment and described everything I'd been experiencing, from insomnia to thyroid issues to anxiety. He listened and ordered blood work. I came back and he walked me through a 3-month treatment plan, including a few supplements, some foods to focus on, and three sessions of energy healing with him. He told me this was all fixable and I would be fine.

When I went for my first energy healing session with him, I was nervous. I laid on the massage table surrounded by crystals and the receptionist told me the doctor would come in, do the healing and leave when it was over.

I raised my head to say hello when he entered and we exchanged a quick greeting before he got to work. He put on music of angels singing and put rose oil on my forehead. Like the Bali healer, he used hand gestures and also, was saying things in all different languages.

I can't even put into words what it felt like, but it seemed I was entering another galaxy. Whatever he did, it made me feel at peace and when I left, I couldn't even describe how truly different I felt. All I knew was the energy healing was working, along with the supplements and the food. This man was truly working magic.

Mostly, he helped me to stop dwelling on what was wrong. He basically handed me a permission slip that said: *You can heal.* What I really needed to learn from all of this was how to slow down and rest. I had to learn that taking care of myself was the most important thing because I wouldn't be able to show up for myself or anyone else unless I was healthy. I also was fully aware of how many people were terminally ill, missing a limb, unable to walk and generally going through much, much worse. It made me feel guilty, like I should be able to power through—but then my body would be like: *No, bitch, that's not the lesson. Sit down and let yourself heal.*

So I did that. When I was halfway through my energy healing sessions with Dr. Walters, I decided I was ready to travel again.

I wanted to visit Karen on the other side of the world. She was my first friend ever in high school, the one who never judged me for anything with my family. She was living in South Korea, with her kids and husband—and I'd been saying I wanted to visit her forever, so I wanted to follow through on all that talk and actually do it.

I'd been canceling plans right and left with my friends, mostly because I couldn't stay up and drink like a fish anymore. My body was recalibrating and needed rest—and oddly, I was labeled a "flake" because I'd always intend to go and then have to bail when I hadn't slept in days or my thyroid was so bad I couldn't function. Now that I was feeling better, instead of just making plans to do something on a Saturday night, I went all in and decided to travel to the other side of the world because why not be as extreme as possible?! *You only live once!*

We decided to meet in Vietnam over Thanksgiving. I landed there a few days before Karen, so I wouldn't be totally jet-lagged. The staff at the hotel really swooped in on me and were almost disturbingly kind.

I slept a lot and during weird hours the first few days, and I'd get woken up every once in a while by a phone call from the front desk or a knock on the door: Miss, you alive? It's like they really genuinely wanted to make sure I was okay—which was both comforting and alarming, because why? *Was I in some kind of danger I didn't know about?*

After three days of doing minimal activity and ordering room service, I realized that I'd flown across the world only to lay in a bed and have food delivered to my room, just as one would do, in say, a hospital.

I took a cab into Hanoi and visited the Temple of Literature. I got there early, so I people watched on the street. A man was trying to sweep the street and I also saw so many businesswomen on scooters. I walked around the temple grounds and admired the lotus flowers. I was feeling really zen.

The streets of Vietnam reminded me of India, with a little less people but still a clusterfuck on the roads (in an almost beautiful way, like beautiful chaos)—and so many people working so hard and tons of stores stacked on top of each other and it made me sad in a way. It was like this westernized culture that's infiltrated these other countries, where you commute and work for barely enough and then, there's all this "shopping"—and it just made me sad. Which was easy for me to feel as I was staying in the lap of luxury at one of the fanciest hotels in the town, eating room service and getting spa treatments.

The spa was on the top level of the hotel, so I sat in a chair overlooking the city as my feet got rubbed. My masseuse's name was Quynh (pronounced Quinn) and it meant "night-blooming flowers." She taught me some Vietnamese (like *Gam Un* means Thank You) and we laughed because my pronunciation was terrible. She told me I sounded like a child and I loved her for that.

We were the same age, and yet she was working her ass off to survive and I was paying her to rub my feet, in her country. I was reminded, yet again, that my own liberation was bound in hers. I left her a whopping tip and had to reassure the front desk that yes, I very much meant to leave that amount. It was surprising to me that in such a fancy hotel, I was obviously tipping the most—and yet so many high-powered business people were staying there. Like there was an entire convention of them. If there's one thing I believe in, it's the importance of tipping well and tipping often. *Maybe I'll host a convention on that?*

Karen finally arrived in the middle of the night on my third day. Three hours later, we got in a van to head to a cruise ship in Halong Bay with a very nice honeymoon couple from London, Nat and Tom, and Leslie from San Diego, the solo traveler.

We started chatting about politics and I was fine with talking about Brexit, but once we got to America, I told them I was on vacation and couldn't go there. On the rest of the drive, we were giddy and excited. We saw pigs in a cage on a scooter and bought leaf hats.

Once we arrived at the dock, Karen pumped breast milk in the public bathroom and the waiter approached us at our table with our new friends and said: It will make me so happy if you order 4 beers and get 2 for free. *We wanted to make him happy.*

After making a dent in our bucket of beer, we took a little boat to the big cruise boat and couldn't stop laughing during the safety presentation. Especially when our captain described, in detail, his romantic relationship with the boat. I literally screamed WHAT?! when he referred to the boat as his girlfriend. We headed to lunch on the deck and we giggled like two schoolgirls at a pajama party for the entire five-course meal. The couple next to us asked: Who will be driving your kayak this afternoon? We weren't entirely sure.

We kayaked through limestone islands and continued to soak up all the beautiful scenery in Halong Bay, all while making fun of each other the entire time. Karen wanted to ditch the cruise and just live on an island but I reminded her that we had no water or food. She kept referring to me as "the big guy in the back" and I asked her to please stop objectifying me by a gender, it was 2018. Miraculously, we did not tip our kayak, which felt like a win.

We paddled back to the boat (after drifting away from the group) and jumped in the sea. The water was refreshing. Karen "lost her sunglasses." We got ready for dinner and Karen refused to be fancy. Mostly because she only brought two outfits—her shorts from high school and her other shorts from high school.

On our way to dinner, we went to the top deck and picked up drinks from our best friend, the boat bartender, on the way. He asked me if I wanted my mind to be blown and Karen said: *No, she wants a Screaming Orgasm and I'll take a Slippery Nipple.* He insisted we try the Kama Sutra drink instead—and Karen didn't know what that even was, so he happily Googled it for us—and showed us all the sexual positions, as I reminded him that it was

2018 and he wasn't allowed to do that anymore, please and thank you.

Four courses later, we were having the time of our lives and everyone else was ignoring us so we decided to order Mai Tais because we thought that more drinks would make us more friends? Instead, we became more annoying. The Mai Tais were delicious.

Then, the real fun began. At the end of dinner, there was a magic show—and Karen happily volunteered a.k.a. I pushed her into the table. The magician asked if we wanted to see "his deck" and someone in the crowd thirstily yelled *YES!* The rest of the night was blurry. Things were foggy, the air quality was bad and we went to bed.

We woke up after a three-hour nap and did Tai Chi, amazingly without laughing. Then we accused the entire boat of stealing Karen's sunglasses. We were begging the crew:

Please let us on that little boat! We know her sunglasses are on there!

Nope.

We're going to talk to the bartender about this!!

But, whoops! They were in Karen's very cool fanny pack the whole time. Then we ate our feelings and had french fries. This was when our idea of creating a kid's TV show starring our new friends, the honeymoon couple from London, Tom and Nat, was born. We told them that they'd see it on TV and we'd give them no credit at all.

After saying goodbye to our new friends who looked relieved to never have to see us again, we took a van to a little village in the middle of nowhere. We got to watch a puppet show with bull-riding

243

and ducks and a bare-chested woman and a man in a thong chasing the woman and more ducks. This was when we realized the Vietnamese must have an interesting sex life? There was a buffet and I grabbed some slices of melon that turned out to be cake and we couldn't let it go to waste, so we had to eat it. The puppet show ended (drats!)—and everyone else in the audience got back on a bus and left. Except us and another couple.

We got on a golf cart to go to our sleeping quarters with a man and a woman from California who clearly had a cold, but kept saying it was from the wildfires. All we knew was we did not want to catch whatever they had.

We arrived at the homestay and sat down at a table with our host, a woman around our age—and we were asked where we were from and why we chose this overnight trip. We realized the answer was: *It was a mistake.*

Activities included: Meeting a village family and eating with them; Catching a cold from the California Wildfire couple; Catching fish with our bare hands in a pond with snakes.

Karen talked about her fishing experience during our intake conversation:

Host: So you fish?

Karen: *I fished once.*

Host: So you love fish?

Karen: *No, I fished once.*

Host: So you're a fisherwoman?

Karen: *No, I fished once. Fish terrify me.*

Our host showed us to our bedroom, where the electricity was out and there were no walls around the toilet. It just went out, that never happens.

I looked at Karen: *We need to get the fuck out of here.*

Karen replied: Let's be rational.

No, it's now or never. There's no time to waste. Grab your shit and let's go.

Our host came back and quickly decided that I had a stomach ache and that's why we had to leave in such a rush. We got in another van and went to Hanoi, got a room at a hotel (where we belonged), and went to eat by the pool. An intoxicated "business" man kept harassing me and at first, Karen was jealous. He was trying to get me to come into his car.

I will take you to the mountains if only you will get in my car.

I'm not getting into your car with you, Sir.

Hotel security made him leave our table and he sat a few tables away, staring at me with a passion I've yet to experience from any man since. Afterward, we watched some great Vietnamese TV channels before Karen milked herself and we fell asleep.

On our last day, we saw the Train Street and the Turtle Temple. We went shopping at the markets and I told Karen: *Don't worry, I've got this. I know how to use the dong.* But weirdly, when we were haggling, all the vendors were telling us no, even when we walked away. Karen crunched some numbers and realized I was way off. We went back and actually were able to buy things.

While sitting by the pool that afternoon, our waiter was very nice and bringing us everything we could possibly ever want or need. We realized our waiter was probably gonna write about us in his journal that night:

Those two bitches thought they were Kardashians.

We did have some serious moments, between the fits of laughter. Karen talked about living in South Korea and how it was just better to live somewhere new. She said she still loved everyone, but she got to do her own thing. It sounded fabulous.

I knew she wasn't going to get a ton of visitors from back home while living in Korea, so that's why I knew I had to come see her. Even though we were being extremely immature, it was so nice to let the seriousness of life melt away for a weekend and just GIGGLE. The trip was really about being silly for a bit, because life can be way too fucking serious and painful sometimes. And honestly, it was the best medicine I'd tried in years!

When we were sitting on top of the cruise ship, looking at the scenery, I literally turned to Karen and said:

What did we do to deserve this?

She looked at me like I was crazy and said: *Nothin'!*

And that's really how life can be. Sometimes, you roll the dice and it's amazing. Other days, it's not so amazing. You never know what you're gonna get, but you might as well take a roll because it could be WONDERFUL!

Karen left and I spent one more day in Vietnam, shamefully sitting by the pool in the same chairs we'd been horribly obnoxious in the day before, only without my sidekick. I felt incredibly grateful to have a friend like her.

My trip with Karen refueled my soul in a way I had been craving. I could spend all the money I had on trying to cure myself, and most of it helped—but it really seemed like the cure I needed most was laughter and fun. Or maybe all those things helped me to laugh again. Who knows.

An older gentleman was sitting next to us at the pool right before Karen left, and he commented on his way out on just how much we were enjoying ourselves:

You two are enjoying yourselves.

Yes sir, YOLO.

Yoyo?

No, YOLO!

View from the top deck in Halong Bay, Vietnam November 2018.

18
MIDDLE AMERICA: SLEEPYHEAD
(joy)

You will ride life straight to perfect laughter.
It's the only good fight there is.

- *Charles Bukowski*

After Vietnam, I'd gotten to the point in my life where I was so fed up that I got in my car and hit the road one day—and did not look back. I threw some shit in my trunk, made the backseat as comfortable as possible for my dog, and drove right across the damn country.

I didn't know where I'd end up (probably California though), I had no set timeline or destination (except California), just a vague idea of where I wanted to go (did I mention California?). But I knew when I got on the highway that it was the first time I'd felt like I was on the right path, maybe in months (or years or decades, who's counting?!).

Before I left, my life had started to feel like it was one hot mess after the next. It turns out when you "surrender" that means letting go of allllllll the things that are not actually good for you, including things you may hold dear. Everything fell apart (multiple times) and trust me, I tried to keep it together. I found myself having conversations like this with the universe:

So, funny thing, I know I said, like, I "surrender" to like my purpose or highest calling or whatever is in my best interest, but what I actually meant was like to go through a soft, quiet inner transition that won't affect my outer world at all—and again, I'd like to do that quietly and gently while still maintaining all my usual comforts and without making any actual big change. Mmmkay?! We're on the same page? Cool. Great. Thanks.

LOL. We were not on the same page. Turns out, most of the things in my life that I'd clung to, like my identity of living in Chicago, so many of my friendships, the guys I'd chased after, my role as the stilts propping things up in my family, how much I valued myself and my work and my ability to make everyone else happy—I'd made those agreements and created that life when I wasn't exactly in the best place...

Now that I was growing up, I was outgrowing who I used to be. My old life just wasn't a match anymore with who I was becoming. I grew right out of it, like a plant that needed to be replanted in a bigger pot.

All my friends were still doing the same things and getting into the same trouble—but I couldn't keep going to the same bars with the same people, every single weekend. I wanted off that party merry-go-round. It was fun while it lasted but I was feeling the same sense of nausea you get when you're stuck on a ride and just want to get off. I was over it and ready to do something different with my life. I just wasn't clear on what that was, exactly.

Also, I was flailing in my love life. Like a persistent shark, Preston kept circling back, trying to find any way to re-enter my world whenever he felt like it, even while blocked on every possible platform. He'd use an old iCloud email address, dump whatever issue was going on in his life on my shoulders, and then repeat the same old patterns—and I'd be reminded why I'd blocked him in the first place.

I also went on a little streak of dating guys who all had one thing in common: they were younger. And it was truly a joy—until Timmy. I met Timmy at a bar in my hometown and he was extremely attractive. Like an Abercrombie & Fitch model. Someone you don't want to be attracted to, because of the douchebag factor, but you can't deny the eye candy factor. He asked me if I wanted to leave with him and my answer was: *Um, duh.*

We got in a cab and went to his place. I wasn't paying attention to where we were headed, but we finally pulled up to a suburban home.

Timmy, you live here?

Yeah, with my roommates. Just be quiet when we go in.

Ok! It seemed a little weird, but we went to Timmy's room.

The next morning, I woke up to a knock on his door.

Timmy, Timmy...I'm going to let Spot in.

The door opened and Spot, his family dog, jumped on the bed and directly on top of my torso, trying to lick my face.

I paused for ten seconds and counted one Mississippi, two Mississippi...

And then I elbowed the shit out of Timmy.

Um, your MOM just opened the door.

Haha really?

YES!

That's funny...

Uh uh (pushing his hot grabby hands away). I need you to get your dog, go downstairs and distract your mom. When the coast is clear, let me know and I will leave.

Whoa, relax. She knows I have friends over.

I'm sorry, but I'm not ready to meet your mother right now. Can you please go?

Yeah, sure, whatever.

Within three minutes, I was dressed and in an Uber. I realized I was looking for a self-esteem boost in the wrong form, yet again. I was forced to reevaluate my life a bit.

I put myself on a man-tox—meaning I was no longer going to seek validation from dudes. I inadvertently became a born-again virgin.

Basically, I'd lost myself—in others, in drinking, in searching for love in the wrong places. I struggled to walk away from that old life and into my new one.

That is, until I reached my boiling point and decided to get in my car and go. I'd had ENOUGH and was finally ready to be better and do better.

I wish I could take full credit for this decision but the universe gave me a few hints (that I swatted away) and then, it gave me a shove out the door. I spent months facing blocked paths and getting repeated signs (that I stubbornly ignored).

I kept trying to make things work, as they were. I was still avoiding dealing with the hard stuff in my life, including the fact that I didn't want to live full-time in the Midwest. Or that I might have some issues around things like intimacy and being truly vulnerable. I didn't want to face the reality that I might have things to work through and so did the people around me.

I wish I could pinpoint one big trigger but it was really a collective mess that I couldn't believe I was even a part of. From the shit with my family to the audacity of Preston to getting dragged into everyone else's drama, I was Over it, with a capital O.

I was so pissed off by everything—the snarky comments, the audacity, the drama, the constant construction everywhere I moved, the culmination of years of trying to be someone I wasn't. And that's when I finally slowed down (ahem...got frustrated enough) and gave a long, side glance to the universe when I realized what it had been trying to tell me:

Wait..what's that? I should put myself first and do what I want and MOVE. Like out of Illinois. Ohhhhhhhhh. THANKS FOR LETTING ME KNOW!!!

The second I got on the highway, it felt like a huge sigh of relief. Ahhh yes, I'm on my way forward again. How refreshing. The biggest source of my frustration really wasn't with anything else but myself. I was so mad at myself for still trying to force and mold a life out of things that weren't a good fit for me anymore. For trying to stay comfortable in familiar discomfort.

This was actually a common practice in my life, the one known as self-sabotage. When we reach a new level in life (often called an "upper limit"—a level of growth we've never experienced yet, like outgrowing friends or finding our self-worth), we often sabotage ourselves, even unconsciously, to stay in our comfort zone, even if it's actually unhealthy. *Not that I would know anything about that!*

My frustration was because I'd outgrown my surroundings but I wasn't letting myself do anything new. I was different but I was trying to stay the same. It wasn't until I got so frustrated that I was about to lose my damn mind that I finally made a move and then, felt the thrill and joy that's on the other side of the fear. *There's actually joy in the unknown. It's wild!!*

Even though I had so many people I loved in Illinois, I had to move, to follow this wind of change, or else, life was only going to keep trying to get my attention. And I didn't even want to see what it was going to throw at me next!! *I get it, I'm ON MY WAY!*

While I was packing all my stuff, I was cleaning my desk and had hundreds of little papers with ideas scribbled on them, almost like a scene from *A Beautiful Mind*. I started throwing them all in the recycling, but one landed right at my feet. I picked it up and saw what I'd written:

Road Trip.

Huh. I had no memory of writing that. But I guess it wasn't a totally new idea.

My first stop outside of Illinois was St. Louis. I'd never been and my cousin lived there—so I stopped to visit her, mostly because I would have felt like a real asshole if I drove right by her and didn't even stop to say hello!

On my way into town, I decided to be a tourist and see the Arch. I saw a sign that said it was a marker, a symbol of being the "Gateway to the West"—where white people finalized the "relocation" of the Native Americans. I didn't like that, but I did like the idea of it being the front door to where I was trying to go. Like most things in the U.S. (and life), there was both a good and a bad side.

The woman who checked me into my hotel was named "Lovely." She told me she could check me in early if I sang a song (I smiled instead) and then she asked me why I was there and what I do. I didn't tell her my whole life story, but I mentioned that I'm a writer and turns out, she was one too.

She looked me right in the eye and said:

Keep on writing and stick with it and remember that someone needs to hear what you have to say because it's healing for them.

Thank you, Lovely. I ordered an Uber to go meet my cousin at her work and was picked up in a white Hummer (appropriate). In any hired ride I've ever been in, I usually know the person's life history and deepest wound within the first two minutes. In this case, my driver was from St. Louis and her husband had died the year before. They lived in Texas for a while where he was a doctor but they had to leave because there wasn't much integration.

This was an ironic story to hear because the first thing my cousin took me to see was Delmar Boulevard, also known as the Delmar Divide. Her office was right in the middle of it—the most acute racial divide in any city in America. The North is 98% black with 80% vacancy (meaning abandoned, unlivable homes) and the South is white, with a Lululemon and condo developments and all.

We walked through the North part, by Fountain Park and my cousin explained all about the segregation plus lack of integration she sees in her work—and how the vacant homes are on sale for $1, just like on Chicago's South Side.

We walked to get Ethiopian food and then we got ice cream in a neighborhood she described as "anarchist hipster with antique shops"—a.k.a. my dream.

On the ride back to my hotel, my driver was a nice older gentleman in his 60's and he had a daughter around my age who had decided to have a kid via insemination. He suggested I freeze my eggs, and as any woman will tell you, there's nothing better than a man telling a woman what to do with her body! *Freeze yours, Sir!*

The next morning, I packed up my stuff and went to meet my cousin at the local Catholic Worker House, where she volunteered every Saturday morning, much like a living saint.

Dorothy Day was the founder of the Catholic Worker Houses and I'd read her autobiography and became obsessed with her, mostly because of her dedication to equality, so I had to go see what this was all about.

The house was a women's shelter in an old convent—and it felt really relaxed and open, welcoming to all and built on the values of respect, dignity and love. A true gem in middle America. I got a tour and met one of the young women living there.

My cousin had to like actually do things—so I started browsing magazines and found a story, written by one of the former residents of the House, and the ending really hit home:

Growing up, I was angry and embarrassed and ashamed. Now I know that it's my journey and it was necessary. Necessary to make me strong enough for where I'm going. Because of my past, I'm strong enough for my future. I am humbled.

I went to the office to look for my cousin and instead, sat down to chat with the young girl who was living there. I asked her why she was there and she told me how her grandmother and mother both abused her—and she referred to them both by their first names, which I respected as a boss power move.

She told me how she was writing and how life is all about the energy you give out. It's always comical to me the way the world plants the most humble, beautiful people in the places we least expect. A teenage runaway living in a charity home was filled with more wisdom than the gaggles of sheep-people I'd met with big titles elsewhere.

I drove away filled with a sense of pride for my twenty-something cousin and the life she made for herself. I used to babysit her and now she was out there, changing the world. I knew our grandparents would be so proud of her too.

When I left St. Louis, I drove through a trifecta of rain, sleet, and snow to get to Kansas City. When I finally got there, I realized my hotel was in the midst of a very interesting combination of things...

There was the KC Speedway and a sprawling shopping mall with a VERY interesting statue out front. I couldn't help but wonder: *Who the fuck's idea was it to put that there*?! I can only imagine they thought something like: *Ok...We've got stolen land, NASCAR, and stores...I know what this place needs...a statue of a NATIVE AMERICAN CHIEF!* Sometimes America really is the land of the ignorant and the tone-deaf.

Luckily, I did spend some time in other areas of Kansas City (like the library with all the book spines) and I was charmed. The sun was shining, I saw the *Queer Eye* loft, and bought some trinkets from Raygun. Really, I was excited about going to Tulsa the next day (a sentence I will only utter once in my life).

For years, I'd been listening to a podcast that was like weekly spiritual teachings. I even talked to my Gram about it, because I knew she'd like what it was all about. Like how Jesus made the poor, the outcast, the whore, the blind, and the forgotten, the primary audience for his teachings. He got mad and tore up a

257

market in a temple, condemning the government for taking advantage of the poor. He preached a new, inclusive way. My Gram loved talking about that—the underlying meaning of what's inside those Bible stories, why she told me to keep the faith over and over and over again. It had everything to do with the rebellious act of loving and living outside the norms, of making your own rules and constantly evolving. And that's basically what this podcast was all about, so I stopped in my tracks when I heard:

And if you happen to be passing through Oklahoma at the end of March, there will be a live show in Tulsa.

I thought: *Wow, that's, like, so funny, because I actually will be...I will be passing through Oklahoma...I will be in Tulsa...then...too...*

If there's anything I believe in, it's serendipity. If you'd asked me two months before when I'd be in Oklahoma, my response would have been: NEVER! I knew I had to go this live show. The stars were aligning.

It was perfect timing because doubt had started to creep in more and more, like a fog hanging over my head. I'd only been on the road for a few days and as I got further away from the Midwest, I started to seriously doubt what the f I was doing.

When I left Kansas City, I was already worn out. I chatted with my little niece and she asked me if I was coming over and I had to tell her no for the first time. I got prank voicemail messages from my cousins who I knew I wouldn't be able to see for a while.

I stopped to get BBQ somewhere in Kansas (delicious). Most of the drive was peaceful and I did also stop for an ice cream cone. But when I got to Tulsa, I got off at the wrong exit and I was lost for a hot second—and I was fried and tired and anxious. By the time I got to my hotel, I started to feel like:

What am I even doing with my life?!?! Did I make the right call? Was this all a huge mistake?

Even though I was feeling like a weary traveler, I still went to see this podcast show, all by myself, anyway. Because I just happened to be passing through Oklahoma, at just the right time.

The only way to describe what happened in that room was "something magical." It was as if I'd been planted in that seat, where I learned exactly what I needed to, right there and then, in that moment.

The two main things I walked away with were:

One: There's a big difference between "I get to" and "Do I gotta?"

Instead of drowning myself in a sea of self-doubt (something I'd grown quite good at), I had to instead say:

I get to do this. I get to do this. I get to do this. This is my life. I get to put all my things in my car and drive across the country and enjoy myself and nature. I get to do this.

Two: The purpose of life is to find joy.

This was a big lesson for me. To let myself experience all the JOY, minus the guilt.

Because finding joy doesn't erase all the bad. It's going through the other side of pain and feeling a certain lightness because we know how quickly life can change. We're here for a second and then we're gone—so it's our duty to enjoy it while we're here.

I thought about how my Gram would say to me, from her wheelchair, towards the end: *Are you taking notes?* Which meant:

Do you see? Do you see how life can change in an instant? Don't waste it. Don't waste a moment of it.

I know I was meant to be in that room and hear that message and receive the blessing to go forward. With JOY.

When I got back to my hotel room, I cried, not because I was sad, but because it's all just so damn beautiful. And I felt so lucky, to have the opportunity for something new.

What I went through in my past, before my decision to leave, was like an initiation of sorts. It plunged me into a deep, dark grief—a place I'd been avoiding for most (all) of my life. And yet—it opened me up too. I was on the other side of that now, and I was meant to fill my life with as much joy as possible. And the best way for me to do that was to get out there in the world, on my own. To drive my car across the damn country to an unknown destination (called California).

Because no matter what I did, it was all ok. There was no "right" choice or one "right" way to do things. I had to follow my heart and do what was best for me.

As I carried on through Middle America, I spent another night in Oklahoma. I was staying in a small town, outside of Oklahoma City—and I was very out of place as a single lady, just passing on through. My accent instantly gave me away, and so did my Illinois license plates. I did not belong there.

To be honest, I was used to the streets being filled with homes, bustling businesses, people honking at each other for driving too slow, and at least two Starbucks on every block. In Elk City, tumbleweeds and dust were more abundant than retail franchises— and that scared me. There wasn't a can of LaCroix to be found for miles and miles. I needed more people and less pick-up trucks around me to feel safe.

Not to mention, the huge rural-urban divide that was only growing deeper in the country at the time. I knew I was in a state where red hats were worn proudly. I tried to make myself look as gender neutral as possible, hair in a bun, no make-up, big hoodies, only carrying a wallet. I wore a baseball hat and sunglasses on the highways, hoping my disguise would keep creepy men from getting any ideas. A few still gave me the eye and I refused to look. *If I can't see you, you can't see me.*

I had no idea how many Native American reservations existed throughout Oklahoma because I'd never really seen any around Chicago. There was a noticeable difference when the highway cut through one. There weren't as many exits, not as many stores and places to stop, the speed limit was lower, and there was almost an eerie silence, like I was passing through land that I didn't belong in, the land that somehow survived all the violence that happened before and I was only allowed through if I promised to keep going. Reservations were a reminder that as much as we want to push things to the side, the truth never dies. It remains.

Back in the U.S. of good ol' A., small town Oklahoma also felt desolate, like parts of it were now just for ghosts. Abandoned factories, rotting farm equipment, empty strip malls—I couldn't help but wonder:

Where did the people that used to live here go? Did they all get recruited by Amazon?

And sadly, it felt that way along most of Route 66. So many of the "classic" stops were now not much of anything. Left behind, aging after their heyday.

In the town I chose to spend the night in, there was an actual oil rig in the center, with a Family Video store down the block—meaning people still used DVDs and worse, VCRs. I saw a sign for a storage business that read: "Well-Lighted Storage Spaces." I felt a shiver run down my spine. *Well-Lit. WELL-LIT!!!*

I spotted a statue of a white man and a Native American shaking hands and thought: *Oh that's sweet!!* Until I read what was written underneath: *Binding Contract*. I knew my time in that town couldn't be short enough. I did appreciate being called Ma'am though. It was starting to have a nice ring to it. *Howdy and G'day to you too.*

Even though I was in the same country, it felt like I'd entered another world out there in the middle of it all. I could see with my own two eyes, the enormous divide between two ways of life in America: the country and the city folk, the conservative and the liberal, the Elk City kind and the Chicago kind.

The disparity was so obvious to me—how the ones who've made enough money and gained enough privilege so often become out-of-touch with reality. I can say this as someone who has benefited from living in places with an abundance of resources my entire life.

I went to bed that night, wearing socks, sweatpants, a hoodie with the hood over my hair, and gloves, trying to protect my body from the brittle bedding in the worn-down "hotel" (motel) I was staying in. I could hear the buzz of the streetlights in the parking lot and that's about it. Everything else was silent.

The next morning, I woke up bright and early, filled up at the gas station, and got the fuck out of Oklahoma. I had to cross through the top of Texas—and it was the only part of the trip I was afraid of. Let me just say, there was a VIBE there. There were signs that said: *Don't Mess with Texas* everywhere. *No worries, I don't wanna!*

I only stopped once and everyone was friendly, in almost an angry way. I saw a cattle ranch with cows living right on top of each other and none of them could move. All I could think was: *I probably need to try going vegan again now, fuck!* I also saw a cross that was probably 50 feet tall on the side of the highway. *Is this Handmaid's Tale?*

I assumed everyone had a shotgun and made eye contact with no one. I'd spent years in Chicago's most dangerous neighborhoods, but it was nothing compared to the fear I experienced in all-white, middle America.

I counted the seconds (one-Elk City, two-Elk City, three-Elk City) until I saw my salvation:

Welcome to New Mexico
The Land of Enchantment.

Halle-fucking-lujah. I'd made it to the Southwest.

North of the Delmar Divide, St. Louis, MO | March 2019

19
SANTA FE: FUNERAL SINGERS
(déjà vu)

Oh, if I'd followed people's advice, it would have been hopeless.
-Georgia O'Keefe

As a kid, I had déjà vu all the time. I'd dream about something—
and then I'd be living it, a few weeks later.

The first time I had the full-on experience was at my uncle's
wedding when I was a toddler. I was sitting at a table, eating dinner
with my family, in a big banquet hall with pink walls—and in an
instant, I knew I'd already lived in that moment, just at night about a
week earlier. I got so excited and I turned to my dad and told him:
Dad, I dreamt this last week! I was here before!

He laughed a little and told me to lay off the wedding cake, but I
felt like I had a new superpower. I could dream something before it
happened!

When I saw a cemetery for the first time, also with my dad, I burst
into tears because I was so sad for all those people. And their
families!! And as I got older, I realized I could sense what people
were feeling, just by being around them. These moments and
heightened senses were signs of a high sensitivity to the world, but I
quickly realized: it didn't always make me feel good.

Sometimes, it was too much to be able to feel so much.

As time went on and I grew up, this sensitive part of me I'd tried to
bury started to come alive again—and grab my attention. It came in

flashes of knowing, in more vivid dreams, and in the experiences I couldn't describe in words, but could feel in my heart.

And often, I tried to ignore it, especially when it was telling me to do something I knew would be tough. Like when it told me to drive across the country alone.

When I pulled into Santa Fe (after hauling ass through the top of Texas), I had a strong sense of déjà vu from the moment I got there. I could smell all the fireplaces and since the city was higher up, the air felt more crisp and clean, especially at night. I had the same feeling there that I had in Peru: a taste of freedom, of being on the right path.

I was staying at the Hotel St. Francis, the oldest hotel in the oldest state capital in the U.S. The city of Santa Fe (which means "holy faith") was founded in 1610 by Spanish colonists. Even though I'd been taught that Jamestown was the first settlement on the East Coast, there was actually a lot more (colonial) activity happening in the south. The Spanish colonists were swiftly making their way from South to Central to North America, like a hot European fire.

My hotel room was like a simplistic convent, with white walls, old wooden floors, a sink and a bed, reminiscent of the monastery I'd visited in Arequipa. I took my dog for a walk and felt like I'd really accidentally driven back to Peru. From the narrow streets to the mountains and the sun and the temperature, it all felt the same.

I realized I was also in the same stage of life as I was when I went to South America: I was back on my own, arriving in a new place and stepping into my own life again after getting a little lost along the way—only this time, I had done it before so it was an easier groove to find. I was slipping right back into it—and it felt really good.

Back then, I couldn't believe I'd left my life behind to go to South America by myself. And being in New Mexico, I couldn't believe I'd left my life behind (again) to drive across the country. Of course, there was still a part of me that had doubts and worries. But the good thing was I was better at catching it now. I'd survived before, so I would again.

What I loved about being back out on my own again was having the freedom to explore. The energy in Santa Fe felt like Peru to me—this deep sense of ancient culture, of creativity. It felt heavenly, like it was up above the rest of humanity. Maybe that was just the elevation, but I don't think so.

I drove to Taos and the drive was so beautiful. It was a perfect day out, blue skies and a decent temperature. The road went through the mountains, but towards the bottom. I'd nearly conquered my fear of heights, but it was still in me and popped up from time to time.

When I got to the top of the mesa, the views were incredible. So expansive. It's hard to capture in pictures, you can only really feel how BIG it is when you're there. Kinda like the Grand Canyon.

But when I got to the famous pueblo in Taos, I only stayed for ten minutes. I felt dizzy and out of it, something about that place was not sitting right with me. Maybe that really was the elevation again. *Where were my coca leaves?*

There was an actual village still in the pueblos with actual people living inside the clay pueblo homes. They set up little shops and sold trinkets and baked goods—and were basically functioning as a real-life museum, only it was the 21st century and the pueblos were very old and the whole thing just felt...exploitative?

I don't know what I was expecting, but that was not it. I wanted to see the empty, preserved pueblo, not the descendants still trying to live a way of life that was now being treated like an exhibit. I got right out of there, after of course buying some art to support them.

As I drove back through the mountains to Santa Fe, it was just so damn pretty. I felt alive, even though I was tired. Like I was re-energized. I had no idea where I would be in two weeks, let alone two months, or even two years. I was alone, on the road, and happy. I know science hasn't proven it yet, but there's a healing side of travel. Something about soaking up the energy of new places changes us.

Back in Santa Fe, I treated myself to the Javanese Royal Treatment at the local spa. I learned it was actually a ritual done for brides— which felt both ironic and fitting. I guess I'd decided to marry (and commit to) my life (not everyone else's ideas for my life).

I was now my own bride.

The treatment began with a rose petal bath with special oils, then a body scrub with turmeric and honey, and then like a warm yogurt rub. And then a shower and then...a Balinese massage! It was HEAVEN.

I spent the rest of my time in Santa Fe exploring everything it had to offer. Like Meow Wolf, an art and play center funded by the author of *Game of Thrones*. It was trippy, with lots of neon lights and made me feel like I was on drugs. I went to a local bookstore (that I loved) and the cashier told me about "rockhounding" while her friend smoked a joint.

By far, my favorite thing was the Georgia O'Keeffe Museum. My Gram loved art, so I felt like she was right there with me, admiring all the paintings.

I didn't know how much Georgia traveled. And she loved her dogs. Her life felt revolutionary, given when she was born. She was an artist and followed what she wanted and lived in New York and New Mexico.

I got chills when I went into a room and learned she'd traveled to Peru. She did paintings of Machu Picchu and the El Misti volcano from Arequipa.

It felt very full circle, being in Santa Fe. Wandering alone in a mountain city, just like I'd done years ago in Peru. Like I'd been in one big cycle of transformation, learning how to let go and follow my own path.

There was one thing I saw at the Georgia O'Keeffe Museum that practically popped off the wall. There was a plaque that described what her friend said to her when she moved to New Mexico:

You have finally achieved a dream of yours — maybe your chief dream...
You have a house you can call your own.

Georgia had been living in Taos (near the pueblo) and learned how to drive a car. She started exploring, driving the same roads I drove between Taos and Santa Fe, and she came across an old, nearly washed-up adobe home in a village called Abiqui—and she knew she wanted it. It took her over a decade to get it, purchasing it from the Catholic Church. There was a spectacular view looking down into the valley that inspired much of her art. She also bought another home called the Ghost Ranch, surrounded by exotic lands that she described as: *Red hills of apparently the same sort of earth that you mix with oil to make paint.*

New Mexico felt like art magic. That's probably why it's called the Land of Enchantment. And celebrating the life of a woman who made her art her life, who traveled and created beautiful homes, who lived amongst nature and shared her creativity with the world—it all felt incredibly inspiring.

I couldn't help but think what a waste it would have been if Georgia had never had the courage to pursue her art. If she'd followed the custom of her day, which was to get married and support her husband. Instead, she allowed him to support her and her work.

What I loved about Georgia's life was how she seemed to experience the world in her own unique way.

I was realizing that happiness, for me, meant a way of being, not something I had to earn. It meant art, laughter, sharing, meeting new people, and experiencing the world. It meant love as something to be participated in, not desperately searched for. It meant knowing there are a thousand Ones out there and letting myself fall in love— and moving on if it wasn't returned. It was all the things that made life rich, varied and wonderful. Happiness was staying open to possibilities.

Back where I was from, I had been trying to fit in with all my friends and I'd been limiting my own possibilities. And I guess, deep down, a part of me believed that I didn't really fit in...anywhere.

But New Mexico made me see that I could create a home for myself, in one place or many, but it could be mine. And I could be happy, in whatever way felt best to me.

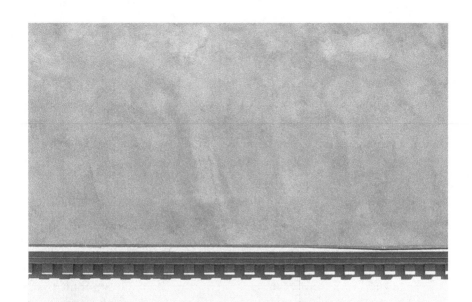

Spotted: One of my favorite Rumi quotes on a storefront "Let the beauty of what you love be what you do."
– Rumi | Santa Fe, April 2019

20
TEMPE: SEPTEMBER
(alchemy)

They always say that time changes things, but you actually have to
change them yourself.

-Andy Warhol

The last time I was in Arizona was on Spring Break (as an adult)
with my family. It was the first time I admitted, out loud, to anyone
in my family, that I might want to move somewhere else.

I told my sister as she was driving us on a highway (I'd gone on a
Party Bike tour with my cousin and was a little tipsy). I also told her
to take the next exit towards Jack in the Box for curly fries. I realized
after my confession how much moving away might alienate my
family—and might even make them mad? I mean, my sister took it
well (to my face)—but I had a hard time imagining telling anyone
else.

And then, three years later, there I was, on the same highway again,
only I was in the driver's seat this time and I was alone. And I'd
picked Tempe as a place to stop for a reason. It's where my parents
met decades ago—a place where they'd been young and happy and
spoke to each other.

Imagining them living a totally different life in a different state
(literally and figuratively) made me feel closer to them. Like
whatever it was inside me that made me want to get out of Illinois,
they had it at one point too. And it brought them both, separately, to

Arizona State University in the '70s, also known as the prime college experience.

They met while working on the student newspaper. My dad was a photographer and a writer who mainly wrote concert reviews, getting to see Bob Dylan and like every other amazing band in the seventies. Literally the coolest college job ever. My mom was a sorority girl who was determined to be a journalist.

I took my dog for a walk down Mill Avenue, the main strip in Tempe. It was 95 degrees and as I looked around at all the students, I had a weird moment where I realized: *Wow, my parents were just like these students walking down this street.*

And I realized just how young they were when they met. Now that I was an adult, I realized that they were just baby adults back then. Being there gave me a sense of compassion for them that I think I lacked when I was younger— that just like me, they were young once and they had hopes and dreams and they lived in this place that was so far away from home. I realized they were just two young kids who were making their way in life. And look at what they gave me:

Freedom to make my own choices.

Autonomy, a way with words, an education. And maybe their relationship was fated to never last but they must have done something right because my siblings and I all turned out better than pretty good. *Amazing, actually.*

They'd lived in a time where you found a spouse and you got married, end of story—and I was so goddamn fortunate that I had the luxury to be able to do something different. To wait. To take my time. To rewrite the rules for my own future. It felt like being there, I was remembering what I forgot when I was younger: my parents were just people too.

The next morning, I wanted to see where they each used to live. I stopped to get a refreshing lemonade and asked two girls who were sitting outside to make sure no one stole my dog. I tied her leash to a bench—and when I came back out two minutes later, both girls were sitting on the bench, petting and cuddling her, while she looked at me like: *Um, do I know you? Sorry, these are my new moms now.*

The girls were really friendly and I chatted with them for a minute and mentioned how lucky they were to go to school in such a beautiful place. They asked for my name and then introduced themselves (Daniella and Leslie).

They said they were actually originally from the area and gave me some recommendations on things to do. And then Daniella said:

You know I'm really into God and I'm just wondering: Is there anything we can pray for you for?

My first thought was: Oh great, I'm about to get converted.

I tried to just stay with her and keep eye contact:

Um, yeah. I'm on a road trip, so maybe like so I'll stay safe?

Would it be okay if we say the prayer together now?

(Shit.) Yeah, totally.

The two young college co-eds both bowed their heads and closed their eyes—as I stood there in front of them, allowing them to say a blessing over me:

Dear God, please watch over this woman on her road trip and keep her safe and let her have great human interactions along the way and let her know how deeply loved she is.

I felt like a jackass. They were so sweet.

I replied with:

WOW! Thank you! You guys are so mature and wise. I was partying my brains out at your age, I'm so impressed by your maturity!

(Awkward pause) *There's always time to develop your faith.*

Right. For sure. A part of me still wanted to laugh at how ridiculous this scenario must have looked, but another part of me couldn't believe how kind and compassionate these young girls were and how much confidence they must have to approach strangers and pray not only for them, but WITH them and OVER them.

As I walked away, I couldn't help but feel they were right about something: I WAS feeling very loved.

Remembering the original good between my parents was reminding me of their best qualities—and how who they were and where they met is a part of my story too.

As I was walking back to my hotel, I walked across two bricks that had quotes on the ground.

The first one said:

You are here to heal the past.

And the second one was:

You are here to rewrite the future.

Um, excuse me, who put these here?! Like, what?!?

That's exactly what it felt like though. Like I was letting go of the old story in my family and writing a new one for my future—where I decide the new ending.

The stories we tell ourselves hold great power in our lives, and we have to be willing to heal in order to rewrite the future.

The process of reinvention involves clearing, releasing, and finally, transmuting. Like the process of alchemy, it felt like I was taking what was once dense and dark and finding the gold that was really there all along. And that's really just how much love I have, for myself and the people in my life. We can all move on in life—and I only wanted to move forward with a baseline of love, because that's all that ever mattered to begin with.

On the night before I left Tempe, it was so hot so I decided to go see a movie at this little theater. It was a French film entitled *Slut in a Good Way*. The main character, Charlotte, was a teen girl who breaks up with her boyfriend and starts working at a toy store, where she proceeds to sleep with almost every guy who works there (except the one who really likes her). It made me fall in love with movies all over again. And there was even Bollywood music in it!!?!

I remembered how much I loved movies (enough to study them in college). Before I left on my road trip, the only movie I'd watched was *Moana*, just a few (ten) times with my niece and nephew. I'd watched it for the first time the weekend after my grandma died—and one can imagine what an emotional event that was. My niece loved watching it and every time the grandma part came on, I'd have to turn my head and try to hold back the tears. *I'm not crying, these are my allergies!*

The message Moana gets from her family (except her grandmother - sob) was:

The people before us left home so we could have all this and you're safe now and have everything you need so why would you leave??

I'd always felt the pull to leave, ever since I was young. But for so long, I tried to stay. Or I'd leave, only to circle back, trying again.

I heard an interview with Bruce Springsteen where he talked about his (challenging) upbringing and how he always felt this pull to go back. He said: *"Something went wrong there and I just kept going back, thinking I could fix it. Circling back around, trying to make things different."*

The hardest thing was accepting that all of it has been totally out of my control, since day one. I've always wanted everyone to get along. I worked so hard and put so much effort into fixing my family as I got older, making everyone happy, often at my own expense. Until I'd tried everything and had to put myself first, instead.

Because as an adult, I get to decide how I'm treated, moving forward. With honesty, respect, accountability, and love. I can't be the scapegoat, and I certainly don't deserve it. At a certain point, I had to hand the responsibility back to the other adults and say: *"This is yours. I can't carry it for you anymore."*

The only thing I had control over was creating a different future, for myself. And to be in a place, from my parent's past, one where I imagined things were better between them, that made me happy. And that's all I ever wanted, was just peace, for them and with them. I will always love my parents, no matter what they do. That's what unconditional love is. But the war ended, for me. I was stepping off the battle field. And it felt nice to walk around a place, and imagine a time when that war never even existed. When there was peace and my existence was only an idea, a possibility for the future.

Before I left on my road trip across the country, I, of course, had an intense spiritual reading with an intuitive based in Switzerland, as one does. She told me that from here on out, my life was about moving forward. To think of a river because a river never flows backwards. A river flows forward, to the ocean.

Arizona State University in Tempe, Arizona | April 2019.

21
MORONGO VALLEY: FIGHT TEST
(owning it)

Why will you take by force what you may have quietly by love? My daughter speaks with a wisdom beyond her years. We have all come here with anger in our hearts but she comes with courage and understanding. From this day forward if there is to be more killing it will not start with me.

- Chief Powahatan

I spent my first night in California in a town called Blythe. It was...not ideal. Even the two women I met who lived there agreed. They both hated it.

I checked into a hotel—and it was so bad, but I didn't have the heart to cancel the room because the lady who checked me in was so nice. She'd just moved there from Hawaii and in the three minutes it took to get my room key, I learned her whole life story.

She still had family back in Hawaii but her dad passed away a couple years ago and her mom died a couple of days after she was born. She was adopted by her grandmother and her grandmother went back to the Philippines, so she moved to Blythe with her son, following her husband—and she was not a fan of the town.

I could see why. It was just like the other small towns I'd stayed in along my drive, only this time, you knew you were so close to something better. It seemed almost cruel to be living in California, only there were dusty roads and two gas stations and fast-food drive-thrus —and that's about it.

When I got to my hotel room and it was a shit hole, I decided to sneak out and go to another hotel, which was also a shit hole, only a better shit hole.

When I checked in to Hotel #2, I met another friendly receptionist who also shared her life story. Within two minutes, we bonded over the fact that we were the same age and felt like we needed to get some distance from our hometowns because we couldn't live our own lives without getting stuck in everyone else's stuff.

I sat in my hotel room, with an office chair jammed under the door, and thought about how crazy it was that I could drive across the country to two shitty hotels and within 120 seconds, instantly bond with two women over our shared experiences. Even though it might look different on the outside, in essence, we're all going through the same things.

The next morning was Easter—and I rose right out of that cave of a hotel, as Jesus rose from the dead, and did not look back. *Thank you, next.*

Even though I was no longer a practicing Catholic, Easter still felt like a holiday, mostly because my family would all be getting together back home. I wanted to do something special on this holy day—so I decided to go to Joshua Tree National Park.

The weather was cool, the sky was a crisp blue, and I took my sweet ass time driving through the park, stopping to look at cacti and big rocks and this landscape that felt like it was from another world. It looked like the rocks had been perfectly placed there a very long time ago.

As I was moseying around the Cholla Cactus Garden, I started thinking about how Joshua was similar to Yeshua, which was actually Jesus's name (like in Hebrew, the language he spoke). And I had this thought that dropped into my mind and I knew it was true:

That the whole point of this life is to know that pain = growth.

I thought about what I'd left behind—the shitty hotel I woke up in, the shitty living situations, the painful endings to relationships, the person I used to be, and everything in the past. It was painful but in letting go I was truly being reborn—and my life was so beautiful right there, at that moment. Better than I could have ever imagined.

And that's the thing about life. It really does keep getting better and better as we go on, even if we can't see it in the moment. There's a big picture and a big force and it's always expanding. And everything that's happening, isn't some form of punishment for an innate badness in us. It's the exact opposite. It's all happening to help us grow.

It felt weirdly important that I was there, in Joshua Tree, on the day that celebrates coming back to life. Because I, too, felt like I was coming back to life. If anything, Jesus showed us that through suffering and letting go of all the labels, all the things we identify ourselves with and staying true to our values and standing up for what's right that it may cause us pain in this world—but it's ultimately how we find redemption.

When we die to the old way of doing things, when we allow death to occur, it ultimately leads to new life. We have to let one thing die in order to let a new thing grow.

I drove out of there feeling like a goddamn modern-day prophet.

And because life is filled with polarities, I went from this beautiful, ethereal experience in the park and straight into Palm Springs, on what was the last (and most popular) night of Coachella, starring Ariana Grande.

For the first time in my life, I spent Easter by myself. I finished the day sitting by the pool in Palm Springs with the mountains in the background and a good book in my hands. It was peaceful and beautiful and serene.

On my way out of town the next morning, I stopped at the post office to send treats to my little nuggets back home. I was talking with the postal worker and he was telling me how he went on big, long road trips and we chatted about how much land there was out there and yet, we somehow feel like we don't have enough space for everyone. Once you see it, it's kinda like seeing an abundance of money and someone still insisting there's not enough. *But yes there is...just print more?!*

I left and drove up the road to Morongo Valley where I'd decided to spend some time in the desert alone, ironically, just like Jesus. I'd been scouring Airbnb, looking for places to stay in southern California for months. And I kept coming across the same little cabin, which appeared to be in the middle of nowhere. It looked like the perfect place to isolate myself from the world and immerse myself in nature.

When I pulled onto the dirt road and started driving into the canyon, losing cell service, I thought: *This will either be a delightful surprise or I will be murdered. Let's see which one!*

I was greeted at the gate of the compound by a lovely woman, a groundskeeper if you will, who later took me on a golf cart tour and explained the history of the canyon and the little homes, one of which I'd be spending almost a week in.

The cottage I was staying in was built by pioneers, who lived there without running water or electricity, using only lanterns for light and fireplaces for heat. And these weren't like old-school pioneers, this was happening in the 1950's. The West was still being explored and claimed (colonized) only a few decades ago.

In 1938, the U.S. government was looking to get rid of "useless" western property and in exchange for building a home and living in it for three years, a person could purchase up to 5 acres of land for about $10 to $20 per acre. This was called homesteading, a very American pursuit to claim land and build some property on it, even if it was deemed worthless by the government. A local hardware store sold home kits for $1500—and that's what provided the basic structure for the cottages.

Each cottage was given a Greek name because the couple who bought these properties thought the topography was dramatic and similar to the Acropolis, surrounded by steep mountain walls that create a sense of protection and safety. Clio, the cottage I was staying in, was named after one of the nine Muses, the patron of history and writing.

I did not leave the cottage for five days. I soaked up everything I could in that canyon. I felt like I could relax there. Like I could finally let my shoulders down and just be.

I was still trying to decide where to go next, and more specifically, where to live next. I still had no idea where I wanted to end up. (Except that it would definitely be in California).

What I was really looking for in that canyon was clarity. I wanted to know, clearly, where I was meant to land next. (In California).

What happened in that desert, where I spent time alone, was I realized, by the end of my time there, that whenever the timing was right, I'd figure it out and the perfect place to live would show up (probably while I continued driving through California). I also realized just how LONG a day can be when I'm not filling it with constant work and distractions.

I read in the sun and played fetch with my dog. I sat by the pool and enjoyed the air conditioning. I still had a bit of anxiety, underneath it all, mainly because I was out of my comfort zone, out on my own—and I'd never made it this far before. I'd always turned back after a few months.

I knew I was not going back this time, though. It wasn't totally perfect, but I did feel happy. And more at peace. And I knew it would keep getting better. I just had to keep moving forward and not let anything else drag me down. I had to stay focused on what I wanted.

All the people I met on the road, when I told them what I was doing, they'd always respond using the same word. *Wow, you are so brave. What a brave woman. That is so brave of you.*

I looked up the definition and the original meaning was a Native American warrior. And it's also being able to face pain and discomfort, which I guess I was doing. But it's only because I'd felt pain and discomfort before too, so it was nothing new to me. Being brave meant more than just handling being uncomfortable—it meant being able to listen to—and trust in—myself.

When I'd gotten my tour of the canyon, the groundskeeper woman explained how it's nestled between two snowcap mountains, San Jacinto and San Gorgonio. The Native Americans who lived on the land were very rich traders and artisans—and they believed that the very first people on Earth came from those mountains. They talked about the "people who came before" and it was said these ancient ancestors could fly. They landed on the two mountains, considered to be Brothers, the oldest beings on Earth. The Natives came to these mountains to get food, medicinal plants, basket making material and to hunt. A way of life that almost feels idyllic now.

For everything we've gained in comfort, we've paved over our connection with the Earth. It seems so radical to connect with spirits and gain wisdom from rocks, but most radical things are actually ancient. People so often cling to religious ideals and value systems (especially about Jesus) because in (an often) twisted way, it's a way to feed the soul. But what I realized in the desert was that connection to something deeper is right beneath our feet and right above our heads—and it has been the whole time.

I came out of the desert replenished and filled with fire. I'd gotten a bit of my warrior spirit back and she was ready to take down injustice. Swiftly. And this newfound strength was immediately put to the test. As I drove between the two mountain Brothers, my own brother called me.

Even though I'd often tortured him as a kid, we were always close, mostly because we'd been through such rocky times growing up together. When I left for college, my brother became the oldest one at home—and it was not easy, at all, for him. The dysfunction got even worse (didn't think that was possible) and he was the brunt of much of it.

Even though he got through it and came out a respectable citizen, father, and husband, he (often) got a lot of flack from our own dad's wife who carried resentment that her first few years of marriage with our father were overshadowed by all the shit that was pre-existing in our family.

We were made well-aware how the issues that happened then, were still an issue for her in the present. And even though it was over a decade later, we were reminded, regularly, of how many sacrifices she'd made because of us older kids. (Meaning, just the fact that we existed at all).

The hardest part was she was over-the-top friendly in front of others and went out of her way to show everyone how much she "included" us...in our own family?

We weren't part of the original dream she'd had for the family she wanted—and it was obvious from day one. Like when we went on a "family" trip to NYC and she asked my youngest sister to step out of the picture and take the camera so she could have a picture of "just us" when my brother and I had snuck away to have a cig. Great self-esteem booster for a tween girl: *Hey get out of the family picture, you don't belong in this one! Just us!*

But it was the moments when no one was watching that the truth really leaked out.

I'd learned from my grandmother just not to engage. How to say "oh" in response. How sometimes the high road means turning the other cheek. And that mostly worked—but it seemed the back-handed comments and the constant gossiping and judgment of others were exponentially increasing as the years went on. And they were becoming really, really hard to ignore. The list of insults was stacking up, really high at this point.

As my brother relayed what happened in his most recent run-in with her, I could feel the fire in my belly rising up to fill my entire being. My blood was boiling.

He'd taken the time to drop-off a birthday present for her—with two of his children, both under the age of 5—and she covered a variety of topics inappropriate for my niece and nephew's ears, including how he had once known someone who'd died from heroin?! She stuck her landing by declaring how her son (our littlest brother) would never "be like you older kids" because <u>she</u> was his parent and she would never allow him to become like us. *Wait, like a kind-hearted adult?! You lost me at talking about heroin in front of a 2 year old, lady.*

And of course, my brother walked away without defending himself, letting her talk about drugs in front of his toddlers and shaming him for his teenage years, because we'd all become conditioned to just

286

accepting being talked to that way, even though it was getting worse and worse.

I pulled into a parking lot, in the 100 degree desert heat, and thought about what I wanted from this situation. My brother was a good man and an excellent father. He worked his butt off and spent his days off with his children, only taking a moment for himself to go running. And he'd taken the time to do something kind for her— giving this person a gift—and he received a response he absolutely did not deserve. And my line had been crossed: it was happening in front of the children.

I knew my dad's wife had her own things to deal with in life—but the constant jabs and put downs, hidden between fake kindness, were just not necessary. And they'd gone unchecked for far too long. I'd kept my mouth shut in order to "keep the peace." But for who? I definitely didn't feel any sense of peace around her. The comments and the chilly behavior usually only happened when no one else was around to see it. And somehow, the narrative always ended in her being a victim. *How convenient!*

I sat and thought about what to do—and immediately was like:

No way. Fuck this. Not in front of the kids.

I took some deep breaths, thought about the outcome I wanted, and knew I had to handle it directly, as an adult. So, I sent the following text:

Hi, I just heard from my brother that he stopped by to drop off your birthday gift and somehow, the convo ended really inappropriately. Please don't say that stuff to him or in front of his kids. There's absolutely no reason for it. Thank you!

I was clear, I was calm, I was cool, I was collected, and even though I wanted to open my mouth and breathe fire, I hit send and put away my phone for two hours.

By the time I checked again, my brother had gotten the apology he deserved and I had a voicemail, assuring me it would "never happen again." (Spoiler alert: It continued to happen again.)

Even though I was relieved by the temporary positive outcome, it was still disappointing that it was ever an issue. That the past was constantly being held over our heads as if we were the adults back then, not the children.

It was a turning point. I stood up for my brother for the first time ever, probably because I was now far enough away to see how not okay the situation was. I realized family doesn't mean tolerating being treated with disrespect. That we can live in a way that forces others to rise to our level, not lower ourselves to theirs. Sometimes people need a reminder not to take their crap out on others, especially when it happens for over a decade. And sometimes, we have to be strong enough to stand up and put an end to the dysfunction, even if no one else will.

I spent the night in Desert Hot Springs, soaking in the magical hot spring water. I talked to the owner of the hotel I was staying in who had bought the place only a few months before and renovated it. She moved from Michigan with her partner and told me once she came out to California, everything started coming together—and she said she never gave up hope and told me I had a lot of courage, which felt nice to hear because I knew it took more bravery for me to finally stand up to my dad's wife than it did to drive across the country alone.

The last thing I ever wanted was more family conflict—but I was old enough now that I had a choice. And unless my family treated each other with a baseline of honesty, love, and respect, I just wasn't participating anymore. I was no longer going to allow myself (or my siblings) to be hurt in order to please anyone else. The medieval times were over, marriage did not give anyone a free pass to treat other adults with blatant rudeness and disrespect. Consistently.

As I sat in the hot tub, looking up at the stars before bed, I thanked the heavens for what a goddamn miracle that day was. Justice was (finally) being served. And I had a whole ocean of possibility (and freedom) ahead of me.

Joshua Tree National Park | April 2019

22
JULIAN: GYPSY
(purpose)

Once you learn what life is about, there is no way to erase the knowledge. If you try to do something else with your life, you will always sense that you are missing something.

- James Redfield

I'll never forget the feeling I had when I finally made it to the West Coast. I stopped at a park where I saw a couple, with their dogs off leash under a sign that forbade it, while doing yoga and hugging between each pose. That moment really summed up the vibe in southern California and I was LOVING it.

My pup and I walked by the ocean, soaking in the beautiful views. Anytime I'd walked on a beach, I always looked for seashells (even along a lake). As I was dipping my feet in the ocean, I looked down and found a shell I'd always wanted but had never found. It was a perfect pair of angel wings that were totally intact and held together. *Thank you, mighty Pacific.*

My dog escaped from her harness as we walked back to our hotel, only to chase after a cute skater and I tried to "stop" her. *Sorry, I don't know what got into her. Anyway, what's your number?*

I could taste freedom on my tongue (or maybe it was just the salt in the air). Deep down, I knew this was where I was meant to be. Something I'd known all along, but could finally now admit.

As someone who had always obsessively planned my life, driving around without a plan or knowing when (or where) my road trip would end was extremely uncomfortable for me. (Except I did have a vague idea, but still stressful).

Comfort, to me, was planning every minute and never, ever losing control. That felt comfortable because it was not a challenge, it was the norm. What kept me safe was always running, jumping to the next thing and making a goddamn plan.

It was uncomfortable to let go. To stop pushing. To stop trying to make everyone happy. And to start making myself happy. It was uncomfortable to stand up for myself, to tell people "no," to let go of friendships, to let go of who I used to be. To be on the road with no clue when it would be over while knowing it was only temporary and enjoying it while also feeling overwhelmed by making this life change. To know I had so many open slots in my life and to hope that only better things fell in place and to know that any doubt was futile and a waste of time.

All I kept thinking was:

How can this be my life? I am so lucky and it feels like heaven on Earth and it comes down to a question of worthiness. Do I feel worthy enough to accept this new life?

All I knew was I'd already made my choice. And for some reason, it made me both happy and sad. Because I knew I wanted to stay in California (duh!) and I also knew that I missed my loved ones, even though many of them could be real nuts sometimes.

So, I decided to do what I knew would help me clear my head. I went to the mountains.

Anytime I'd ever been driving in mountains before, I'd always conveniently asked to "switch" right before the windy, ascending roads began so I could shut my eyes and pretend I was somewhere else. I couldn't shut my eyes this time and even though my knuckles were whiter than usual, I did appreciate the scenery.

As I browsed around the town of Julian, I stopped in a little antique shop and met the storekeeper, Grace. She was a real kick and asked where I was from, which turned into an hour long discussion.

She'd lived with her second husband in a home nearby overlooking a lake and a winery, and also, helped alcoholics. She worked with delinquent teens, the ones who were rebelling against everything outside them (doesn't sound familiar, don't know the type). She explained that you have to reach them on some level where they trust you.

She told me a story about a tenant she once had, a woman who stopped paying her rent. Grace sold the place and transferred the lease to the neighbor that the woman hated instead. She looked me right in the eye and said:

What goes around comes around.

I liked Grace and she reminded me of my grandmothers. I walked out of her store and around the corner where I came across a psychic in a bell tower. And by that I mean, it was an old bell tower from a church that a psychic was now doing readings in. *Perfect.*

When it was time for my appointment, I was immediately put off by the cat and the clutter. I tried to practice non-judgment as I sat in the chair and she closed her eyes. And then she started to explain:

You are an old soul. And you understand that you're here to learn lessons. You have a big heart and I want to acknowledge that first. It's huge. Take that as a compliment.

You might believe that everything happened for a reason. And because of that, the things that happened to you, you take ownership of them, thinking you created all this, and it's happening to you for a reason.

The things that happened in the past were not always your lessons. You might have been plowed over by other people's lessons, but it wasn't yours to learn. It's not always your lesson.

I want you to try thinking this way. Instead of everything happening for a reason, think instead: Everything is on purpose. Figure out how it's helping you. And then let it go.

As an old soul, you agreed to be a point of light.

Those weren't your lessons. It's okay for you to move on and let it all go.

Tears ran down my cheeks as I listened to her speak. It didn't matter where this information came from, she was giving me a gift: my very own *Good Will Hunting* moment.

She was telling me, essentially, what I always needed to hear, but refused to actually acknowledge: *The past was not my fault.*

I had a very strong urge to get a hug from Robin Williams at that moment. And Matt Damon too. And Ben Affleck.

For as strong and as brave as I could be, inside, I still couldn't shake the feeling that I was to blame for everything that hurt. That if only I'd been different then the pain would be different too. That there must be something wrong with me that I deserved the bad things that happened.

I'd also learned that like attracts like, that if I think negative things, negative things would happen. That maybe this was karma from a past life when I was a terrible person and now I needed to make up for it. And that meant that all the negative things that happened to me in the past must have been my fault in some way, whether it was something I did centuries ago or the night before.

But what she was telling me was: *That's not true!*

Life's challenges still come, no matter what. It is an inevitable part of being human—but it doesn't mean I did anything wrong or that I deserved to be treated with anything less than love.

I needed to learn that sometimes the painful things that happen are not even about me at all (still a shocking discovery—not everything is about me. Whoa. Truly mind-blowing).

I just happened to be a bystander, a piece of the puzzle, a part in the play, and because we all have free will, sometimes bad things can come down on us that have nothing to do with us whatsoever, it's someone else's choice and someone else's lesson. Of course, we're going to walk away with more understanding and compassion (if we're lucky) but it doesn't mean we deserved for that thing to happen to us, which explains why terrible things happen to truly wonderful people.

This tiny town in the mountains absolved me of the sins I was carrying, but didn't even commit. I finally felt ready to really keep going and look for somewhere to live that rented in terms of months, instead of by the night.

294

I found a place in Laguna Beach, which at first, I was embarrassed by because of the reality TV show. But I fell in love with the coastal scenery. It was gorgeous and the most beautiful place I'd ever been in the States—so I figured: *This must be the place!*

I moved into a small backhouse right up the street from Victoria Beach, a beach that's Insta-famous because of a tower. Definitely go there, the local residents love to welcome visitors.

I'd see pods of dolphins during my morning walks and I'd watch each sunset with total wonder and awe. I couldn't believe people, myself included, lived amongst such beauty!

Except many of those people were two things: rich and entitled.

Like the oil tycoon who spent his summers at his second home (across the street from mine). One night, probably after many bottles of wine, he rammed my (parked) car down the street, leaving me a very aggressive note, simply because he didn't like where it was parked. *Sir, have you heard of anger management?*

Don't worry, the police handled it. Just kidding they not only did nothing, but kept taking me outside their station to "talk it through" (where there were no cameras) and proceeded to mansplain to me why it was actually totally legal to move someone else's car like a psychopath. *Oh, okay, thank you! Would you be willing to put that in writing? No?!? Hmmm..why not?!*

But I wasn't going to let one aggressive man ruin my dream of being in California. *I mean, it's people like him that are the reason this country even exists! Just kidding, kinda.*

I did once hear someone say: *I came to this place and I just knew I would do more with my life there.* That's how I felt in California.

California has always shown me that the life of my dreams was attainable. And that it won't be perfect, but it's my choice.

One thing I kept thinking when I first was getting settled, especially when things weren't working out perfectly, was like: *Hey, grandmas, um, what's going on up there? Because I keep asking you for help. Where the heck is all this leading me?!?!*

The gift my grandmothers gave me was both nothingness and everything. They cleared the way for endless possibilities for me, in how they lived and how they loved, and they constantly reminded me that I was enough, just as I was.

They guided me to see that there were no rules for me, that I didn't have to follow the same ones they did. That I had more options— and what a shame it would be if I didn't at least explore them. And they had this thing that most Elders have called "perspective."

After they had lived through so much, they'd nod while I was caught up in whatever crisis of the moment, knowing that whatever thing I was going through, that it would never be the thing that really mattered, it would just be the thing that pushed me more towards myself. That all that mattered was me being brave enough to become me.

They gave me a space that only I could fill. I was gifted a clean plate—things broke down and were cleared away so I could have a new canvas to build on and put my heart and soul into. There's really no greater gift in this world than a fresh start—and it felt like that's what they were giving me.

Oddly enough, I wrote a paper in high school about the evolution of women, from obedient ladies to empowered humans. My teacher put a star next to this paragraph:

A Renaissance court lady may have been frustrated with her situation, but she also had clear guidelines to follow of what was acceptable and what was not. A modern woman does not have this. She must create for herself what she wants her life to be.

I finally realized I can be whatever the heck I want. That there is no right or wrong way of living. That part of being human is being multifaceted, not this or that. I can be a writer, an artist, an astronaut, a sister, a daughter, a granddaughter, a partner, a mother, a neighbor, a wife, a goddess, a caregiver, a leader, a teacher— whatever the fuck I want to be and all of it is me and all of it is more than okay.

There's something very unique and special about each of us. And we are also just a speck of dust in the universe and this life will be over in a flash.

While I was in the mountain town of Julian, I found an old picture in an antique shop. It's of a woman riding a surfboard in a flooded street, being pulled behind a car by a tow rope. I loved it so much because it just captures exactly what life can be. The town can flood, disaster can strike, things happen that are outside our control—and yet, we always have the option to make the best of it. To find joy. To pull out a damn surfboard and get tugged through the flooded streets with a smile. To go with the flow. Enjoy the moment. Notice the hummingbirds and the butterflies and the flowers. Watch the sun go down. Feel the beauty. Absorb the salt in the air. To live, here and now, and to let the sun shine right down on our faces, from up above.

Beautiful day in Laguna Beach, California. Even better than early '90's reality TV | May 2019.

23
LAKE GENEVA: FLOAT ON
(happy)

I didn't run away from life,
I went deeper into it.

- Cheryl Strayed

It had always been my grandpa's dream to own a lake house for his family, even though he didn't (technically) know how to swim. He named the house FLOWERS, because he wanted to give us all something we could enjoy together now, instead of after he died.

The house was 100ish years old and the bedrooms were packed with (bunk) beds. As kids, it was like heaven on earth. We got to swim and play ALL DAY and even, walk to the local hotel by ourselves.

As adults, we still did all the same things, only now a lot of that fun was also happening at nighttime and involved walking to Chuck's, the local bar—a place we (miraculously) were never banned from.

My cousins and I bonded hard there every summer. As kids, we'd spend our days playing lifeguard off the pier, and our nights prank calling the Sugar Shack. *Hello, do your dancers wear undies?!?* As adults, we spent our days hanging on the pier and our nights still making prank calls. *Hello, are you hiring?!*

On this lake, my grandparent's home had become such a place of joy and happiness for us. For me, it was a constant, the one home I always could go to, no matter what. I'd tell my Gram: *You know, this is the only house that's been in my life all my life, since I was little?*

And she'd nod with conviction and say:

Oh, I know and I've thought about that a lot.

We'd sit on the porch swing and talk about life. She always wanted to know what we thought about things and what we wanted to do next. She'd ask:

Do you know what you want to be when you grow up?

Um, not really...

Well, good, neither do I! Now go jump in the lake!

At night, we would all eat a big dinner on the wraparound porch, and Gram made sure everyone had a shirt on, that no one was dripping wet from the lake, and that no one got seconds before everyone got firsts. Grandpa would lead us in prayer and ask us to remember all the soldiers who sacrificed their lives for us, all the sick who were suffering, and all the poor who did not have enough to eat.

After dinner, he'd sometimes sit down at the piano and we'd all play little instruments and sing songs. One of my most treasured memories was sitting next to my Grandpa on the piano bench as he tried to teach me how to play (and I'd tell him I'd been practicing even though I really hadn't). Sometimes he'd get out his slides and we'd look at old family pictures together. He was so gentle and loving—and really set the bar (very) high for what I expected out of a man in life.

At night, we'd get into our PJ's and fight over who got to sit next to Grandpa on the porch swing. As all the grandkids surrounded him, he made up tales, ironically, about the Native Americans who'd lived there before and what life used to be like on the lake. We went to sleep in our bunk beds, after our Gram confirmed the sleeping arrangements at least 15 times to ensure everyone had a clean bed to sleep in. The time I spent there, at any age, it always felt like the troubles of the world just melted away for a bit.

Lake Geneva was a sanctuary, an escape from the chaos, a slice of Heaven, a place filled with family and connection and shared meals and so many memories.

When I landed back at O'Hare, the first summer after I'd moved away, it was like a whirlwind. I crossed the stateline between Illinois and Wisconsin four times in less days, and tried to see every family member I could, on both sides. It wasn't perfect, but it was better. Or maybe I was just better because I knew I had a life of my own outside it all.

I couldn't wait to see my siblings. I never wanted them to think I'd abandoned them. In my perfect world, I would have packed up my car for California and tossed them (and their children) in my trunk too. Which would have gotten me arrested (again) because they had no desire to leave the state. But I knew I could leave because they were now grown up too. My little ducklings were now swans and it was so beautiful to see them fly, like as adults.

Other perks of going back: I got to surprise my brother's kids and borrow my sister's clothes again. The drive up to Wisconsin felt nostalgic and sweet, and I watched the fireworks on the pier, over the lake, with my cousins, like I had since I was little.

When I was able to be there, fully present, I had a wonderful time, which was ironic because earlier that year, I couldn't get out of there fast enough. Being away for a while had given me a new perspective. And I felt (mostly) really, really grateful to be with the people I love. Until the last 24 hours, when I was exhausted from constant socializing and couldn't wait to get back to California.

Even though I'd had to leave on my own, coming back reminded me that I had so many people who did love me and support me, but they couldn't figure out my life for me. Only I could do that.

And even though my family had been through hell and back in the past, my entire family as a whole—like all the extended parts including my nuggets, siblings, cousins, aunts, uncles, grandparents in heaven—were like my saving grace. And I knew my grandparents would be so proud of us for actually enjoying one another.

And even though my Gram had passed on, I could still sit on the porch and close my eyes and picture her with me—talking to her, knowing when she'd smile, swinging on the porch swing, and taking a sip of tea as we enjoy each other's company. The memories all my grandparents left me were always in my heart.

I decided to write my Gram one last letter because I didn't get the chance to give her one while she was still alive and could actually read it, so I hoped she could see it, from wherever she was:

Dear Gram,

I miss you so much. I hope you are in a better place and that you are with Grandpa. What is it even like? I wish you could tell me. You haven't missed much here yet. The summer is coming to an end and Fall is starting soon. Guess what? We kept the Lakehouse. I know you'd want to know that.

Well, I guess I just need to tell you how much you mean to me and how grateful I am for you. I don't even know where to begin.

You've taught me so much and I'm so grateful I was able to spend so much TIME with you. You and Grandpa have been such loving positive influences on my life. You gave me the gift of an education, you helped me to read and learn and love books, you taught me how to have a good conversation, to love everyone and to believe in myself.

Mainly, you've just always understood me and made me feel like my ideas weren't crazy. That it's ok to be me and to travel where I want to go—even if no one else agrees. That has meant more to me than I can even put into words. You also showed me how to cook and clean and take a leadership role. I know you were not perfect, but guess what, neither am I. I hope I can be as strong as you were one day.

Most of all, I wanted you to know this: THANK YOU.

Thank you, thank you, thank you for showing me the way. Thank you for always being there. Thank you for loving me. Thank you for making this big, beautiful family. Thank you for ALL OF IT. I hope you are having fun, wherever you are. I promise I will have fun too. I LOVE YOU SO MUCH.

Say hi to Issy and Grandpa and Pa.

Thank you Gram. For everything.

I didn't say it back, so: After a while, Crocodile.

Love,
Caitlin

Before I left to go back to California, I was in one of my (many) childhood bedrooms and I saw a copy of *The Ugly Duckling* on the shelf. I pulled it down and thought:

Whatever happened to that girl?

The last line stopped me in my tracks. The Ugly Duckling, once she realized she was actually a beautiful swan and had found her place in the world, said:

I couldn't imagine I could be this happy.

I realized that's exactly what my life felt like. I could never have imagined I could be that happy—and really, free.

Lake Geneva, Wisconsin.

EPILOGUE:
CARMEL: CALIFORNIA STARS
(better)

Tame birds sing of freedom. Wild birds fly.
- John Lennon

After about a year of living in California, I took another road trip, this time up the coast. I found myself driving on the same roads that I'd driven when I was staying in San Francisco years earlier, when I was circling around the northern part of the state, looking for a place to call home.

Back then, I was mad at myself for not having it all figured out, so I forced myself to go back to the Midwest because I wasn't "doing it right" and I didn't "have an address"—and who the fuck was I to think I could just up and move to California? That I could just hit the road and explore?!? *Scoff.*

As I was going over the same roads, I realized what a dick I'd been to myself before and how much better it felt to actually be...nice to myself? To let myself make mistakes and to just give myself a break for being human. To go where I wanted to go, unapologetically.

Throughout all my travels and my search for somewhere to live, I was really stepping *away* from all the conditioning I'd been given, and *into* my own life. Slowly but surely, with every place I went, I became a little bit more myself.

I always thought change happened sharply, in a straight line, but it doesn't happen like that; it happens in cycles, in circles, in a spiral. I found myself circling the same path until I reached the end of the pattern. Until it became time for me to create a new one, not keep repeating the one that had been grooved and laid before me.

On this California road trip, I stayed along the Russian River and it was truly gorgeous. Until the second night, when I came face-to-face with an actual bat, in the cabin I was staying in. I'd prided myself on being Miss Independent, someone who could do it *all* on her own. Except I realized I did need a little help every once in a while. And maybe it would have been nice to have someone with me, especially when it came to bats flying indoors.

I obviously researched a bit about bats afterwards, making sure rabies was not airborne. Instead, what I found felt a little too symbolic. During the day, bats go into their caves and then they appear in the dark, each night. They represent letting go of the old and bringing in the new. When a person sees one, it's often the start of a new beginning.

I'd planned to stay in that cabin for a week so when I left after Bat Night, on my way back down the coast, I decided to stop in Carmel-by-the-Sea. I'd been there twice before. The last time was ten years earlier, right after being a maid of honor. That trip was like a treat to myself, a carrot at the end of the wedding duty stick.

But the first time ever was about a decade before that, one of my only early memories with both of my parents. We'd come out to California to stay with Aunt Sheila and took a road trip from San Francisco down to the Monterey Bay area. We went to the Aquarium (well before the "thicc" tweet) and I remember thinking how Carmel looked like it belonged somewhere in France. My siblings and I searched the tide pools on Spanish Bay and it was the first time I ever got to see a sunset over the Pacific Ocean. It was also the last family vacation we ever took, all together.

The only other truly pleasant memories I had from my childhood were mostly from home videos. My grandpa started the first tape, right when I was born. Every time he saw me, he brought his video camera and filmed. It was the sweetest thing in the world and I never wanted to lose the footage, so I had it digitized. I sent it to my other family members, and I found myself creating three versions: 1. the full, unedited version; 2. the version where mom gets edited out for dad; 3. the version where dad gets edited out for mom. And that's what my life had become, three different filters that I was constantly shifting between. Until I decided to just choose one: the full, unedited one, also known as: reality.

The structure and the pressure of the nuclear family (the basis of the American dream) had often been pretty painful, in my experience. I was stuck on the battleground for so many years, trying to get the tension to ease, the war to end between opposing sides. There was also this box with my name on it, created by society, telling me: *This is life for you, woman. And by the way, woman, you are not to be trusted, so don't get any crazy ideas! This is where you belong, now get in!* And I tried very hard to bend down, contort myself, put myself in a pretzel, so I could fit in that box, mostly because I thought it was the only way I could be loved. Until I realized, maybe I was born inside the box so I could learn how to break out of it?

Being back in Carmel, as an adult on my own, I sat with my feet in the sand, both exhausted and refreshed, and smelled the ocean air and watched my dog spastically playing fetch and I just felt like *me* again. Like I'd found a piece of my dreams for the future that had been left there when I came the very first time, with my mom and my dad and my aunt, when everyone got along and we stayed at a fancy hotel and we saw these beautiful places and life was so sweet and simple and kind and beautiful—and I just loved it all so much and I took one million pictures on disposable cameras and I thought the world could only be sweet, could only be giving, until I went home and everything changed. The memories that felt good started to sting, instead, because it hurt to think of how good it had once been, before it all fell apart. Because if things had never been that good, then I would have had nothing to lose and it wouldn't have hurt.

There were many things I savored about my past, many people I loved, many memories I would always cherish. There was a sweetness that existed right in the middle of everything else, the only thing that balanced out all the other stuff.

I'd found myself drawn to caring for kids, my whole life. Babysitting, volunteering, writing sharp soapbox social media posts about injustices towards children. And ultimately, the thing that changed everything for me, the absolute sweetest part of my life, was the kids I had the honor of spending time with, especially the ones in my family.

From the moment I became a sister and an auntie, I just knew that my life was no longer just about me. There was now a future that I wouldn't live to see, but I would have an influence on it. I knew I had to show the kids in my life not just what I won't be a part of, but what is possible: another option, outside of the box. That there is another way, if they want it.

The patterns of silence, stonewalling, ostracising, tension, unhappy relationships, creative dreams unrealized, playing small, victimhood, ignorance, fear, addiction, shame, hiding the truth, secrets, all the things so many families struggle with, I made the decision that: it stops with me. I will not participate in any of those things from here forward. And let me tell you, breaking ancestral patterns is not for the faint of heart! But it not only heals us, but everyone, when we do.

Instead, I wanted clear communication, inclusivity, compassion, ease, happy relationships, living out creative dreams, shining big, responsibility, activism, knowledge, courage, wellness, pride, embracing the truth, and being transparent. And the only way I could do that was by walking that path first, even if I had to do it alone.

Even sitting on any beach in California, it was impossible not to acknowledge the families that used to live there that were destroyed by violence. The indigenous people who were pushed out of their home. In a way, I decided I cannot participate in violence of any kind and I only agreed to be a part of the healing, of all of it: in the world, in my country, and the people I call family.

I had to find the strength to say one of the most powerful words in the universe: No. I won't let you treat me this way. I won't keep participating in the dysfunction, the gossip, the blame, and the shame. And when the doors slammed shut in my face, I had to learn how to stop knocking, stop begging to be seen, stop looking for acceptance in a place that withheld it.

Even though it felt like an acutely isolating experience, I was very much not alone. In families, there's often a person (usually a "black sheep") who gets met with distance, anger and resistance from their family when they start choosing a healthier life. This is because, in

308

families, we're often taught: This is just the way things are and they are *unchangeable*. Until someone comes along and says: *Eh, I bet I could change it, actually*.

I'd decided to create different standards for how I expect to be treated and how I expect my life to feel. I didn't have to be married off to enjoy financial freedom, I didn't have to pop out some kids by a certain age to be treated with respect, and I didn't have to tolerate mistreatment, even from family. I could choose to live my life in a way that only made room for love.

I saw my grandparents suffer at the end, and I knew I had no choice but to live *now* and to not wait for someone to tell me it's okay. To give myself the permission, to grab hold of my own freedom and take my power back. My therapist once told me that when someone does this, in a family, it shifts the dynamics. Like a mobile over a baby's crib, when one piece decides to rotate in a different direction, it throws the rest off-balance for a bit.

Separating from our family, even just physically, is a major part of finding our own individuality. For me, I had to step away from trying to protect everyone. I thought I was doing something good, with only pure intentions, trying to "help" and "please" anyone and everyone—family, friends, strangers, whether they wanted it or not. But actually, when I was blocking people from experiencing their own hardship, I was doing more harm than good. Hardship is how we grow. By staying silent and denying reality, never forcing anyone to have the hard and necessary conversations, I was the walking definition of codependency. And the only way to get better, was if I stopped taking on everyone's pain, as my own. Stopped meddling, stopped trying to help, stopped fixing and protecting. Even though it felt like some noble thing to do, to put everyone else first, it was not. I finally had to say: Enough is enough.

I found this fun fact once: The entire human population would only be as large as one sugar cube if there were no space between atoms.

Meaning, if there's no space between us, we'd all be globbed together and we wouldn't be able to move or live. So, the only way to be ourselves, to individuate, to expand, to evolve, is to allow for space. And sometimes, we need to step into a totally new space, in order to keep growing.

Suffering in life is a given. It's truly living that takes bravery. It's opening up, being seen, sharing who you are and living to the fullest, holding both extremes: the pain and the beauty. Knowing that there's something inside that can never be broken. That sometimes things aren't always this or that, or perfect, or totally binary.

California reminds me that the world is good too. That the reason we are here is for love. Even if that love is as simple as watching a sunset. Or smiling at a stranger. Or putting yourself first, signaling to others that they can too.

My grandmothers didn't have much choice in their life. They were the first generation to end the cycle of poverty, to get an education, to find stability in a capitalist society and a family system deeply entrenched in religion. I had more options, because of them. And the generation after me will have even more options.

So, the very best thing I could do, as a future ancestor, was push my life to be the fullest, the least limited; hoping that will let the ones after me, who I love so much, both in my family and in the world, feel even more free, more alive, more whole. So that, maybe one day, they'll stand on the beach in Carmel and think: Wow, my ancestors were here once and look how much life has improved since then. I guess it really does keep getting better and better.

YOUR LIFE IS YOUR LIFE.
KNOW IT WHILE YOU HAVE IT.
YOU ARE MARVELOUS
THE GODS WAIT TO DELIGHT
IN YOU.

Charles Bukowski

PLAYLIST

Hospital Beds - Cold War Kids

Criminal - Fiona Apple

Crystal Village - Pete Yorn

Chicago - Sufjan Stevens

Polyester Bride - Liz Phair

Girl from the North Country - Bob Dylan + Johnny Cash

Back Down South - Kings of Leon

Blank Maps - Cold Specks

Sad Dream - Sky Ferreira

Everybody's Changing - Keane

Blood - The Middle East

As - Stevie Wonder

My Sweet Lord - George Harrison

(Sittin On') The Dock of the Bay - Otis Redding

Signals - Junius Meyvant

Downtown - Majical Cloudz

Brace - Twin Shadow

Sleepyhead - Passion Pit

Funeral Singers - Sylvan Esso

September - Earth, Wind & Fire

Fight Test - The Flaming Lips

Gypsy - Fleetwood Mac

Float On - Modest Mouse

California Stars - Wilco

THANK YOU

Gratitude is contagious. We can spread it to as many people as we want. It opens our hearts. And if we all share our gratitude, freely, it wouldn't take very long to spread it to everyone on the planet!

This is a bit of my gratitude, from my heart to yours:

DOODLE: This book would not exist without you. I'm eternally grateful for your willingness to read all my shitty drafts and your patience in helping me bring this to life. I'm not sure where I'd be without you, Sissy.

THOMAS: Thank you for being the kind of man I'm so honored to call my brother. I'd like to take this chance to publicly apologize for terrorizing you as a child—you are better for it. Our grandparents would be so proud of you.

RYAN: Thank you for being the best little brother we could ask for. It's so fun to watch you grow up.

KAREN: Thank you for being my friend even when I was a huge loser and for always making me laugh until I pee my pants. I'm so lucky to be friends with a model like you, and you'll always be my role model in life.

PRIYA: Thank you for taking me to India and for always being there. You're one of my favorite human beings ever. I cannot wait to keep wearing Volturi robes with you.

CAROLLYNE: Thank you for all your support and guidance. It has meant so much to me.

KY: Thank you for being such a love. I'm so deeply honored to know you.

IDA: Thank you for being so gentle and loving to me. You taught me so much. Ganesha comes with me everywhere I go!

BETTY: Thank you for being such a good friend and for always being so supportive. I always smile when I think about you!

ALDO: Thank you for laughing at me when I said I was ready to "settle down" at 22. I love you friend!

KATIE: Thank you for being my cube mate and roommate—and for making cube life enjoyable. I treasure your friendship!

JULIE R.: Thank you for taking me under your wing. You showed me the beauty of print and what it means to be fully committed to your work and your family.

LINDA T.: Thank you for mentoring me and helping me to own my worth. I'm forever grateful for all the time you spent teaching me.

ERIKA: You are the best boss I ever had. Thank you for supporting me, for encouraging me and for always giving me a break.

SATVINDER: Thank you for taking me under your wing and showing me around. I'll always remember how kind you were to me.

PHOENIX: Thank you for sticking with me in the Colca Canyon, I would have literally died without you.

THE NEW ZEALANDERS: Thank you for letting me hang by you on the Inca Trail and introducing me to Monopoly Deal.

RAQUEL: Thank you for giving me the opportunity to work in your home. It changed my life forever and I am so in awe of you and the work you do.

MRS. COLEMAN: I've wanted to write you a thank you for the longest time. Thank you for being my teacher during the hardest year of my life. I will always remember how kind you were to me and I am so incredibly grateful I had you as my teacher.

MRS. PARSONS: Thank you for teaching me how to correctly use words and for driving me home from school when I lied that I didn't have a ride home because I was afraid to take the bus.

MRS. NOTTER: Thank you for teaching me the importance of good handwriting and being kind to other girls.

MRS. BEE: Thank you for caring and for taking the time to help the Rainbows kids.

MR. NALL: Thank you for teaching me how to think outside the box for the first time in my life.

CATONYA: You inspire me so much.

WANDA: You are the strongest person I've ever met. Thank you for being my friend.

LIZ: Your faith and confidence are magnetic. Thank you for being my friend.

JULIE H.: Thank you for always giving me opportunities and for being so kind to me. I learned so much by just seeing how you operate in the world. Thank you for teaching me to fill up my well first.

DAVID: Thank you for your constant support and encouragement. It really means a lot and I learned so much about being a good neighbor from you.

TIM: The time you spent mentoring and teaching me was invaluable. Your willingness to stand up for what's right and your encouragement was truly a gift. Thank you, from the bottom of my heart.

JANET: Thank you for being so beyond kind and generous to me. I'm so thankful for everything you did for me.

LAELA: Thank you for being such a great friend. Your support and kindness means the world to me.

SERA: Thank you for all your time and kindness. I really hope to come visit you one day!

MIKE(Y): Thank you for showering me with presents and for being so kind to me and my family.

NANCY: Thank you for always being so sweet to me. I'm so inspired by how lovely you are and all the work you do to help others.

CARLOS: Thank you for always making me feel at home at the pantry. I admire everything you do and your commitment to helping others.

PONCIANA: Thank you for bringing me gifts and always making me smile. You always brightened my days.

JEFF B.: Thank you for all you do to help other people. I'm so lucky to know you.

JOYCE: Thank you, thank you, thank you for all your guidance. You are definitely an Earth Angel.

KIPLEY: Thank you for taking me under your wing. I loved spending time with you and really appreciate all you did for me.

KAREN (my therapist): Thank you for holding the space for me to talk through all my issues. You helped me tremendously and I cannot put into words how grateful I am.

MARIE: Thank you for everything. I can't even begin to express how much your kindness has changed my life.

RENEE: Thank you for encouraging me to write this book and for all your help and guidance.

AURORA: Thank you for the gift of your time. You came into my life exactly when I needed you most and I will never forget how much you helped me.

DR. MASSEY: Thank you for helping me truly heal.

COUSINS: I don't know where I'd be without you guys. #loveyoucuz

BRADLEY: Thank you for stalking us down through 23andme. Our lives will never, ever be the same.

MICHAEL: Thanks for being such a great cousin. I'm excited to see where life takes you!

GRANNY NANCY: Thanks for always being interested in my travels.
MARY ELLEN: Thank you for always being so supportive.

DOROTHY: Thank you for always listening and for all your kindness.

AUNT SHEILA: Thank you for spoiling me rotten, for always listening, and for showing me California.

AUNT PATRICE & UNCLE DOUG: Thank you for always being so kind to all of us and for everything you've done for me.

AUNT PAM & UNCLE MIKE: Thanks for adopting my sister when she was little. I can't wait to loop one day :)

AUNT DAWN & UNCLE MATT: Thank you for taking me out in California and for always being so supportive!

AUNT CAMILLE & UNCLE DAVE: Thank you for always being so supportive and for always checking in on us. I'm really grateful for everything!

AUNT LISA & UNCLE GREG: Thank you for being so cool and for always being so good to my siblings and I. And for always listening!

AUNT BETH & UNCLE PAUL: Thank you for always showing up and being so supportive of all of us. It means the world.

DAD: Thank you for always being there, for all the concerts and trips, and for putting up with me as a teenager.

RYLEE: Thank you for making me an auntie. I love you so much.

TOMMY: Thank you for being the sweetest little guy in this world. I love you so much.

KEIRA: Thank you for FaceTiming me more than anyone else. I love you so much.

GRANDPA DUDE: Thank you for the lake house, the piano lessons, the videos, and for being such a wonderful grandpa. I'm so lucky to be your granddaughter.

PA: Thank you for all the rides, the lunches, the bike, the dresses, and for being such a wonderful grandpa. I'm so lucky to be your granddaughter.

ISSY & GRAM: Thank you doesn't feel like enough but I will say it anyway. Thank you.

And to all the places where this book was written, including: Bali, the Faroe Islands, Peru, Vietnam, Costa Rica, Iceland, Illinois, Arizona, New Mexico, Oklahoma, Missouri, Florida, and California. Thank you, I thoroughly enjoyed most of you.

INSPIRATION

One thing I love more than anything is books. They are like my best friends. I've always relied on them (a little too heavily) for support and even, for companionship. Whether I want to relax and unplug, or I'm just having a shit day (sometimes both), I can always pick up a book and be taken away.

Words are how we tell the tales of what we've survived. How we share our hopes and dreams and stories with each other. Every person is born with a heart beating inside them that knows the way for their one life. It's our job to slow down and hear it. To listen to where it wants us to go next. A book can help us do that. These are some of the books that have helped me, along the way:

The Alchemist by Paulo Coehlo

A Ring of Endless Light by Madeleine L'Engle

The Book of Secrets by Deepak Chopra

Born a Crime by Trevor Noah

The Celestine Prophecy by James Redfield

The Disobedience of the Daughter of the Sun by Martín Prechtel

Eat Pray Love by Elizabeth Gilbert

Fear of Flying by Erica Jong

The Forty Rules of Love by Elif Shafak

The Four Agreements by Don Miguel Ruiz

The Girl Who Drank the Moon by Kelly Barnhill

Holy Cow by Sarah Macdonald

I Know Why the Caged Bird Sings by Maya Angelou

The Last Black Unicorn by Tiffany Haddish

Let My People Go Surfing by Yvon Chouinard

The Light Between Us by Laura Lynne Jackson

Light is the New Black by Rebecca Campbell

Little Princes by Conor Grennan

Milk and Honey by Rupi Kaur

A People's History of Chicago by Kevin Coval

Rules for the Unruly by Marion Winik

Shopgirl by Steve Martin

There Are No Children Here by Alex Kotlowitz

The Time Traveler's Wife by Audrey Niffenegger

Untamed by Glennon Doyle

Walk Two Moons by Sharon Creech

Wild by Cheryl Strayed

Yes Please by Amy Poehler

ABOUT THE AUTHOR

Caitlin Elizabeth is a writer and overly proud aunt, amongst many other things. *Everything in Between* is her first book, and it won't be her last. She lives in southern California with her most loyal companion, her dog.

Instagram: @lovecaitlinelizabeth
Website: caitlinelizabeth.me

CPSIA information can be obtained
at www.ICGtesting.com
Printed in the USA
BVHW061520200622
640203BV00008B/886